Jeremiah Chaplin

Chips from the White House; or, Selections from the speeches

Jeremiah Chaplin

Chips from the White House; or, Selections from the speeches

ISBN/EAN: 9783337057008

Printed in Europe, USA, Canada, Australia, Japan

Cover: Foto ©Suzi / pixelio.de

More available books at **www.hansebooks.com**

CHIPS

FROM THE

WHITE HOUSE

OR, SELECTIONS FROM THE

SPEECHES, CONVERSATIONS, DIARIES, LETTERS, AND
OTHER WRITINGS, OF ALL THE PRESIDENTS
OF THE UNITED STATES.

COMPILED BY

JEREMIAH CHAPLIN.

BOSTON:
D. LOTHROP AND COMPANY,
32 FRANKLIN STREET.
1881.

COPYRIGHT,
1881,
BY D. LOTHROP & CO.

PRINTED BY DUFFY, CASHMAN & Co.
603 Washington St., Boston.

STEREOTYPED AT THE BOSTON STEREOTYPE FOUNDRY,
NO. 4 PEARL STREET.

TO

JAMES A. GARFIELD,

**WORTHY SUCCESSOR
TO THE BEST WHO HAVE PRECEDED HIM IN THE
HIGHEST OFFICE OF THE REPUBLIC,**

This Volume

IS RESPECTFULLY DEDICATED.

MARCH 4, 1881.

THE PRESIDENTS.

FROM 1789 TO 1881 — 92 YEARS.

GEORGE WASHINGTON, Virginia, 1789-1797 — 8 years.
JOHN ADAMS, Massachusetts, 1797-1801 — 4 years.
THOMAS JEFFERSON, Virginia, 1801-1809 — 8 years.
JAMES MADISON, Virginia, 1809-1817 — 8 years.
JAMES MONROE, Virginia, 1817-1825 — 8 years.
JOHN QUINCY ADAMS, Massachusetts, 1825-1829 — 4 years.
· ANDREW JACKSON, Tennessee, 1829-1837 — 8 years.
MARTIN VAN BUREN, New York, 1837-1841 — 4 years.
WILLIAM HENRY HARRISON, Ohio, 1841 — 1 month.
JOHN TYLER, Virginia, 1841-1845 — 3 years and 11 months.
JAMES K. POLK, Tennessee, 1845-1849 — 4 years.
ZACHARY TAYLOR, Louisiana, 1849-1850 — 1 year, 4 months, 5 days.
MILLARD FILLMORE, New York, 1850-1853 — 2 years, 7 months, 22 days.
FRANKLIN PIERCE, New Hampshire, 1853-1857 — 4 years.
JAMES BUCHANAN, Pennsylvania, 1857-1861 — 4 years.
ABRAHAM LINCOLN, Illinois, 1861-1865 — 4 years, 1 month, and 11 days.
ANDREW JOHNSON, Tennessee, 1865-1869 — 3 years, 10 months, and 17 days.
ULYSSES S. GRANT, Illinois, 1869-1877 — 8 years.
RUTHERFORD B. HAYES, Ohio, 1877-1881 — 4 years.
JAMES A. GARFIELD, 1881-

PREFACE.

THE present volume is not intended to be so much a contribution to political science, as to exhibit an interesting phase in American history, as it appears in the opinions, upon a variety of subjects of general interest, political and otherwise, of the men who, during the period of nearly a century, have successively reached the highest position in the Republic. It is an occasion for just pride for ourselves, and cheering anticipations for mankind, that, beyond all precedent in ancient and modern times, in the regular succession of rulers, the chief magistrates of the United States have all been men of fair reputation and abilities, and many of them men of superior intellectual capacity and singular devotion to the interests of humanity and freedom. This fact speaks loudly in favor of popular self-government, as opposed to hereditary rule. In this important respect, as in other ways, the people have never failed to show their capacity to manage their own affairs. And the history of the past furnishes a guarantee, that no man of feeble ability or questionable morality can hereafter gain the suffrages of the free citizens of America, to represent and execute their will in the highest office in their gift.

In the case of two or three of the Presidents, the selections from their writings are necessarily brief and unsatisfactory; but for the rest, more abundant material has enabled us to present their opinions with sufficient fulness.

It is proper to state that for the conversations of General Grant, we are indebted to a work of much interest and value — "*Around the World with General Grant in* 1877–1879," by JOHN R. YOUNG.   J. C.

CONTENTS.

CHAPTER.		PAGE.
I.	GEORGE WASHINGTON	11
II.	JOHN ADAMS	45
III.	THOMAS JEFFERSON	88
IV.	JAMES MADISON	111
V.	JAMES MONROE	127
VI.	JOHN QUINCY ADAMS	133
VII.	ANDREW JACKSON	176
VIII.	MARTIN VAN BUREN	186
IX.	WILLIAM HENRY HARRISON	195
X.	JOHN TYLER	202
XI.	JAMES K. POLK	205
XII.	ZACHARY TAYLOR	210
XIII.	MILLARD FILLMORE	212
XIV.	FRANKLIN PIERCE	217
XV.	JAMES BUCHANAN	219
XVI.	ABRAHAM LINCOLN	223
XVII.	ANDREW JOHNSON	284
XVIII.	ULYSSES S. GRANT	292
XIX.	RUTHERFORD B. HAYES	347
XX.	JAMES A. GARFIELD	388

"There is not, perhaps, one sovereign of the Continent who, in any sense of the word, can be said to honor our nature, while many make us almost ashamed of it. The curtain is seldom drawn aside without exhibiting to us beings, worn out with vicious indulgence, diseased in mind if not in body, the creatures of caprice and insensibility.

"On the other hand, since the foundation of the American Republic, the chair has never been filled by a man for whose life, to say the least, any American need to blush." — *London Morning Chronicle, after the death of Adams and Jefferson.*

"Every four years there springs from the vote created by the whole people a President over that great nation. I think the world affords no finer spectacle than this: I think it affords no higher dignity — that there is no greater object of ambition on the political stage on which men are permitted to move. You may point, if you like, to hereditary royalty, — to crowns coming down through successive generations in the same families, to thrones based on prescription or on conquest, to sceptres wielded over veteran legions or subject realms, — but to my mind there is nothing more worthy of reverence or obedience, nothing more sacred, than the authority of a freely chosen magistrate of a great and free people." — JOHN BRIGHT, *Speech at Rochdale, Eng.*, Dec. 4, 1860.

CHIPS FROM THE WHITE HOUSE.

GEORGE WASHINGTON.

BORN 1732; DIED 1799, AGED 67.—MAJOR IN 1751.—MEMBER OF PROVINCIAL ASSEMBLY OF VIRGINIA.—COMMANDER-IN-CHIEF OF THE CONTINENTAL ARMY, JUNE 15, 1775.—RESIGNED HIS COMMAND, DECEMBER 23, 1783.—MEMBER OF THE CONVENTION WHICH FRAMED THE CONSTITUTION, 1787.—PRESIDENT, 1789-1797.

[To Captain Robert Mackenzie, of Virginia, who had written to Washington from Boston, September 13, 1774, complaining of the province of Massachusetts as aiming at "total independence," and that "the rebellious and numerous meetings of men in arms, their scandalous and ungenerous attacks upon the best characters in the province, obliging them to save themselves by flight, and their repeated but feeble threats to dispossess the troops, have furnished sufficient reasons to General Gage to put the town in a formidable state of defence, about which we are now fully employed, and which will be shortly accomplished, to their great mortification."]

PHILADELPHIA, 9 October, 1774.

DEAR SIR: Your letter of the 13th ultimo, from Boston, gave me pleasure, as I learnt thereby that you were well, and might be expected at Mount

Vernon, in your way to and from James River, in the course of the winter.

When I have said this, permit me, with the freedom of a friend, to express my sorrow that fortune should place you in a service that must fix curses to the latest posterity upon the contrivers, and, if success (which, by the by, is impossible) accompanies it, execrations upon all those who have been instrumental in the execution.

I do not mean by this to insinuate that an officer is not to discharge his duty, even when chance, not choice, has placed him in a disagreeable situation; but I conceive, when you condemn the conduct of the Massachusetts people, you reason from effects, not causes; otherwise you would not wonder at a people, who are every day receiving fresh proofs of a systematic assertion of an arbitrary power, deeply planned to overturn the laws and constitution of their country, and to violate the most essential and valuable rights of mankind, being irritated, and with difficulty restrained from acts of the greatest violence and intemperance. For my own part, I confess to you candidly, that I view things in a very different point of light from the one in which you seem to consider them; and though you are led to believe by venal men, — for I must take the liberty of so calling those new-fangled counsellors who fly to and surround you, and all others who for honor or pecuniary gratification will lend their aid to overturn the constitution, and introduce a system of arbitrary government, — although you are taught, I say, by discoursing with such men, to believe that the people of Massachusetts are rebellious, setting up for independency, and what not, give me leave, my good friend, to tell you that you are abused, grossly abused. This I advance with a degree of confidence and boldness which may claim your belief, having better opportunities of knowing the real sentiments of the people you are among, from the leaders of them, in opposition to the present measures of the administration, than you have from those whose business it is not to disclose truths, but to misrepresent facts in order to justify as much as possible to the world their own conduct. Give me leave to add, — and I think I can announce it as a fact, — that it is not the wish or interest of that government, or any other upon this continent, separately or collectively, to set up for independence; but this you may at the same time rely on, that none of them will ever submit to the loss of those valuable rights and privileges which are essential to the happiness of every free state, and without which, life, liberty, and property are rendered totally insecure.

[From a reply to a Congratulatory Address by the President
of the New York Congress, 1775.]

As to the fatal but necessary operations of war, when we assumed the soldier we did not lay aside the citizen; and we shall most sincerely rejoice with you in that happy hour when the establishment of American liberty on the most firm and solid foundations shall enable us to return to our private stations, in the bosom of a free, peaceful, and happy country.

[From a letter to his wife, on his appointment to the command of the American army, 1775.]

You may believe me when I assure you, in the most solemn manner, that, so far from seeking this appointment, I have used every endeavor in my power to avoid it, not only from my unwillingness to part with you and the family, but from a consciousness of its being a trust too great for my capacity, and I should enjoy more real happiness in one month with you at home than I have the most distant prospect of finding abroad, if my stay were to be seven times seven years. But as it has been a kind of destiny that has thrown me upon this service, I shall hope that my undertaking it is designed to answer some good purpose. . . . . I shall rely confidently on that Providence which has heretofore preserved and been bountiful to me, not doubting but that I shall return safe to you in the fall. I shall feel no pain from the toil or danger of the campaign; my unhappiness will flow from the uneasiness I know you will feel from being left alone. I therefore beg that you will summon your whole fortitude, and pass your time as agreeably as possible. Nothing will give me so much sincere satisfaction as to hear this, and to hear it from your own pen.

[From a letter to his brother John Augustine, on the same occasion.]

I am now to bid adieu to you, and to every kind of domestic ease, for awhile. I am embarked on a wide ocean, boundless in its prospect, and in which, perhaps, no safe harbor is to be found. I have been called upon by the unanimous voice of the colonies to take the command of the continental army; an honor I neither sought after nor desired, as I am thoroughly convinced that it requires great abilities, and much more experience than I am master of. . . . I shall hope that my friends will visit, and endeavor to keep up the spirits of, my wife as much as they can, for my departure will, I know, be a cutting stroke upon her; and on this account alone I have many disagreeable sensations.

[Letter to George William Fairfax, England. The fight at Concord, here referred to, occurred April 19, 1775.]

PHILADELPHIA, 31st May, 1775.

DEAR SIR: Before this letter will come to hand you must undoubtedly have received an account of the engagement in the Massachusetts Bay between the ministerial troops (for we do not, nor can we yet prevail upon ourselves to, call them the king's troops) and the provincials of that government. . . .

General Gage acknowledges that the detachment under Lieutenant-Colonel Smith was sent out to destroy private property, or, in other words, to destroy a magazine which self-preservation obliged the inhabitants to establish. And he also confesses, in effect, at least, that his men made a very precipitate retreat from Concord, notwithstanding the reinforcement under Lord Percy; the last of which may serve to convince Lord Sandwich, and others of the same sentiment, that the Americans will fight for their liberties and property, however pusillanimous in his lordship's eye they may appear in other respects.

From the best accounts I have been able to collect of that affair, indeed from every one, I believe the fact, stripped of all coloring, to be plainly this: That if the retreat had not been as precipitate as it was, and God knows it could not well have been more so, the ministerial troops must have surrendered, or been totally cut off. For they had not arrived in Charlestown (under cover of their ships) half an hour, before a powerful body of men from Marblehead and Salem was at their heels, and must, if they had happened to be up one hour sooner, inevitably have intercepted their retreat to Charlestown. Unhappy it is, though, to reflect, that a brother's sword has been sheathed in a brother's breast, and that the once happy and peaceful plains of America are either to be drenched with blood or inhabited by slaves. Sad alternative! But can a virtuous man hesitate in his choice?

[From a letter to Joseph Reed.]

CAMBRIDGE, 14 January, 1776.

DEAR SIR: The reflection on my situation, and that of this army, produces many an unhappy hour when all around me are wrapped in sleep. Few persons know the predicament we are in on a thousand accounts; fewer still will believe, if any disaster happens to these lines, from what cause it flows. I have often thought how much happier I should have been if, instead of accepting the command under such circumstances, I had taken my musket on my shoulder and entered the ranks, or, if I could have justified the matter to posterity and my own conscience, had retired to the back country and lived in a wigwam. If I shall be able to rise superior to these and many other difficulties which might be enumerated, I shall most religiously believe that the finger of Providence is in it, to blind the eyes of our enemies; for surely, if we get well through this month, it must be for want of their knowing the disadvantages we labor under.

[To Benedict Calvert.]

MOUNT VERNON, 3 April, 1773.

DEAR SIR: I am now set down to write you on a subject of importance, and of no small embarrassment to me. My son-in-law and ward, Mr. Custis, has, as I have been informed, paid his addresses to your second daughter, and, having made some progress in her affections, has solicited her in marriage. How far a union of this sort may be agreeable to you, you best can tell; but I should think myself wanting in candor, were I not to confess that Miss Nelly's amiable qualities are acknowledged on all hands, and that an alliance with your family will be pleasing to his.

This acknowledgment being made, you must permit me to add, sir, that at this, or in any short time, his youth, inexperience, and unripened education, are, and will be, insuperable obstacles, in my opinion, to the completion of the marriage. As his guardian, I conceive it my indispensable duty to endeavor to carry him through a regular course of education, (many branches of which, I am sorry to add, he is totally deficient in,) and to guard his youth to a more advanced age before an event, on which his own peace and the happiness of another are to depend, takes place. Not that I have any doubt of the warmth of his affections, nor, I hope, I may add, any fears of a change in them; but at present I do not conceive that he is capable of bestowing that attention to the important consequences of the married state, which is necessary to be given by those who are about to enter into it, and of course I am unwilling he should do it till he is. If the affection which they have avowed for each other is fixed upon a solid basis, it will receive no diminution in the course of two or three years, in which time he may prosecute his studies, and thereby render himself more deserving of the lady, and useful to society. If, unfortunately, as they are both young, there should be an abatement of affection on either side, or both, it had better precede than follow marriage.

Delivering my sentiments thus freely will not, I hope, lead you into a belief that I am desirous of breaking off the match. To postpone it is all I have in view; for I shall recommend to the young gentleman, with the warmth that becomes a man of honor, (notwithstanding he did not vouchsafe to consult either his mother or me on the occasion,) to consider himself as much engaged to your daughter as if the indissoluble knot were tied; and, as the surest means of effecting this, to apply himself closely to his studies, (and in this advice I flatter myself you will join me,) by which he will, in a great measure, avoid those little flirtations with other young ladies, that may, by dividing the attention, contribute not a little to divide the affection.

It may be expected of me, perhaps, to say something of property; but, to descend to particulars, at this time, must seem rather premature. In general, therefore, I shall inform you, that Mr. Custis's estate consists of about fifteen thousand acres of land, a good part of it adjoining the City of Williamsburg, and none of it forty miles from that place; several lots in the said city; between two and three hundred Negroes; and about eight or ten thousand pounds upon hand, and in the hands of his merchants. This estate he now holds independent of his mother's dower, which will be an addition to it at her death; and, upon the whole, it is such an estate as you will readily acknowledge ought to entitle him to a handsome portion with a wife. But as I should never require a child of my own to make a sacrifice of himself to interest, so neither do I think it incumbent on me to recommend it as a guardian.

At all times, when you, Mrs. Calvert, or the young ladies can make it convenient to favor us with a visit, we should be happy in seeing you at this place. Mrs. Washington and Miss Custis join me in respectful compliments, and

I am, dear sir, your most obedient servant.

[Letter to Miss Phillis Wheatley, a colored poet, who published a volume of poems in 1773, when she was nineteen years of age. She addressed a letter and poem to Washington.]

CAMBRIDGE, 28 February, 1776.

MISS PHILLIS: Your favor of the 26th of October did not reach my hands till the middle of December. Time enough, you will say, to have given an answer ere this. Granted. But a variety of important occurrences, continually interposing to distract the mind and withdraw the attention, I hope will apologize for the delay, and plead my excuse for the seeming but not real neglect. I thank you most sincerely for your polite notice of me, in the elegant lines you enclosed; and however undeserving I may be of such encomium and panegyric, the style and manner exhibit a striking proof of your poetical talents; in honor of which, and as a tribute justly due to you, I would have published the poem had I not been apprehensive that, while I only meant to give the world this new instance of your genius, I might have incurred the imputation of vanity. This, and nothing else, determined me not to give it place in the public prints.

If you should ever come to Cambridge, or near head-quarters, I shall be happy to see a person so favored by the Muses, and to whom nature has been so liberal and beneficent in her dispensations.

I am, with great respect, your obedient humble servant.

[From Orderly Book, August 3d, 1776.]

That the troops may have an opportunity of attending public worship, as well as to take some rest after the great fatigue they have gone through, the General in future excuses them from fatigue duty on Sundays, except at the ship-yards, or on special occasions, until further orders. The General is sorry to be informed that the foolish and wicked practice of profane cursing and swearing, a vice heretofore little known in an American army, is growing into fashion; he hopes the officers will, by example as well as influence, endeavor to check it, and that both they and the men will reflect that we can have little hope of the blessing of Heaven on our arms, if we insult it by our impiety and folly; added to this, it is a vice so mean and low, without any temptation, that every man of sense and character detests and despises it.

[From a letter, August 20, 1778.]

The hand of Providence has been so conspicuous in all this, that he must be worse than an infidel, that lacks faith, and more than wicked, that has not gratitude enough to acknowledge his obligations.

[To Dr. John Cochrane, Surgeon and Physician General.]

WEST POINT, 16 August, 1779.

DEAR DOCTOR: I have asked Mrs. Cochrane and Mrs. Livingston to dine with me to-morrow; but am I not in honor bound to apprise them of their fare? As I hate deception, even where the imagination only is concerned, I will. It is needless to premise, that my table is large enough to hold the ladies. Of this they had ocular proof yesterday. To say how it is usually covered is rather more essential; and this shall be the purport of my letter.

Since our arrival at this happy spot, we have had a ham, sometimes a shoulder of bacon, to grace the head of the table; a piece of roast beef adorns the foot; and a dish of beans or greens, almost imperceptible, decorates the centre. When the cook has a mind to cut a figure, which I presume will be the case to-morrow, we have two beef-steak pies, or dishes of crabs, in addition, one on each side of the centre dish, dividing the space and reducing the distance between dish and dish to about six feet, which without them would be near twelve feet apart. Of late he has had the surprising sagacity to discover that apples will make pies;

and it is a question, if in the violence of his efforts, we do not get one of apples, instead of having both of beef-steaks. If the ladies can put up with such entertainment, and will submit to partake of it on plates once tin but now iron (not become so by the labor of scouring), I shall be happy to see them; I am, dear Doctor.

Yours, etc.

[From a letter to Lafayette, in 1783, four years before the adoption of the Federal Constitution, and six years before his inauguration as President.]

We are now an independent people, and have yet to learn political tactics. We are placed among the nations of the earth, and have a character to establish; but how we shall acquit ourselves time must discover. The probability is (at least I fear it), that local or state politics will interfere too much with the more liberal and extensive plan of government which wisdom and foresight freed from the mist of prejudice, would dictate; and that we shall be guilty of many blunders in treading this boundless theatre before we shall have arrived at any perfection in this art; in a word, that the experience which is purchased at the price of difficulties and distress, will alone convince us, that the honor, power, and true interest of this country must be measured by a continental scale, and that every departure therefrom weakens the

Union, and may ultimately break the band which holds us together. To avert these evils, to form a new constitution that will give consistency, stability, and dignity to the Union, and sufficient power to the great council of the nation for general purposes, is a duty incumbent on every man who wishes well to his country, and will meet with my aid as far as it can be rendered in the private walks of life.

[From a letter to Robert Morris.]

MOUNT VERNON, 12 April, 1786.

. . . . . I hope it will not be conceived from these observations that it is my wish to hold the unhappy people who are the subject of this letter, in slavery. I can only say that there is not a man living who wishes more sincerely than I do to see a plan adopted for the abolition of it; but there is only one proper and effectual mode by which it can be accomplished, and that is by legislative authority; and this, as far as my suffrage will go, shall never be wanting. But when slaves who are happy and contented with their present masters are tampered with and seduced to leave them; when masters are taken unawares by these practices; when a conduct of this kind begets discontent on one side and resentment on the other; and when it hapens to fall on a man whose purse will not measure with that of the society, and he loses his property for want of means to defend it; it is oppression in such a case, and not humanity in any, because it introduces more evils than it can cure.

[From a letter to Lafayette.]

MOUNT VERNON, 10 May, 1786.

. . . . . The benevolence of your heart, my dear Marquis, is so conspicuous upon all occasions that I never wonder at any fresh proofs of it; but your late purchase of an estate in the colony of Cayenne, with a view of emancipating the slaves on it, is a generous and noble proof of your humanity. Would to God a like spirit might diffuse itself generally into the minds of the people of this country. But I despair of seeing it. Some petitions were presented to the Assembly at its last session for the abolition of slavery, but they could scarcely obtain a reading. To set the slaves afloat at once would, I really believe, be productive of much inconvenience and mischief; but by degrees it certainly might, and assuredly ought to, be effected, and that, too, by legislative authority.

[From a letter to John F. Mercer.]

September 9, 1786.

. . . . . I never mean, unless some peculiar circumstances should compel me to it, to possess another slave by purchase, it being among my first wishes to see some plan adopted by which slavery in this country may be abolished by law.

[From a letter to Henry Knox, 1787.]

It is among the evils, and perhaps not the smallest of democratical governments, that the people must always *feel* before they will *see*. When this happens they are roused to action. Hence it is that those kinds of government are so slow.

[From a letter to David Stuart.]

PHILADELPHIA, July 1, 1787.

. . . . . Happy, indeed, will it be, if the convention shall be able to recommend such a firm and permanent government for this Union, that all who live under it may be secure in their lives, liberty, and property; and thrice happy would it be if such a recommendation should obtain. Everybody wishes, everybody expects something from the convention; but what will be the final result of its deliberation, the book of fate must disclose. Persuaded I am that the primary cause of all our disorders lies in the different state governments, and in the tenacity of that power which pervades the whole of their systems. Whilst independent sovereignty is so ardently contended for; whilst the local views of each state, and separate interests by which they are too much governed, will not yield to an enlarged scale of politics, incompatibility in the laws of different states, and disrespect to those of the general government, must render the situation of this great country weak, inefficient, and disgraceful. It has already done so, almost to the final dissolution of it.[*]

[From a letter to the Marquis de Chastellux.]

MOUNT VERNON, 25 April, 1788.

MY DEAR MARQUIS: In reading your very friendly and acceptable letter, which came to hand by the last mail, I was, as you may well suppose, not less delighted than surprised to meet the plain American words, "My wife." A wife! Well, my dear Marquis, I can hardly refrain from smiling to find you are caught at last. I saw by the eulogium you often made on the happiness of domestic life in America that you had swallowed the bait, and that you would as surely be taken, one day or another, as that you were a philosopher and a soldier. So your day has at length come. I am glad of it with all my heart and soul. It is quite good enough for you. Now you are well served for coming to fight in favor of the American rebels all the way across the Atlantic

---

[*] The present constitution went into full operation in 1789.

Ocean, by catching that terrible contagion, domestic felicity, which, like the smallpox, or the plague, a man can have only once in his life, because it commonly lasts him (at least, with us in America — I know not how you manage these matters in France) for his whole lifetime. And yet, after all, the worst wish which I can find in my heart to make against Madame de Chastellux and yourself is, that you may neither of you ever get the better of this same domestic felicity during the entire course of your mortal existence.

If so wonderful an event should have occasioned me, my dear Marquis, to write in a strange style, you will understand me as clearly as if I had said, what in plain English is the simple truth, "Do me the justice to believe that I take a heartfelt interest in whatsoever concerns your happiness." And, in this view, I sincerely congratulate you on your auspicious matrimonial connexion. I am happy to find that Madame de Chastellux is so intimately connected with the Duchess of Orleans; as I have always understood that this noble lady was an illustrious example of connubial love, as well as an excellent pattern of virtue in general. . . .

P. S. May 1st. Since writing the above I have been favored with a duplicate of your letter in the handwriting of a lady, and cannot close this without acknowledging my obligations for the flattering postscript of the fair transcriber. In effect, my dear Marquis, the characters of this interpreter of your sentiments are so much fairer than those through which I have been accustomed to decipher them, that I already consider myself as no small gainer by your matrimonial connexion; especially as I hope your amiable amanuensis will not forget sometimes to add a few annotations of her own to your original text.

[From a letter to Lafayette.]

MOUNT VERNON, 28 April, 1788.

. . . . . On the general merits of this proposed Constitution [adopted in the course of this year], I wrote to you some time ago my sentiments pretty freely. . . . . There are other points in which opinions would be more likely to vary; as, for instance, on the ineligibility of the same person for President after he should have served a certain course of years. Guarded so effectually as the proposed Constitution is, in respect to the prevention of bribery and undue influence in the choice of President, I confess I differ widely from Mr. Jefferson and you as to the expediency or necessity of rotation in that appointment. The matter was fully discussed in the Convention, and to my full conviction, though I cannot have time or room to sum up the arguments in this letter. There cannot, in my judgment, be the least danger that the President will by any practicable intrigue ever be able to continue himself one moment in office, much less to perpetuate himself in it, but in the last stage of corrupted morals and political depravity; and even then there is as much danger that any other species of domination would prevail. Though when a people shall have become incapable of governing themselves, and fit for a master, it is of little consequence from what quarter he comes. Under an extended view of this part of the subject, I can see no propriety in precluding ourselves from the services of any man, who, on some great emergency, shall be deemed universally most capable of serving the public.

In answer to the observations you make on the probability of my own election to the presidency,* knowing me as you do, I need only say, that it has no enticing charms and no fascinating allurements for me. However, it might not be decent for me to say I would refuse to accept, or even to speak much about, an appointment which may never take place; for, in so doing, one might possibly incur the application of the moral resulting from that fable in which the fox is represented as inveighing against the sourness of the grapes, because he could not reach them. All that it will be necessary to add, my dear Marquis, in order to show my decided predilection, is, that at my time

* Washington became President in 1789.

of life,* and under my circumstances, the increasing infirmities of nature and the growing love of retirement do not permit me to entertain a wish beyond that of living and dying an honest man on my own farm. Let those follow the pursuits of ambition and fame who have a keener relish for them, or who may have more years in store for the enjoyment.

[From a letter to Lafayette, 1788.]

It is a wonder to me that there should be found a single monarch who does not realize that his own glory and felicity must depend on the prosperity and happiness of his people. How easy is it for a sovereign to do that which shall not only immortalize his name, but attract the blessings of millions.

[From the same.]

You see I am not less enthusiastic than I ever have been, if a belief that peculiar scenes of felicity are reserved for this country is to be denominated enthusiasm. Indeed, I do not believe that Providence has done so much for nothing. It has always been my creed, that we should not be left as a monument to prove "that mankind, under the most favorable circumstances for civil liberty and happiness, are unequal to the task of governing themselves, and therefore made for a master."

* He was now fifty-six.

[From a letter to John Lathrop, 1788.]

How pitiful, in the eye of reason and religion, is that false ambition which desolates the world with fire and sword for the purposes of conquest and fame, when compared to the milder virtues of making our neighbors and our fellow-men as happy as their frail conditions and perishable natures will permit them to be!

[To Charles Pettit, 16 August, 1788.]

. . . . . The great Searcher of hearts is my witness that I have no wish which aspires beyond the humble and happy lot of living and dying a private citizen on my own farm.

[To Count de Moustier, 15 December, 1788.]

. . . . . In whatever country useful inventions are found out, and improvements made, I rejoice in contemplating that those inventions or improvements may, in some way or other, be turned to the common good of mankind.

[To Rev. John Lathrop, 22 June, 1788.]

In truth, it appears to me, that, should the proposed government be generally and harmoniously adopted, it will be a new phenomenon in the political and moral world, and an astonishing victory gained by enlightened reason over brutal force.

[To Benjamin Lincoln, 29 June, 1788.]

. . . . . No one can rejoice more than I do at every step the people of this great country take to preserve the Union, to establish good order and government, and to render the nation happy at home and respectable abroad. No nation upon earth ever had it more in its power to attain these blessings than United America. Wondrously strange, then, and much to be regretted indeed would it be, were we to neglect the means, and to depart from the road, which Providence has pointed out to us so plainly. I cannot believe it will ever come to pass. The great Governor of the universe has led us too long and too far on the road to happiness and glory, to forsake us in the midst of it. By folly and improper conduct, proceeding from a variety of causes, we may now and then get bewildered; but I hope and trust that there is good sense and virtue enough left to recover the right path before we shall be entirely lost.

[To Lafayette, 29 July, 1789.

. . . . . If I know my own heart, nothing short of a conviction of duty will induce me again to take an active part in public affairs; and in that case, if I can form a plan for my own conduct, my endeavors shall be unremittingly exerted, even at the hazard of former fame or present popularity, to extricate my country from the embarrassments in which it is entangled through want of credit; and to establish a general system of policy, which, if pursued, will ensure permanent felicity to the commonwealth. I think I see a path as clear and as direct as a ray of light, which leads to the attainment of that object. Nothing but harmony, honesty, industy, and frugality are necessary to make us a great and happy people.

[To Benjamin Harrison.]
9 March, 1789.

. . . . . Men's minds are as variant as their faces, and, where the motives of their actions are pure, the operation of the former is no more to be imputed to them as a crime, than the appearance of the latter; for both, being the work of nature, are alike unavoidable. Liberality and charity, instead of clamor and misrepresentation, ought to govern in all disputes about matters of importance.

[To Henry Knox.]
MOUNT VERNON, 1 April, 1789.

. . . . . I feel for those members of the new Congress who hitherto have given an unavailing attendance at the theatre of action.* For myself, the delay may be compared to a reprieve; for, in

* New York was now, temporarily, the capital. Washington was inaugurated April 30.

confidence I tell you, (with the world it would obtain little credit,) that my movements to the chair of government will be accompanied by feelings not unlike those of a culprit who is going to his place of execution; so unwilling am I, in the evening of a life nearly consumed in public cares,* to quit a peaceful abode for an ocean of difficulties, without that competency of political skill, abilities and inclination, which are necessary to manage the helm. I am sensible that I am embarking the voice of the people, and a good name of my own, on this voyage; but what returns will be made for them, Heaven alone can foretell. Integrity and firmness are all that I can promise. These, be the voyage long or short, shall never forsake me, although I may be deserted by all men: for of the consolations which are to be derived from these, under any circumstances, the world cannot deprive me.

[From his Inaugural Address.]

April 30, 1789.

FELLOW-CITIZENS OF THE SENATE AND OF THE HOUSE OF REPRESENTATIVES:—

Among the vicissitudes incident to life, no event could have filled me with greater anxieties than that of which the notification was transmitted by your order, and received on the fourteenth day of the present month. On the one hand I was

* He was now fifty-seven years old.

summoned by my country, whose voice I can never hear but with veneration and love, from a retreat which I had chosen with the fondest predilection, and, in my flattering hopes, with an immutable decision, as the asylum of my declining years; a retreat which was rendered every day more necessary, as well as more dear to me, by the addition of habit to inclination, and by frequent interruptions of my health, from the gradual waste committed on it by time. On the other hand, the magnitude and difficulty of the trust to which the voice of my country called me, being sufficient to awaken in the wisest and most experienced of her citizens a distrustful scrutiny into his qualifications, could not but overwhelm with despondence one who, inheriting inferior endowments from nature, and unpractised in the duties of civil administration, ought to be peculiarly conscious of his own deficiencies. In this conflict of emotions, all I dare aver is, that it has been my faithful study to collect my duty from a just appreciation of every circumstance by which it might be affected. All I dare to hope is, that if, in executing this task, I have been too much swayed by a grateful remembrance of former instances, or by an affectionate sensibility to this transcendent proof of the confidence of my fellow-citizens, and have thence too little consulted my incapacity as well as disinclination for the weighty and untried cares before me, my error will be palliated by the motive which misled me, and its consequences be judged by my country with some share of the partiality in which they originated.

[To his nephew George S. Washington.]

MOUNT VERNON, 23 March, 1789.

DEAR GEORGE : — As it is probable that I shall soon be under the necessity of quitting this place, and entering once more into the bustle of public life, in conformity to the voice of my country, and the earnest entreaty of my friends, however contrary it is to my own desires or inclinations, I think it a duty incumbent on me, as your uncle and friend, to give you some advisory hints, which, if properly attended to, will, I conceive, be found very useful to you in regulating your conduct, and giving you respectability, not only at present, but through every period of life.

You have now arrived at that age when you must quit the trifling amusements of a boy, and assume the more dignified manners of a man. At this crisis your conduct will attract the notice of those who are about you; and, as the first impressions are generally the most lasting, your doings now may mark the leading traits of your character through life. It is, therefore, absolutely necessary, if you mean to make any figure upon the stage [of action], that you should take the first steps right. What those steps are, and what general line is to be pursued to lay the foundation of an honorable and happy progress, it is the part of age and experience to point out. This I shall do as far as is in my power, with the utmost cheerfulness, and I trust that your own good sense will show you the necessity of following it.

The first and great object with you at present is, to acquire, by industry and application, such knowledge as your situation enables you to obtain, and as will be useful to you in life. In doing this, two other important advantages will be gained, besides the acquisition of knowledge, namely, a habit of industry, and a disrelish for that profusion of money and dissipation of time which are ever attendant upon idleness. I do not mean by a close application to your studies, that you should never enter into those amusements which are suited to your age and station; they can be made to go hand in hand with each other, and, used in their proper seasons, will ever be found to be a mutual assistance to one another. But what amusements, and where they are to be taken, is the great matter to be attended to. Your own judgment, with the advice of your *real* friends, who may have an opportunity of a personal intercourse with you, can point out the particular manner in which you may best spend your moments of relaxation, better than I can at a distance. One thing, however, I would strongly impress upon you, namely, that when you have leisure to go into company, it should always be of the best kind that the place you are in will afford; by this means you will be constantly improving your manners, and cultivating your mind, while you are relaxing from your books; and good company will ever be found much less expensive than bad. . . . . .

I cannot enjoin too strongly upon you a due observance of economy and frugality, as you well know yourself the present state of your property and finances will not admit of any unnecessary expense. The article of clothing is now one of the chief expenses that you will incur, and in this I fear you are not so economical as you should be. Decency and cleanliness will always be the first objects in the dress of a judicious and sensible man. A conformity to the prevailing fashion in a certain degree is necessary; but it does not from thence follow, that a man should always get a new coat or other clothes upon every trifling change in the mode, when perhaps he has two or three very good ones by him. A person who is anxious to be a leader of the fashion, or one of the first to follow it, will certainly appear in the eyes of judicious men, to have nothing better than a frequent change of dress to recommend him to notice. I would always wish you to appear sufficiently decent to entitle you to admission into any company where you may be; but your own knowledge must convince you, that you should be as little expensive in this respect as you properly can. You should always keep some clothes to wear to church or on particular occasions, which should not be worn every day; this can be done without any additional expense, for whenever it is necessary to get new clothes, those which have been kept for particular occasions will then come in as every-day ones, unless they should be of superior quality to the new. . . . . .

Much more might be said to you as a young man, upon the necessity of paying a due attention to the moral virtues; but this may, perhaps, more properly be the subject of a future letter when you may be about to enter into the world. If you comply with the advice herein given, . . . you will find but few opportunities and little inclination, while you continue at an academy, to enter into those scenes of vice or dissipation which too often present themselves to youth in any place, and particularly in towns. If you are determined to neglect your books, and plunge into extravagance and dissipation, nothing I could now say would prevent it; for you must be employed, and if it is not in pursuit of those things which are profitable, it must be in pursuit of those things which are destructive.

[Letter to General Armstrong.]

March 14, 1792.

I am sure there never was a people who had more reason to acknowledge a divine interposition in their affairs, than those of the United States;* and I should be pained to believe that they have forgotten that agency which was so often manifested during our revolution, or that they failed to consider the omnipotence of that God who is alone able to protect them.

[To the Members of the New Church in Baltimore.]

January, 1793.

We have abundant reason to rejoice that, in this land, the light of truth and reason has triumphed over the power of bigotry and superstition, and that every person may here worship God according to the dictates of his own heart. In this enlightened age, and in this land of equal liberty, it is our boast, that a man's religious tenets will not forfeit the protection of the laws, nor deprive him of the right of attaining and holding the highest offices that are known in the United States.

[From a Speech to both Houses of Congress.]

December 8, 1795.

. . . . . While we indulge the satisfaction which the actual condition of our western borders so well

* Referring to the successful progress of the war.

authorizes, it is necessary that we should not lose sight of an important truth, which continually receives new confirmation; namely, that the provisions heretofore made with a view to the protection of the Indians from the violence of the lawless part of our frontier inhabitants are insufficient. It is demonstrated that these violences can now be perpetrated with impunity; and it can need no argument to prove that, unless the murdering of Indians can be restrained by bringing the murderers to condign punishment, all the exertions of the government to prevent destructive retaliations by the Indians will prove fruitless. The frequent destruction of innocent women and children, who are chiefly the victims of retaliation, must continue to shock humanity, and an enormous expense to drain the treasury of the Union.

To enforce upon the Indians the observance of justice it is indispensable that there should be competent means of rendering justice to them. . . . I add, with pleasure, that the probability even of their civilization is not diminished by the experiments which have been thus far made under the auspices of government. The accomplishment of this work, if practicable, will reflect undecaying lustre on our national character, and administer the most grateful consolation that virtuous minds can know.

[From the Farewell Address to the people of the United States, September 17, 1796.]

Of all the dispositions and habits which lead to political prosperity, religion and morality are indispensable supports. In vain would that man claim the tribute of patriotism who should labor to subvert these great pillars of human happiness, these firmest props of the duties of men and citizens. The mere politician, equally with the pious man, ought to respect and to cherish them. A volume could not trace all their connections with private and public felicity. . . . And let us, with caution, indulge the supposition that morality can be maintained without religion. Whatever may be conceded to the influence of refined education on minds of peculiar structure, reason and experience both forbid us to expect that national morality can prevail in exclusion of religious principle.

JOHN ADAMS.

BORN, 1735; DIED, 1826, AGED 91. — GRADUATED AT HARVARD COLLEGE, 1755. — TAUGHT A GRAMMAR SCHOOL, 1755. — BEGAN PRACTICE OF LAW, 1758. — REPRESENTATIVE IN THE GENERAL COURT OF MASSACHUSETTS, 1770. — DELEGATE TO THE CONGRESS OF 1774. — TO THE CONTINENTAL CONGRESS, 1775. — PRESIDENT OF BOARD OF WAR AND ORDINANCE, 1776. — COMMISSIONER TO FRANCE, 1777. — MEMBER OF CONVENTION TO FRAME A CONSTITUTION FOR MASSACHUSETTS, 1778. — MINISTER TO GREAT BRITAIN, 1779 — MINISTER TO HOLLAND, 1780. — MINISTER TO GREAT BRITAIN, 1785. — MEMBER OF THE CONTINENTAL CONGRESS, 1788. — VICE-PRESIDENT, 1789. — RE-ELECTED, 1792. — PRESIDENT, 1797-1801.

[From a letter to Mrs. Adams, at Braintree.]

BOSTON, 12 May, 1774.

..... WE live, my dear soul, in an age of trial. What will be the consequence, I know not. The town of Boston, for aught I can see, must suffer martyrdom. It must expire. And our principal consolation is, that it dies in a noble cause — the cause of truth, of virtue, of liberty, and of humanity, and thus it will probably have a glorious resurrection to greater wealth, splendor, and power than ever.

Let me know what is best for me to do. It is expensive keeping a family here, and there is no prospect of any business in my way in this town this whole summer. I don't receive a shilling a week. We must contrive as many ways as we can to save expenses: for we may have calls to contribute very largely, in proportion to our circumstances, to prevent other very honest, worthy people from suffering for want, besides our own loss in point of business and profit.

Don't imagine from all this that I am in the dumps. Far otherwise. I can truly say that I have felt more spirits and activity since the arrival of this news than I had done before for years. I look upon this as the last effort of Lord North's despair, and he will as surely be defeated in it as he was in the project of the tea.

[From a letter to James Waterhouse.]

It has been, in all times, the artifice of despotism and superstition to nip liberty, truth, virtue, and religion in the bud, by cutting off the heads of all who dared to show regard to either. But when a process so summary could not be effected, the next trick was to blast the character of every rising genius who excited their jealousy, by propagating lies and slanders to destroy his influence.

[From a letter to J. H. Tiffany.]

I would define liberty to be a power to do as we would be done by.

I advise every young man to keep school. I acquired more knowledge of human nature while I kept school than while I was at the bar, than while I was in the world of politics or at the Courts of Europe. It is the best method of acquiring patience, self-command, and a knowledge of charter. JOHN ADAMS.

[Letter to Mrs. Adams, at Braintree. Reference is had to serious interruptions in his legal business, in Boston, from his political principles.]

YORK [MAINE], 1 July, 1774.

I am so idle that I have not an easy moment without my pen is in my hand. My time [at home] might have been improved to some purpose in mowing grass, raking hay, or hoeing corn, weeding carrots, picking or shelling pease. Much better should I have been employed in schooling my children, in teaching them to write, cipher, Latin, French, English, and Greek.

I sometimes think I must come to this — to be the foreman upon my own farm, and the schoolmaster to my own children. I confess myself to be full of fears that the ministry and their friends and instruments will prevail, and crush the cause and friends of liberty. The minds of that party are so filled with prejudices against me that they will take all advantages, and do me all the damage they can. These thoughts have their turns in my mind, but in general my hopes are predominant.

Dr. Gardiner arrived here to-day from Boston, brings us news of a battle at the town meeting, between Whigs and Tories, in which the Whigs, after a day and a half's obstinate engagement, were finally victorious by two to one. He says the Tories are preparing a flaming protest.

I am determined to be cool, if I can. I have suffered such torments in my mind heretofore as have almost overpowered my constitution, without any advantage. And now I will laugh and be easy if I can, let the contest of parties terminate as it will; nay, whether I stand high or low in the estimation of the world, so long as I keep a conscience void of offence towards God and man. And this I am determined, by the will of God, to do, let what will become of me or mine, my country or the world.

I shall arouse myself ere long, I believe, and exert an industry, a frugality, a hard labor, that will serve my family, if I can't serve my country. I will not lie down in despair. If I cannot serve my children by the law, I will serve them by agriculture, by trade, by some way or other. I thank God I have a head, and heart, and hands, which if once fully exerted altogether, will succeed in the world as well as those of the mean-spirited, low-minded, fawning, obsequious scoundrels who have long hoped that my integrity would be an obstacle in my way, and enable them to outstrip me in the race. But what I want in comparison of them of villany and servility, I will make up in industry and capacity. If I don't, they shall laugh and triumph. I will not willingly see blockheads, whom I have a right to despise, elevated above me and insolently triumphing over me. Nor shall knavery, through any negligence of mine, get the better of honesty, nor ignorance of knowledge, nor folly of wisdom, nor vice of virtue.

I must entreat you, my dear partner in all the joys and sorrows, prosperity and adversity of my life, to take a part with me in the struggle. I pray God for your health — entreat you to rouse your whole attention to the family, the stock, the farm, the dairy. Let every article of expense which can possibly be spared be retrenched; keep the hands attentive to their business, and the most prudent measures of every kind be adopted and pursued with alacrity and spirit.

[To Mrs. Adams, at Braintree; written while on his way to Philadelphia, as a delegate to Congress.]

PRINCETON, NEW JERSEY, 28 August, 1774.

I received your kind letter at New York, and it is not easy for you to imagine the pleasure it has given me. I have not found a single opportunity to write you since I left Boston, excepting by the post, and I don't choose to write by that conveyance for fear of foul play. But as we are now within forty-two miles of Philadelphia, I hope there to find some private hand by which I can convey this.

The particulars of our journey I must reserve, to be communicated after my return. It would take a volume to describe the whole. It has been, upon the whole, an agreeable jaunt. We have had opportunities to see the world, and to form acquaintance with the most eminent and famous men in the several colonies we have passed through. We have been treated with unbounded civility, complaisance, and respect. We yesterday visited Nassau Hall College, and were politely treated by the scholars, tutors, professors, and president, whom we are this day to hear preach. To-morrow we reach the theatre of action. God Almighty grant wisdom and virtue sufficient for the high trust that is devolved upon us. The spirit of the people, wherever we have been, seems to be very favorable. They universally consider our cause as their own, and express the firmest resolution to abide by the determination of the Congress.

I am anxious for our perplexed, distressed province; hope they will be directed into the right path. Let me entreat you, my dear, to make yourself as easy and quiet as possible. Resignation to the will of heaven is our only resource in such dangerous times. Prudence and caution should be our guides. I have the strongest hopes that we shall yet see a clearer sky and better times.

Remember my tender love to little Abby; tell her she must write me a letter, and inclose it in the next you send. I am charmed with your amusement with our little Johnny.* Tell him I am glad to hear he is so good a boy as to read to his mamma for her entertainment, and to keep himself out of the company of rude children. Tell him I hope to hear a good account of his accidence and nomenclature when I return. . . . Your account of the rain refreshed me. I hope our husbandry is prudently and industriously managed. Frugality must be our support. Our expenses in this journey will be very great. Our only [recompense will] be the consolatory reflection that we toil, spend our time, and [encounter] dangers for the public good, — happy, indeed, if we do any good.

The education of our children is never out of my mind.* Train them to virtue. Habituate them to industry, activity, and spirit. Make them consider every vice as shameful and unmanly. Fire them with ambition to be useful. Make them disdain to be destitute of any useful or ornamental knowledge or accomplishment. Fix their ambition upon great and solid objects, and their contempt upon little, frivolous, and useless ones. It is time, my dear, for you to begin to teach them French. . Every decency, grace, and honesty should be inculcated upon them. . . . I am, with the tenderest affection and concern,

Your wandering
JOHN ADAMS.

* John Quincy Adams.

[Letter to Mrs. Adams, at Braintree.]

PHILADELPHIA, 16 September, 1774.

Having a leisure moment while the Congress is assembling, I gladly embrace it to write you a line.

When the Congress first met, Mr. Cushing made a motion that it should be opened with prayer. It was opposed by Mr. Jay of New York, and Mr. Rutledge of South Carolina, because we were so divided in religious sentiments, — some Episcopalians, some Quakers, some Anabaptists, some Presbyterians, and some Congregationalists, — that we could not join in the same act of worship. Mr. Samuel Adams arose and said he was no bigot, and could hear a prayer from a gentleman of piety and virtue, who was at the same time a friend to his country. He was a stranger in Philadelphia, but had heard that Mr. Duché (Dushay, they pronounce it) deserved that character, and therefore he moved that Mr. Duché, an Episcopal clergyman, might be desired to read prayers to the Congress to-morrow morning. The motion was seconded, and passed in the affirmative. Mr. Randolph, our president, waited on Mr. Duché, and received for answer that if his health would permit he certainly would. Accordingly, next morning, he appeared with his clerk, and in his pontificals, and read several prayers in the established form; and then read the Collect for the seventh day of September, which was the thirty-fifth psalm. You must remember that this was the next morning after we heard the horrible rumor of the cannonade of Boston. I never saw a greater effect upon an audience. It seemed as if heaven had ordained that psalm to be read on that morning.

After this, Mr. Duché, unexpected to everybody, struck out into an extemporary prayer, which filled the bosom of every man present. I must confess I never heard a better prayer, or one so well pronounced. Episcopalian as he is, Dr. Cooper* himself never prayed with such fervor, such ardor, such earnestness and pathos, and in language so eloquent and sublime, — for America, for the Congress, for the Province of Massachusetts Bay, and especially the town of Boston. It has had an excellent effect upon everybody here. I must beg you to read that psalm. If there was any faith in the Sortes Biblicæ, it would be thought providential.

It will amuse your friends to read this letter and the thirty-fifth psalm to them. Read it to your father and Mr. Wibird. I wonder what our Braintree churchmen will think of this! Mr. Duché is one of the most ingenious men, and best characters, and greatest orators in the Episcopal

---

* Pastor of the Brattle Square church, Boston, and a zealous patriot.

order, upon the continent, yet a zealous friend of liberty and his country.*

I long to see my dear family. God bless, preserve, and prosper it. Adieu.

[From a letter to Mrs. Adams.]

7 October, 1775.

. . . The situation of things is so alarming, that it is our duty to prepare our minds and hearts for every event, even the worst. From my earliest entrance into life, I have been engaged in the public cause of America, and from first to last, I have had upon my mind a strong impression that things would be wrought up to their present crisis. I saw, from the beginning, that the controversy was of such a nature that it never would be settled, and every day convinces me more and more. This has been the source of all the disquietude of my life. It has lain down and risen up with me these twelve years. The thought that we might be driven to the sad necessity of breaking our connection with Great Britain, exclusive of the carnage and destruction which, it was easy to see, must attend the separation, always gave me a great deal of grief. And even now, I would cheerfully retire from public life forever, renounce

* Three years later, Mr. Adams wrote: "Mr. Duché, I am sorry to inform you, has turned out an apostate and traitor. I pity his weakness, and detest his wickedness."

all chance for profits or honors from the public, nay, I would cheerfully contribute my little property to obtain peace and liberty. But all these must go, and my life too, before I can surrender the right of my country to a free constitution. I dare not consent to it. I should be the most miserable of mortals ever after, whatever honors or emoluments might surround me.

[Letter to George Wythe.]

January, 1776.

You and I, my dear friend, have been sent into life at a time when 'the greatest lawgivers of antiquity would have wished to live. How few of the human race have ever enjoyed an opportunity of making an election of government more than of air, soil, or climate, for themselves or their children? When, before the present epocha, had three millions of people full power and a fair opportunity to form and establish the wisest and happiest government that human wisdom can contrive?

Genius, in a general, is oftener an instrument of divine vengeance than a guardian angel.

[To Mrs. Adams.]

PHILADELPHIA, 23 April, 1776.

This is St. George's Day. . . . The natives of Old England in this city heretofore formed a society, which they called St. George's Club. Upon the 23d of April, annually, they had a great feast. But the Tories and politics have made a schism in the society, so that one part of them are to meet and dine at the City Tavern, and the other at the Bunch of Grapes. Israel Jacobs and a third party go out of town. One set are stanch Americans, another stanch Britons, and a third half-way men, neutral beings, moderate men, prudent folks; for such is the division among men upon all occasions and every question. This is the account which I have from my barber, who is one of the society, and zealous on the side of America.

This curious character of a barber I have a great inclination to draw for your amusement. He is a little, dapper fellow, short and small, but active and lively. A tongue as voluble and fluent as you please, wit at will, and a memory or an invention which never leaves him at a loss for a story to tell you for your entertainment. He has seen great company. He has dressed hair and shaved faces at Bath, and at court. He is acquainted with several of the nobility and gentry, particularly Sir William Meredith. He married a girl, the daughter of a Quaker in this place, of whom he tells many droll stories. He is a sergeant in one of the companies of some battalion or other here. He frequents, of evenings, a beer-house kept by one Weaver, in the city, where he has many curious disputes and adventures, and meets many odd characters.

I believe you will think me very idle to write you so trifling a letter, upon so uninteresting a subject, at a time when my country is fighting *pro aris et focis*. But I assure you I am glad to chat with this barber while he is shaving and combing me, and to divert myself from less agreeable thoughts. He is so sprightly and good humored that he contributes more than I could have imagined to my comfort in this life. Burne has prepared a string of toasts for the club to drink to-day at Israel's: "The Thirteen United Colonies," "The Free and Independent States of America," "The Congress for the time being," "The American Army and Navy," "The Governor and Council of South Carolina," etc., etc., etc. "A happy election for the Whigs on the 1st of May," etc.

PHILADELPHIA, 23 April, 1777.

My barber has just left the chamber. The following curious dialogue was the amusement during the gay moments of shaving:

"Well, Burne, what is the lie of the day?"

"Sir, Mr. —— told me that a privateer from Baltimore has taken two valuable prizes with sixteen guns each. I can scarcely believe it."

"Have you heard of the success of the *Rattlesnake*, of Philadelphia, and the *Sturdy Beggar*, of Maryland, Mr. Burne? These two privateers have taken eleven prizes, and sent them into the

West India Islands; nine transports and two Guinea-men."

"Confound the ill luck, sir; I was going to sea myself on board the *Rattlesnake*, and my wife fell a yelping. These wives are queer things. I told her I wondered she had no more ambition. 'Now,' says I, 'when you walk the streets, and anybody asks who that is, the answer is "*Burne the barber's wife*." Should you not be better pleased to hear it said, "*That is Captain Burne's lady*, the captain of marines on board the *Rattlesnake?*"' 'Oh,' says she, 'I would rather be called Burne the barber's wife than Captain Burne's widow. I don't desire to live better than you maintain me, my dear.' So it is, Sir, by this sweet, honey language, I am choused out of my prizes, and must go on with my soap and razors and pincers and combs. I wish she had my ambition."

If this letter be intercepted by the Tories, they will get a booty. Let them enjoy it. If some of their wives had been as tender and discreet as the barber's, their husbands' ambition would not have led them into so many salt-ponds. What an *ignis fatuus* this ambition is! How few of either sex have arrived at Mrs. Burne's pitch of moderation, and are able to say, "I don't desire to live better, and had rather be the barber's wife than the captain's widow!" Quite smart, I think, as well as philosophical.

[From a letter to Mrs. Adams.]

BALTIMORE, 15 Feb. 1777.

..... We have, (in Congress,) from New Hampshire, a Colonel Thornton, a physician by profession, a man of humor. He has a large budget of droll stories, with which he entertains company perpetually. I heard, about twenty, or five-and-twenty, years ago, a story of a physician in Londonderry, who accidentally met with one of our New England enthusiasts, called exhorters. The fanatic soon began to examine the doctor concerning the articles of his faith, and what he thought of original sin. "Why," says the doctor, "I satisfy myself about it in this manner. Either original sin is divisible or indivisible. If it is divisible, every descendant of Adam and Eve must have a part, and the share which falls to each individual at this day is so small a particle that I think it is not worth considering. If indivisible, then the whole quantity must have descended in a right line, and must now be possessed by one person only; and the chances are millions and millions and millions to one that that person is now in Asia or Africa, and that I have nothing to do with it." I told Thornton the story, and that I suspected him to be the man. He said he was. He belongs to Londonderry.

[To Mrs. Adams.]

PHILADELPHIA, 20 August, 1777.

This day completes three years since I stepped into the coach at Mr. Cushing's door, in Boston, to go to Philadelphia in quest of adventures; and adventures I have found. I feel an inclination sometimes to write the history of these last three years, in imitation of Thucydides. There is a striking resemblance in several particulars between the Peloponnesian and the American war. The real motive to the former was a jealousy of the growing power of Athens by sea and land. The genuine motive to the latter was a similar jealousy of the growing power of America. The true causes which incite to war are seldom professed or acknowledged.

We are now upon a full sea; when we shall arrive at a safe harbor, no mariner has skill and experience enough to foretell. But by the favor of Heaven we shall make a prosperous voyage, after all the storms and shoals are passed.

[To Patrick Henry.]

PHILADELPHIA, 3 June, 1776.

..... The dons, the bashaws, the grandees, the patricians, the sachems, the nabobs, call them by what name you please, sigh, and groan, and fret, and sometimes stamp, and foam, and curse, but all in vain. The decree is gone forth, and it cannot be recalled, that a more equal liberty than has prevailed in other parts of the earth, must be established in America. That exuberance of pride which has produced an insolent domination in a few, a very few, opulent, monopolizing families, will be brought down nearer to the confines of reason and moderation, than they have been used to. This is all the evil which they themselves will endure. It will do them good in this world, and in every other. For pride was not made for man, only as a tormentor.

3 July, 1776.

..... But the day is past. The second day * of July, 1776, will be the most memorable epocha in the history of America. I am apt to believe that it will be celebrated by succeeding generations as a great anniversary festival. It ought to be commemorated, as the day of deliverance, by solemn acts of devotion to Almighty God. It ought to be solemnized with pomp and parade, with shows, games, sports, guns, bells, bonfires, and illuminations, from one end of this continent to another, from this time forward, for evermore.

You will think me transported with enthusiasm, but I am not. I am well aware of the toil, and blood, and treasure, that it will cost us to maintain

---

* The Declaration of Independence was agreed to on the second day of July, but not formally approved and signed till the fourth.

this declaration, and support and defend these states. Yet, through all the gloom, I can see the rays of ravishing light and glory. I can see that the end is worth more than all the means, and that posterity will triumph in that day's transactions, even although we should rue it, which I trust in God we shall not.

[To Mrs. Adams.]

PASSY, 3 June, 1778.

On the 13th of February I left you.* It is now the 3d of June, and I have not received a line nor heard a word, directly or indirectly, concerning you, since my departure. This is a situation of mind in which I never was before, and I assure you I feel a great deal of anxiety at it; yet I do not wonder at it, because I suppose few vessels have sailed from Boston since ours. . . . . It would be useless to attempt a description of this country. It is one great garden. Nature and art have conspired to render everything here delightful. . . . . There is so much danger that my letter may fall into malicious hands, that I should not choose to be too free in my observations upon the customs and manners of this people. But thus much I may say with truth and without offence,

* He had been appointed Commissioner at the Court of Versailles, to act in conjunction with Dr. Franklin and Arthur Lee.

that there is no people in the world who take so much pains to please, nor any whose endeavors in this way have more success. Their acts and manners, taste and language, are more respected in Europe than those of any other nation. Luxury, dissipation, and effeminacy are pretty nearly of the same degree of excess here and in every other part of Europe. The great cardinal virtue of temperance, however, I believe flourishes here more than in any other part of Europe.

My dear countrymen! how shall I persuade you to avoid the plague of Europe? Luxury has as many and as bewitching charms on your side of the ocean as on this; and luxury, wherever she goes, effaces from human nature the image of the Divinity. If I had power I would forever banish and exclude from America all gold, silver, precious stones, alabaster, marble, silk, velvet, and lace.

Oh, the tyrant! the American ladies would say. What! Ay, my dear girls, these passions of yours, which are so easily alarmed, and others of my own sex which are exactly like them, have done and will do the work of tyrants in all ages. Tyrants different from me, whose power has banished, not gold indeed, but other things of greater value, wisdom, virtue, and liberty.

My son * and servant are well. I am, with an ardor that words have not power to express, yours.

* John Quincy.

Paris, Feb., 1780.

I have the honor to be lodging here with no less a personage than the Prince of Hesse-Cassel, who is here upon a visit. We occupy different apartments in the same house, and have no intercourse with each other; but some wags are of opinion that if I were authorized to open a negotiation with him, I might obtain from him as many troops to fight on our side of the question as he has already hired to the English *against us!*

[To Mrs. Adams.]

Don't disturb yourself about any malicious attempts to injure me in the estimation of my countrymen. Let them take their course, and go the length of their tether. They will never hurt your husband, whose character is fortified with a shield of innocence and honor ten thousand fold stronger than brass or iron. The contemptible essays, made by you know whom, will only tend to their own confusion. My letters have shown them their own ignorance, a sight they could not bear. Say as little about it as I do. I laugh, and will laugh before all posterity at their impotent rage and envy.

[To Mrs. Adams, June 9, 1783, referring to French intrigues, difficulties in America, and opposition in England to a treaty of peace with Great Britain.]

I am weary, worn, and disgusted to death. I had rather chop wood, dig ditches, and make fence upon my poor little farm. Alas, poor farm! and poorer family! what have you lost that your country might be free! and that others might catch fire and hunt deer and bears at their ease!

There will be as few of the tears of gratitude, or the smiles of admiration, or of the sighs of pity for us, as for the army. But all this should not hinder me from going over the same scenes again, upon the same occasion — scenes which I would not encounter for all the wealth, pomp, and power of the world. Boys! if you ever say one word, or utter one complaint, I will disinherit you. Work! you rogues, and be free. You will never have so hard work to do as papa has had. Daughter! get you an honest man for a husband, and keep him honest. No matter whether he is rich, provided he be independent. Regard the honor and the moral character of the man more than all circumstances. Think of no other greatness but that of the soul, no other riches but those of the heart.

[To Secretary Livingston; Paris, 23 June, 1783.]

Wise statesmen, like able artists of every kind, study nature, and their works are perfect in proportion as they conform to her laws.

[To Count Sarsfield, 1785. Dated, Grosvenor Square.]

I believe this many-headed beast, the people, will some time or other, have wit enough to throw their riders; and, if they should, they will put an end to an abundance of tricks, with which they are now curbed and bitted, whipped and spurred.

[To Thomas Jefferson, 1813.]

God has infinite wisdom, goodness, and power; he created the universe; his duration is eternal, *a parte ante and a parte post.* His presence is as extensive as space. What is space? An infinite spherical *vacuum.* He created this speck of dirt and the human species for his glory; and with the deliberate design of making nine-tenths of our species miserable forever for his glory. This is the doctrine of Christian theologians in general, ten to one. Now, my friend, can prophecies or miracles convince you or me that infinite benevolence, wisdom, and power created, and preserves for a time, innumerable millions, to make them miserable forever for his own glory? Wretch! What is his glory? Is he ambitious? Does he want promotion? Is he vain, tickled with adulation, exulting and triumphing in his power and the sweetness of his vengeance?

Pardon me, my Maker, for these awful questions. My answer to them is always ready. I believe no such things. My adoration of the author of the universe is too profound and too sincere. The love of God and his creation — delight, joy, triumph, exultation in my own existence — though but an atom, a *molecule organique* of the universe, are my religion.

[To Thomas Jefferson, 1813.]

I have examined all [religions] as well as my narrow sphere, my straitened means, and my busy life would allow me; and the result is that the Bible is the best book in the world. It contains more of my little philosophy than all the libraries I have seen; and such parts as I cannot reconcile to my little philosophy I postpone for future investigation.

[To Thomas Jefferson, 1813.]

It appears to me that the great principle of the Hebrews was the fear of God; that of the Gentiles, honor the gods; that of Christians, the *love* of God.

[To Thomas Jefferson, 1813.]

The human understanding is a revelation from its Maker, which can never be disputed or doubted.

[To Dr. J. Morse.]

Quincy, 22 December, 1815.

..... In the course of these ten years [from 1765 to 1775], they [the British ministry] formed and organized and drilled and disciplined a party in favor of Great Britain, and they seduced and deluded nearly one third of the people of the colonies. . . . Let me confine myself to Massachusetts. . . . Daniel Leonard was the only child of Colonel Ephraim Leonard, of Norton. He was a scholar, a lawyer, and an orator, according to the standard of those days. As a member of the House of Representatives, even down to the year 1770, he made the most ardent speeches which were delivered in that House against Great Britain, and in favor of the colonies. His popularity became alarming. The two sagacious spirits, Hutchinson and Sewall, soon penetrated his character, of which, indeed, he had exhibited very visible proofs. He had married a daughter of Mr. Hammock, who had left her a portion, as it was thought, in that day. He wore a broad gold lace round the rim of his hat, he had made his cloak glitter with laces still broader, he had set up his chariot and pair, and constantly travelled in it from Taunton to Boston. This made the world stare; it was a novelty. Not another lawyer in the province, attorney or barrister, of whatever age, reputation, rank, or station, presumed to ride in a coach or a chariot. The discerning ones soon perceived that wealth and power must have charms to a heart that delighted in so much finery, and indulged in such unusual expense. Such marks could not escape the vigilant eyes of the two archtempters, Hutchinson and Sewall, who had more art, insinuation, and address than all the rest of their party. Poor Daniel was beset with great zeal for his conversion. Hutchinson sent for him, courted him with the ardor of a lover, reasoned with him, flattered him, overawed him, frightened him, invited him to come frequently to his house. As I was intimate with Mr. Leonard during the whole of this process, I had the substance of this information from his own mouth, was a witness to the progress of the impression made upon him, and to many of the labors and struggles of his mind, between his interest or his vanity, and his duty.

[Letter to William Tudor.]

QUINCY, 24 January, 1817.

Bernard, Hutchinson, Oliver, the commissioners of the customs, and their satellites, had an espionage as inquisitive, as zealous, and as faithful as that in France, before, during, or since the revolution, by which the Tories were betttcr informed of the anecdote which I am about to relate to you, than the Whigs were in general. . . .

The public had been long alarmed with rumors and predictions that the king, that is, the ministry, would take into their own hands the payment of the salaries of the judges of the Supreme Court. The people would not believe it; the most thinking men dreaded it. They said, "With an executive authority in a governor possessed of an absolute negative on all the acts of the legislature, and the judges dependent only on the crown for salaries, as well as their commissions, what protection have we? We may as well abolish all limitations, and resign our lives and liberties at once to the will of a prime-minister at St. James's. You remember the controversy that General Brattle excited concerning the tenor of the judges' commissions, and the universal anxiety that then prevailed on the subject. The despatches at length arrived, and expectation was raised to its highest pitch of exultation and triumph on one side, and of grief, terror, degradation, and despondency on the other. The legislature assembled, and the governor communicated to the two houses his Majesty's commands.

It happened that I was invited to dine that day with Samuel Winthrop, an excellent character, and a predecessor in the respectable office you now hold in the Supreme Court. Arrived at his house in New Boston, I found it full of counsellors, and representatives, and clergy. Such a group of melancholy countenances I had rarely, if ever, seen. No conversation, except some insipid observations on the weather, till the great topic of the day was introduced, and at the same time a summons to the feast. All harps upon the willow, we sat down to a *triste* dinner, which all the delicacies before us could not enliven. A few glasses of good wine, however, in time brought up some spirit, and the conversation assumed a little vigor, but it was the energy of grief, complaint, and despair. All expressed their detestation and horror of the insidious ministerial plot, but all agreed that it was irremediable. There was no means or mode of opposing or resisting it. Indignation and despair, too, boiled in my breast as ardently as in any of them, though, as the company were so much superior to me in age and station, I had not said anything; but Dr. Winthrop, the professor, then of the council, observing my silence, and perhaps my countenance, said: "Mr. Adams, what is your opinion? Can you think of any way of escaping this snare!" My answer was: "No, sir; I am as much at a loss as any of the company. I agree with all the gentlemen, that petitions and remonstrances to king or parliament will be ineffectual. Nothing but force will succeed; but I would try one project before I had recourse to the last reason and fitness of things." The company cried out, almost or quite together, "What project is that? What would you do?" *A.* "I would impeach the judges." "Impeach the judges? How? Where? Who *can* impeach them?" *A.* "The House of Representatives," "The House of Representatives? Before whom? Before the House of Lords in England?" *A.* "No; surely. You might as well impeach them before Lord North alone." "Where, then?" *A.* "Before the governor and council." "Is there any precedent for that?" *A.* "If there is not, it is now high time that a precedent should be set." "The governor and council will not receive the impeachment." *A.* "I know that very well, but the record of it will stand upon the journals, be published in pamphlets and newspapers, and perhaps make the judges repent of their salaries, and decline them; perhaps make it too troublesome to hold them." "What right had we to impeach anybody?" *A.* "Our House of Representatives have the same right to impeach as the House of Commons has in England, and our governor and council have the same right and duty to receive and hear impeachments as the king and House of Lords have in parliament. If the governor and council would not do their duty, that would not be the fault of the people; their representatives ought nevertheless to do theirs." Some of the company said the idea was so new to them that they wished I would show them some reason for my opinion that we had the right. I repeated to them the clause of the charter which I relied on, the constant practice in England, and the necessity of such a power and practice in every free government.

The company dispersed, and I went home. Dr. Cooper and others were excellent hands to spread a rumor, and before nine o'clock half the town, and most of the members of the general court, had in their heads the idea of an impeachment. The next morning, early, Major Hawley, of Northampton, came to my house under great concern, and said he heard that I had yesterday, in a public company, suggested a thought of impeaching the judges; that report had got about, and had excited some uneasiness, and he desired to know my meaning. I invited him into my office, opened the charter, and requested him to read the paragraphs that I had marked. I then produced to him that volume of Selden's works which contains his treatise on Judicature and Parliament; other authorities in law were produced to him, and the State Trials, and a profusion of impeachments, with which that work abounds. Major Hawley, who was one of the best men in the province, and one of the ablest lawyers and best speakers in the legislature, was struck with surprise. He said, "I know not what to think. This is in a manner all new to me. I must think of it." You, Mr. Tudor, will not wonder at Major Hawley's embarrassment, if you recollect that my copy of Selden's works, of the State Trials, and the Statutes at Large, were the only ones in Boston at that time. . . .

My strange brother, Robert Treat Paine, came to me with grief and terror in his face and manners. He said he had heard that I talked of an impeachment of the judges; that it had excited a great deal of conversation, and that it seemed to prevail, and that, according to all appearances, it would be brought forward in the House; he was very uneasy about it, etc. I knew the man. Instead of entering into particular conversation with him, I took him into my office, and showed him all that I had before shown to Major Hawley. He had not patience to read much, and went away with the same anxious brow. This man had an upright heart, an abundance of wit, and, upon the whole, a deeper policy than I had. He soon found, however, that the impeachment was popular, and would prevail, and prudently acquiesced. Major Hawley, always conscientious, always deliberate, always cautious, had not slept soundly. What were his dreams about impeachment, I know not. But this I know; he drove away to Cambridge, to consult Judge Trowbridge, and appealed to his conscience. The charter was called for; Selden and the State Trials were quoted. Trowbridge said to him what I had said before, that "the power of impeachment was essential to a free government; that the charter had given it to our House of Representatives as clearly as the Constitution, in the common law or immemorial usage, had given it to the House of Commons in England." This was all he could say, though he lamented the occasion of it.

Major Hawley returned full in the faith. An impeachment was voted, a committee appointed to prepare articles. But Major Hawley insisted upon it in private with the committee that they should consult me, and take my advice upon every article before they reported it to the House. Such was the state of parties at that moment, that the patriots could carry nothing in the House without the support of Major Hawley. The committee very politely requested me to meet them. To avoid all questions about time and place, I invited them to my house in the evening. They came, and produced a draft of articles, which were examined, considered, and discussed, article by article, and paragraph by paragraph. I objected to some, and proposed alterations in others. Sometimes succeeded, and often failed. . . . The result, upon the whole, was not satisfactory to me in all points, but I was not responsible.

Next day I met Ben Gridley, who accosted me in his pompous style, "Brother Adams, you keep late hours! Last night I saw a host of senators vomit forth from your door after midnight." Now, brother Tudor, judge you whether this whole transaction was not as well known at head-quarters, and better too, than in the House of Representatives. This confidence of Major Hawley in me became an object of jealousy to the patriots. Not only Mr. Paine, but Mr. [Samuel] Adams and Mr. Hancock, could not refrain from expressing, at times, their feeling of it. But they could do nothing without Major Hawley. These little passions, of which even the apostles could not wholly divest themselves, have, in all ages, been small causes of great events; too small, indeed, to be described by historians, or even known to them, or suspected by them.

These articles were reported to the House, discussed, accepted; the impeachment voted, and sent up in form to the governor and council; rejected, of course, as everybody knew beforehand that it would be; but it remained on the journals of the House, was printed in the newspapers, and went abroad into the world. And what were the consequences? Chief Justice Oliver and his Superior Court, your Supreme Judicial Court, commenced their regular circuit.

The Chief Justice opened his court as usual. Grand jurors and petit jurors refused to take their oaths. They never, as I believe, could prevail on one juror to take the oath. I attended at the bar in two counties, and I heard grand jurors and petit jurors say to Chief Justice Oliver, to his face, "The chief justice of this court stands impeached by the representatives of the people of high crimes and misdemeanors, and of a conspiracy against the charter privileges of the people. I therefore cannot serve as juror, or take the oath." The cool, calm, sedate intrepidity with which these honest freeholders went through this fiery trial filled my eyes and my heart.

In one word, the royal government was from that moment laid prostrate in the dust, and has never since revived in substance, though a dark shadow of the hobgoblin haunts me at times to this day.

[From a letter to William Tudor, 1817.]

. . . . . The bloody rencounter between the citizens and the soldiers on the 5th of March, 1770, produced a tremendous sensation throughout the town and country. The people assembled first at Faneuil Hall, and adjourned to the Old South Church, to the number, as was conjectured, of ten or twelve thousand men, among whom were the most virtuous, substantial, independent, disinterested, and intelligent citizens. They formed themselves into a regular deliberative body, chose their moderator and secretary, entered into discussions, deliberations, and debates, adopted resolutions, appointed committees. . . . A remonstrance to the governor was ordained, and a demand that the regular troops should be removed from the town. A committee was appointed to present this remonstrance, of which Samuel Adams was the chairman. . . . In his common appearance he was a plain, simple, decent citizen, of middling stature, dress, and manners. He had an exquisite ear for music, and a charming voice, when he pleased to exert it. Yet his ordinary speeches in town meetings, in the House of Representatives, and in Congress, exhibited nothing extraordinary; but upon great occasions, when his deeper feelings were excited, he erected himself, or rather Nature seemed to erect him, without the smallest symptom of affectation, into an upright dignity and gesture, and gave a harmony to his voice which made a strong impression on spectators and auditors, — the more lasting for the purity, correctness, and nervous elegance of his style.

This was a delicate and a dangerous crisis. The question in the last resort was, whether the town of Boston should become a scene of carnage and desolation or not. Humanity to the soldiers conspired with a regard for the safety of the town, in suggesting the wise measure of calling the town together to deliberate. For nothing short of the most solemn promises to the people that the soldiers should, at all hazards, be driven from the town, had preserved its peace. Not only the immense assemblies of the people from day to day, but military arrangements from night to night, were necessary to keep the people and the soldiers from getting together by the ears. The life of a redcoat would not have been safe in any street or corner of the town. Nor would the lives of the inhabitants have been much more secure. The whole militia of the city was in requisition, and military watches and guards were everywhere placed. We were all upon a level; no man was exempted; our military officers were only our superiors. I had the honor to be summoned, in my turn, and attended at the State House with my musket and bayonet, my broadsword, and cartridge-box, under the command of the famous Paddock. . . . He called me, common soldier as I was, frequently to his councils. I had a great deal of conversation with him, and no man appeared more apprehensive of a fatal calamity to the town, or more zealous by every prudent measure to prevent it.

Such was the situation of affairs when Samuel Adams was reasoning [in the council chamber] with Lieutenant-Governor Hutchinson and Lieutenant-Colonel Dalrymple. He had fairly driven them from all their outworks, breastworks, and intrenchments, to their citadel. There they paused and considered and deliberated. The heads of Hutchinson and Dalrymple were laid together in whispers for a long time; when the whispering ceased, a long and solemn pause ensued, extremely painful to an impatient, expecting audience. Hutchinson, in time, broke silence; he had consulted with Colonel Dalrymple, and the Colonel had authorized him to say that he might order one regiment down to the castle, if that would satisfy the people.

With a self-recollection, a self-possession, a self-command, a presence of mind that was admired by every man present, Samuel Adams arose with an air of dignity and majesty of which he was sometimes capable, stretched forth his arm, though even then quivering with palsy, and with an harmonious voice and decisive tone said, "If the Lieutenant-Governor or Colonel Dalrymple, or both together, have authority to remove one regiment, they have authority to remove two, and nothing short of the total evacuation of the town by all the regular troops will satisfy the public mind or preserve the peace of the province."

These few words thrilled through the veins of every man in the audience, and produced the great result. After a little awkward hesitation, it was agreed that the town should be evacuated, and both regiments sent to the castle.

After all this gravity it is merry enough to relate that William Molineux was obliged to march side by side with the commander of some of these troops, to protect them from the indignation of the people in their progress to the wharf of embarkation to the castle. Nor is it less amusing that Lord North, as I was repeatedly and credibly informed in England, with his characteristic mixture of good humor and sarcasm, ever after called these troops by the title of " Sam Adams' two regiments."

[From a letter to William Tudor, with reference to the offensive " writs of assistance," inquisitorial revenue regulations, sought to be forced upon the people.*].

QUINCY, 29 March, 1817.

. . . . . Whenever you shall find a painter, male or female, I pray you suggest a scene and a subject for the pencil.

The scene is the Council Chamber, in the old Town House, in Boston. The date is in the month of February, 1761. . . . The Council

---

* A special effort to enforce the navigation laws, and to prevent the colonists from trading with other nations, was made by Parliament, in 1761, by means of " Writs of Assistance," or general search-warrants, authorizing any sheriff, or officer of the customs, to enter a store or private dwelling, and search for foreign merchandise, which he *suspected* had not paid duty.

Chamber was as respectable an apartment as the House of Commons, or the House of Lords, in Great Britain, in proportion. . . . In this chamber, round a great fire, were seated five judges, with Lieutenant-Governor Hutchinson at their head as Chief Justice, all arrayed in their new, fresh, rich robes of scarlet English broadcloth; in their large cambric bands and immense judicial wigs. In this chamber were seated at a long table all the barristers-at-law of Boston, and of the neighboring county of Middlesex, in gowns, bands, and tie wigs. They were not seated on ivory chairs, but their dress was more solemn and more pompous than that of the Roman Senate when the Gauls broke in upon them. . . . Two portraits, at more than full length, of King Charles the Second, and of King James the Second, in splendid golden frames, were hung up on the most conspicuous sides of the apartment. . . . One circumstance more. Samuel Quincy and John Adams had been admitted barristers at that term. John was the youngest; he should be painted looking like a short, thick archbishop of Canterbury, seated at a table, with a pen in his hand, lost in admiration, now and then minuting those poor notes which your pupil, Judge Minot, has printed in his history. . . . You have now the stage and the scenery; next follows a narration of the subject — [arguing the question of the legality of the " writs of assistance."]

Now for the actors and performers. Mr. Gridley argued, with his characteristic learning, ingenuity, and dignity, and said everything that could be said in favor of Cockle's [the deputy-collector's] petition [for writs of assistance]; all depending, however, on the " if the Parliament of Great Britain is the sovereign legislature of all the British empire." Mr. Thacher followed him on the other side, and argued with the softness of manners, the ingenuity and cool reasoning, which were remarkable in his amiable character.

But Otis * was a flame of fire! With a promptitude of classical allusions, a depth of research, a rapid summary of historical events and dates, a profusion of legal authorities, a prophetic glance of his eye into futurity, and a torrent of impetuous eloquence, he hurried away everything before him. American independence was then and there born; the seeds of patriots and heroes were then and there sown, to defend the vigorous youth, the *non sine Diis animosus infans*. Every man of a crowded audience appeared to me to go away, as I did, ready to take arms against writs of

* James Otis was the advocate for the Admiralty, whose duty it was to argue in favor of the Writs; but he resigned, in order to plead the cause of the people. "To my dying day," he said, "I will oppose, with all the power and faculties God has given me, all such instruments of slavery on the one hand, and villany on the other." — *Patton's History of the United States.*

assistance. Then and there was the first scene of the first act of opposition to the arbitrary claims of Great Britain. Then and there the child Independence was born. In fifteen years, namely, in 1776, he grew up to manhood, and declared himself free. . . . Mr. Otis's popularity was without bounds. In May, 1761, he was elected into the House of Representatives by an almost unanimous vote. On the week of his election I happened to be at Worcester, attending the Court of Common Pleas, of which Brigadier Ruggles was Chief Justice, when the news arrived from Boston of Mr. Otis's election. You can have no idea of the consternation among the government people. Chief Justice Ruggles, at dinner at Colonel Chandler's on that day, said, "Out of this election will arise a d—d faction which will shake this province to its foundation." Ruggles's foresight reached not beyond his nose. That election has shaken two continents, and will shake all four. For ten years Mr. Otis, at the head of his country's cause, conducted the town of Boston, and the people of the province, with a prudence and fortitude, at every sacrifice of personal interest, and amidst unceasing persecution, which would have done honor to the most virtuous patriot or martyr of antiquity.

The minutes of Mr. Otis's argument are no better a representation of it than the gleam of a glow-worm to the meridian blaze of the sun.

[To Robert I. Evans, 1819.]

I have, through my whole life, held the practice of slavery in such abhorrence, that I have never owned a negro or any other slave, though I have lived for many years in times when the practice was not disgraceful, when the best men in my vicinity thought it not inconsistent with their character, and when it has cost me thousands of dollars for the labor and subsistence of freemen, which I might have saved by the purchase of negroes at times when they were very cheap.

[To Samuel Miller, 1820.]

. . . That you and I shall meet in a better world, I have no more doubt than I have that we now exist on the same globe, if my natural reason did not convince me of this. Cicero's Dream of Scipio, and his essays on friendship and old age, would have been sufficient for the purpose. But Jesus has taught us that a future state is a social state, when he promised to prepare places in his Father's house of many mansions, for his disciples.

[To Thomas Jefferson, 1820.]

When we say God is a spirit, we know what we mean, as well as we do when we say that the pyramids of Egypt are matter. Let us be content, therefore, to believe him to be a spirit, that is, an essence that we know nothing of, in which originally and necessarily reside all energy, all power, all capacity, all activity, all wisdom, all goodness.

[To Richard Rush, 1821.]

Strait is the gate, and narrow is the way that leads to liberty, and few nations, if any, have found it.

[To Thomas Jefferson, 1821.]

I may refine too much, I may be an enthusiast, but I think a free government is a complicated piece of machinery, the nice and exact adjustment of whose springs, wheels, and weights, is not yet well comprehended by the artists of the age, and still less by the people.

[To Richard Rush, 1821.]

Never before, but once, in the whole course of my life, was my soul so melted into the milk of human kindness; and that once was when four or five hundred fine young fellows appeared before me in Philadelphia, presenting an address, and receiving my answer. On both occasions I felt as if I could lay down a hundred lives to preserve the liberties and promote the prosperity of so noble a rising generation.

[To Thomas Jefferson, 1823.]

Right and justice have had hard fare in this world, but there is a Power above who is capable and willing to put all things right in the end.

[To Thomas Jefferson, 1825.]

The substance and essence of Christianity, as I understand it, is eternal and unchangeable, and will bear examination forever; but it has been mixed with extraneous ingredients, which I think will not bear examination, and they ought to be separated.

THOMAS JEFFERSON.

BORN, 1743; DIED, 1826, AGED 83.—ENTERED WILLIAM AND MARY COLLEGE, VA, 1760.—BEGAN PRACTICE OF LAW, 1767. —MEMBER OF HOUSE OF BURGESSES, VA., 1769.—MEMBER OF VIRGINIA CONVENTION, 1774.— DELEGATE TO CONGRESS, 1775.—WROTE DECLARATION OF INDEPENDENCE, 1776.—MEMBER OF A CONVENTION TO FRAME A CONSTITUTION FOR VIRGINIA, 1776.—PROCURED PASSAGE OF A BILL PROHIBITING THE FUTURE IMPORTATION OF SLAVES, 1778. GOVERNOR OF VIRGINIA, 1779.—DELEGATE TO CONGRESS, 1783.—MINISTER PLENIPOTENTIARY TO EUROPE, 1784.— MINISTER TO FRANCE, 1785.—SECRETARY OF STATE, 1790.— VICE-PRESIDENT, 1797.— PRESIDENT, 1801-1809.— TOOK ACTIVE PART IN ESTABLISHING THE UNIVERSITY OF VIRGINIA, 1817.

TRAINED in these successive schools, (the Virginia Assembly, the Council of State, and Congress,) he [Madison] acquired a habit of self-possession which placed at ready command the rich resources of his luminous and discriminating mind, and of his extensive information, and rendered him the first of every assembly afterward of which he became a member. Never wandering from his subject into vain declamation, but pursuing it closely, in language pure, classical, and copious, soothing always the feelings of his adversaries by civilities and softness of expression, he rose to the eminent station which he held in the great National Convention of 1787; and in that of Virginia, which followed, he sustained the new constitution in all its parts, bearing off the palm against the logic of George Mason, and the fervid declamation of Mr. Henry. With these consummate powers was united a pure and spotless virtue, which no calumny has ever attempted to sully. Of the powers and polish of his pen, and of the wisdom of his administration in the highest office of the nation, I need say nothing. They have spoken, and will forever speak for themselves. — *Writings*, Vol. I, p. 33.

The bill [in the General Assembly of Virginia] for establishing religious freedom . . . I had drawn in all the latitude of reason and right. It still met with opposition; but, with some mutilation in the preamble, it was finally passed; and a singular proposition proved that its protection of opinion was meant to be universal. Where the preamble declares that coercion is a departure from the plan of the holy author of our religion, an amendment was proposed, by inserting the words "Jesus Christ," so that it should read, "a departure from the plan of Jesus Christ, the holy author of our religion"; the insertion was rejected by a great majority, in proof that they meant to comprehend within the mantle of its protection, the Jew and the Gentile, the Christian and Mahometan, the Hindoo, and Infidel of every denomination.— *Writings*, Vol. I., 36.

[Letter to John Randolph.]

November 29, 1773.

..... Believe me, dear sir, there is not in the British empire a man who more cordially loves a union with Great Britain than I do. But, by the God that made me, I will cease to exist before I yield to a connection on such terms as the British Parliament propose; and in this, I think I speak the sentiments of America.

The passage of the Patowmac [Potomac] through the Blue Ridge is perhaps one of the most stupendous scenes in nature. You stand on a very high point of land. On your right comes up the Shenandoah, having ranged along the foot of the mountain an hundred miles to seek a vent. On your left approaches the Patowmac, in quest of a passage also. In the moment of their junction they rush together against the mountain, rend it asunder, and pass off to the sea. The first glance of this scene hurries our senses into the opinion that this earth has been created in time, that the mountains were formed first, that the rivers began to flow afterwards, that in this place particularly they have been dammed up by the Blue ridge of mountains, and have formed an ocean which filled the whole valley; that continuing to rise, they have at length broken over at this spot, and have torn the mountain down from its summit to its base. The piles of rock on each hand, but particularly on the Shenandoah, the evident marks of their disrupture and avulsion from their beds by the most powerful agents of nature, corroborate the impression.

But the distant finishing which nature has given to the picture is of a very different character. It is a true contrast to the foreground. It is as placid and delightful as that is wild and tremendous. For the mountain being cloven asunder, she presents to your eye, through the cleft, a small catch of smooth, blue horizon, at an infinite distance in the plain country, inviting you as it were from the riot and tumult roaring around to pass through the breach and participate of the calm below. Here the eye ultimately composes itself; and that way too the road happens actually to lead. You cross the Patowmac above the junction, pass along its side through the base of the mountain for three miles, its terrible precipices hanging in fragments over you, and within about twenty miles reach Fredericktown, and the fine country round that. This scene is worth a voyage across the Atlantic.— 1781. *Notes on Virginia.*

The Natural Bridge, the most sublime of nature's works, ... is on the ascent of a hill, which seems to have been cloven through its length by some great convulsion. The fissure, just at the bridge, is, by some admeasurements, two hundred and seventy feet deep, by others only two hundred and five. It is about forty-five feet wide at the bottom, and ninety feet at the top; this of course determines the length of the bridge, and its height from the water. Its breadth in the middle is about sixty feet, but more at the ends, and the thickness of the mass, at the summit of the arch, about forty feet. A part of this thickness is constituted by a coat of earth, which gives growth to many large trees.

The residue, with the hill on both sides, is one solid rock of limestone. The arch approaches the semi-elliptical form; but the large axis of the ellipsis, which would be the chord of the arch, is many times longer than the transverse. Though the sides of this bridge are provided in some parts with a parapet of fixed rocks, yet few men have the resolution to walk to them, and look over into the abyss. You involuntarily fall upon your hands and feet, creep to the parapet, and peep over it. Looking down from this height above a minute gave me a violent headache.

If the view from the top be painful and intolerable, that from below is delightful in an equal extreme. It is impossible for the emotions arising from the sublime to be felt beyond what they are here: so beautiful an arch, so elevated, so light, and springing as it were up to heaven, the rapture of the spectator is really indescribable! — 1781. *Notes, etc.*, p. 34.

THE NEGROES.

Whether further observation will or will not verify the conjecture that nature has been less bountiful to them in the endowment of the head, I believe that in those of the heart she will be found to have done them justice. That disposition to theft with which they have been branded must be ascribed to their situation, and not to any depravity of the moral sense. The man in whose favor no laws of property exist probably feels himself less bound to respect those made in favor of others. When arguing for ourselves, we lay it down as a fundamental, that laws, to be just, must give a reciprocation of right; that without this they are mere arbitrary rules of conduct, founded in force and not in conscience; and it is a problem which I give to the master to solve, whether the religious precepts against the violation of property were not framed for him as well as his slave? and whether the slave may not as justifiably take a little from one who has taken all from him, as he would slay one who would slay him? That a change in the relations in which a man is placed should change his ideas of moral right and wrong is neither new nor peculiar to the color of the blacks. . . . . .

Notwithstanding these considerations, which must weaken their respect for the laws of property, we find among them numerous instances of the most rigid integrity, and as many as among their better instructed masters, of benevolence, gratitude, and unshaken fidelity.

The opinion that they are inferior in the faculties of reason and imagination must be hazarded with great diffidence; . . . let me add, too, as a circumstance of great tenderness, where our conclusion would degrade a whole race of men from the rank in the scale of beings which their Creator may, perhaps, have given them. — 1781. *Notes, etc.* p. 211.

There must, doubtless, be an unhappy influence on the manners of our people produced by the existence of slavery among us. The whole commerce between master and slave is a perpetual exercise of the most boisterous passions, the most unremitting despotism on the one part, and degrading submissions on the other. Our children see this, and learn to imitate it; for man is an imitative animal. This quality is the germ of all education in him. From his cradle to his grave he is learning to do what he sees others do. If a parent could find no motive either in his philanthropy, or his self-love, for restraining the intemperance of passion towards his slave, it should always be a sufficient one that his child is present. But generally it is not sufficient. The parent storms, the child looks on, catches the lineaments of wrath, puts on the same airs to the circle of smaller slaves, gives aloose to the worst of passions, and thus nursed, educated, and daily exercised, cannot but be stamped by it with odious peculiarities. The man must be a prodigy who can retain his manners and morals undepraved by such circumstances. And with what execration should the statesman be loaded, who, permitting one-half the citizens thus to trample on the rights of the other, transforms those into despots, and these into enemies; destroys the morals of the one part, and the *amor patriae* of the other. For if a slave can have a country in this world, it must be any other in preference to that in which he is born to live and labor for another, in which he must lock up the faculties of his nature, contribute, as far as depends on his individual endeavors, to the evanishment of the human race, or entail his own miserable condition on the endless generations proceeding from him.

With the morals of the people their industry also is destroyed. For in a warm climate no man will labor for himself who can make another labor for him. This is so true, that of the proprietors of slaves a very small proportion indeed are ever seen to labor.

And can the liberties of a nation be thought secure when we have removed their only firm basis, a conviction in the minds of the people that these liberties are of the gift of God; that they are not to be violated but with his wrath? Indeed I tremble for my country when I reflect that God is just; that his justice cannot sleep for ever; that considering numbers, nature, and natural means only, a revolution of the wheel of fortune, an exchange of situation is among possible events; that it may become probable by supernatural interference! The Almighty has no attribute which can take side with us in such a contest. — 1781. *Notes, etc.*, p. 240.

What an incomprehensible machine is man! who can endure toil, famine, strife, imprisonment, and death itself, in vindication of his own liberty, and the next moment be deaf to all those motives whose power supported him through his trial, and inflict on his fellow-man a bondage, one hour of which is fraught with more misery than ages of that which he rose in rebellion to oppose. — *Letter to a friend.*

We must wait with patience the workings of an overruling Providence, and hope that that is preparing the deliverance of these our brethren.

When the measure of their tears shall be full, when their groans shall have involved Heaven itself in darkness, doubtless a God of justice will awaken to their distress. Nothing is more certainly written in the Book of Fate than that this people shall be free. — 1778.

I served with General Washington, in the legislature of Virginia, before the revolution, and, during it, with Dr. Franklin, in Congress. I never heard either of them speak ten minutes at a time, nor to any but the main point, which was to decide the question. They laid their shoulders to the great points, knowing that the little ones would follow of themselves. — *Writings*, Vol. I., p. 47.

It is not by the consolidation or concentration of powers, but by their distribution, that good government is effected. Were not this great country already divided into States, that division must be made; that each might do for itself what concerns itself directly, and what it can so much better do than a distant authority. Every State again is divided into counties, each to take care of what lies within its local bounds; each county again into townships, or wards, to manage minuter details; and every ward into farms, to be governed each by its individual proprietor. Were we directed from Washington when to sow, and when to reap, we should soon want bread. It is by this partition of cares, descending in gradation from general to particular, that the mass of human affairs may be best managed, for the good and prosperity of all.— *Writings*, Vol. I., p. 66.

[Letter to Peter Carr, Aug. 19, 1785.]

. . . . . Give up money, give up fame, give up science, give the earth itself and all it contains, rather than do an immoral act. . . . Whenever you are to do a thing, though it can never be known but to yourself, ask yourself how you would act, were all the world looking at you, and act accordingly. . . . If ever you find yourself environed with difficulties and perplexing circumstances, out of which you are at a loss how to extricate yourself, do what is right, and be assured that that will extricate you the best out of the worst situations. Though you cannot see, when you take one step, what will be the next, yet follow truth, justice, and plain dealing, and never fear their leading you out of the labyrinth, in the easiest manner possible. . . . Nothing is so mistaken as the supposition that a person is to extricate himself from a difficulty by intrigue, by chicanery, by dissimulation, by trimming, by an untruth, by an injustice. This increases the difficulties tenfold; and those who pursue these methods get themselves so involved at length, that they can turn no way but their infamy becomes more exposed. It is of great importance to set a resolution not to be shaken, never to tell an untruth. . . . This falsehood of the tongue leads to that of the heart, and in time depraves all its good dispositions. — *Writings*, Vol. I., 285.

[To a friend who had invited him to share in some promising business enterprise, he replied]:

When I first entered on the stage of public life (now twenty-four years ago), I came to a resolution never to engage, while in public office, in any kind of enterprise for the improvement of my fortune, nor to wear any other character than that of a farmer. I have never departed from it in a single instance; and I have, in multiplied instances, found myself happy in being able to decide and to act as a public servant, clear of all interest, in the multiform questions that have arisen, wherein I have seen others embarrassed and biassed by having got themselves in a more interested situation. Then I have thought myself richer in contentment than I should have been with any increase of fortune. Certainly I should have been much wealthier had I remained in that private condition which renders it lawful and even laudable to use proper efforts to better it.

An honest heart being the first blessing, a knowing head is the second. — *Writings*.

The object of walking is to relax the mind. You should therefore not permit yourself even to think while you walk, but direct your attention by the objects surrounding you. Walking is the best possible exercise.—Vol. I., p. 287.

The modern Greek is not yet so far departed from its ancient model, but that we might still hope to see the language of Homer and Demosthenes flow with purity from the lips of a free and ingenious people.—Vol. I., p. 289.

You have formed a just opinion of Monroe. He is a man whose soul might be turned wrong side outward, without discovering a blemish to the world.—Vol. II., p. 15.

I think that by far the most important bill in our whole code, is that for the diffusion of knowledge among the people. No other sure foundation can be devised for the preservation of freedom and happiness. If anybody thinks that kings, nobles, or priests are good conservators of the public happiness, send him here. It is the best school in the universe to cure him of that folly. He will see here, with his own eyes, that these descriptions of men are an abandoned confederacy against the happiness of the mass of the people.— *Letter from Paris,* 1786, Vol. II., 45.

Preach a crusade against ignorance; establish and improve the law for educating the common people.

The Virginia act for religious freedom has been received with infinite approbation in Europe, and propagated with enthusiasm. I do not mean by the governments, but by the individuals who compose them. It has been translated into French and Italian, has been sent to most of the courts of Europe, and has been the best evidence of the falsehood of those reports which stated us to be in anarchy. It is inserted in the new *Encyclopedie* and is appearing in most ot the publications respecting America. In fact, it is comfortable to see the standard of reason at length erected, after so many ages, during which the human mind has been held in vassalage by kings, priests, and nobles, and it is honorable for us to have produced the first legislature who had the courage to declare that the reason of man may be trusted with the formation of his own opinions. — Vol. II., p. 64. 1786.

The rights of conscience we never submitted, we could not submit. We are answerable for them to our God. The legitimate powers of government extend to such acts only as are injurious to others. But it does me no injury for my neighbor to say there are twenty gods, or no god. It neither picks my pocket nor breaks my leg, If it be said his testimony in a court of justice cannot be relied on, reject it then, and be-the stigma on him. Constraint may make him worse by making him a hypocrite, but it will never make him a truer man. It may fix him obstinately in his errors, but will not cure them. Reason and free inquiry are the only effectual agents against error. Give aloose to them, they will support the true religion, by bringing every false one to their tribunal, to the test of their investigation. They are the natural enemies of error, and of error only. — *Notes.*

[From the Declaration of Independence.]

When, in the course of human events, it becomes necessary for one people to dissolve the political bands which have connected them with another, and to assume, among the powers of the earth, the separate and equal station to which the laws of nature and of nature's God entitle them, a decent respect to the opinions of mankind requires that they should declare the causes which impel them to the separation.

We hold these truths to be self-evident, that all men are created equal; that they are endowed by their Creator with certain unalienable rights; that among these are life, liberty, and the pursuit of happiness. That, to secure these rights, governments are instituted among men, deriving their just powers from the consent of the governed; that, whenever any form of government becomes destructive of these ends, it is the right of the people to alter or to abolish it, and to institute a new government, laying its foundation on such principles, and organizing its power in such form, as to them shall seem most likely to effect their safety and happiness. Prudence, indeed, will dictate that governments long established should not be changed for light and transient causes; and, accordingly, all experience hath shown, that mankind are more disposed to suffer, while evils are sufferable, than to right themselves by abolishing the forms to which they are accustomed. But, when a long train of abuses and usurpations, pursuing invariably the same object, evinces a design to reduce them under absolute despotism, it is their right, it is their duty, to throw off such government, and to provide new guards for their future security.

[A passage in the original draft of the Declaration of Independence, which was stricken out by Congress.*]

He [George III.] has waged cruel war against human nature itself, violating its most sacred rights of life and liberty in the persons of a distant peo-

* The clause reprobating the enslaving the inhabitants of Africa was struck out in complaisance to South Carolina and Georgia, who had never attempted to restrain the importation of slaves, and who, on the contrary, still wished to con-

ple who never offended him, captivating and carrying them into slavery in another hemisphere, or to incur miserable death in their transportation thither. This piratical warfare, the opprobrium of INFIDEL powers, is the warfare of the CHRISTIAN king of Great Britain. Determined to keep open a market where MEN should be bought and sold, he has prostituted his negative for suppressing every legislative attempt to prohibit or restrain this execrable commerce. And that this assemblage of horrors might want no fact of distinguished dye, he is now exciting those very people to rise in arms among us, and to purchase that liberty of which he has deprived them, by murdering the people on whom he has obtruded them; thus paying off former crimes committed against the LIBERTIES of one people, with crimes which he urges them to commit against the lives of another.

The man who fights for the country is entitled to vote.

"One must be astonished," says the Abbe Raynal,* "that America has not yet produced a

tinue it. Our northern brethren, also, I believe, felt a little tender under those censures; for though their people had very few slaves themselves, yet they had been pretty considerable carriers of them to others. —THOMAS JEFFERSON, *Writings*, Vol. I., p. 15.

* Died, 1796.

good poet, an able mathematician, one man of genius in a single art or a single science."

"America has not yet produced one good poet." When we shall have existed as a people as long as the Greeks did before they produced a Homer, the Romans a Virgil, the French a Racine and Voltaire, the English a Shakespeare and Milton, should this reproach be still true, we will inquire from what unfriendly causes it has proceeded, that the other countries of Europe and quarters of the earth shall not have inscribed any name in the roll of poets. Has the world as yet produced more than two poets acknowledged to be such by all nations? An Englishman only reads Milton with delight, an Italian Tasso, a Frenchman Henriade, a Portuguese Camoens, but Homer and Virgil have been the rapture of every age and nation; they are read with enthusiasm in their originals by those who can read the originals, and in translations by those who cannot.*

But neither has America produced "one able mathematician, one man of genius in a single art or a single science." In war we have produced a Washington, whose memory will be adored while liberty shall have votaries; whose name will triumph over time, and will in future ages assume its just station among the most celebrated worthies of

* This sentence has been transferred from a note to the text.

the world, when that wretched philosophy shall be forgotten which would have arranged him among the degeneracies of nature.* In physics we have produced a Franklin, than whom no one of the present age has made more important discoveries, nor has enriched philosophy with more, or more ingenious, solutions of the phenomena of nature. We have supposed Mr. Rittenhouse second to no astronomer living; that in genius he must be the first, because he is self-taught. As an artist he has exhibited as great a proof of mechanical genius as the world has ever produced.

. . . .

As in philosophy and war, so in government, in oratory, in painting, in the plastic art, we might show that America, though but a child of yesterday, has already given hopeful proofs of genius, as well as of the nobler kinds, which arouse the best feelings of man, which call him into action, which substantiate his freedom, and conduct him to happiness, as of the subordinate, which serve to amuse him only.

We, therefore, suppose that this reproach is as unjust as it is unkind; and that, of the geniuses which adorn the present age, America contributes its full share. For comparing it with those countries where genius is most cultivated, where are

* Referring to Buffon's theory "of the tendency of nature to belittle her productions on this side of the Atlantic."

the most excellent models of art, and scaffolding for the attainment of science, as France and England, for instance, we calculate thus: The United States contain 3,000,000 of inhabitants; France, 20,000,000; and the British Islands, 10,000,000. We produce a Washington, a Franklin, a Rittenhouse. France, then, should have half a dozen in each of these lines, and Great Britain half that number, equally eminent. — *Notes*, p. 97.

In every government on earth is some trace of human weakness, some germ of corruption and degeneracy, which cunning will discover, and wickedness insensibly open, cultivate, and improve. Every government degenerates when trusted to the rulers of the people alone. The people themselves then are its only safe depositories. And to render them safe, their minds must be improved to a certain degree. — 1781. *Notes*, p. 220.

But are there no inconveniences to be thrown into the scale against the advantage expected from a multiplication of numbers by the importation of foreigners? It is for the happiness of those united in society to harmonize as much as possible in matters which they must of necessity transact together. Civil government being the sole object of forming societies, its administration must be conducted by common consent. Every species of government has its specific principles. Ours, perhaps, are more peculiar than those of any other in the universe. It is a composition of the freest principles of the English constitution with others derived from natural reason. To these nothing can be more opposed than the maxims of absolute monarchies. Yet from such we are to expect the greatest number of emigrants. They will bring with them the principles of the governments they leave, imbibed in their early youth; or, if able to throw them off, it will be in exchange for an unbounded licentiousness, passing, as is usual, from one extreme to another. It would be a miracle were they to stop precisely at the point of temperate liberty. These principles, with their language, they will transmit to their children. In proportion to their numbers, they will share with us the legislation. They will infuse into it their spirit, warp and bias its directions, and render it a heterogeneous, incoherent, distracted mass. . . . If they come of themselves, they are entitled to all the rights of citizenship; but I doubt the expediency of inviting them, by extraordinary encouragements. — 1781. *Notes*, p. 128.

[From his first Inaugural Address, March 4, 1801.]

Every difference of opinion is not a difference of principle. We have called by different names brethren of the same principle. We are all Republicans — we are all Federalists. If there be any among us who would wish to dissolve this Union, or to change its republican form, let them stand undisturbed, as monuments of the safety with which error of opinion may be tolerated where reason is left free to combat it.

Sometimes it is said that man cannot be trusted with the government of himself. Can he then be trusted with the government of others? Or have we found angels in the form of kings to govern him? Let history answer the question.

Peace, commerce, and honest friendship with all nations — entangling alliances with none.

March 23, 1801.

..... I am in hopes . . . they will find that the Christian religion, when divested of the rags in which they have enveloped it, and brought to the original purity and simplicity of its benevolent institutor, is a religion above all others most friendly to liberty, science, and the freest expression of the human mind.

March 29, 1801.

Civil Service. — The right of opinion shall suffer no invasion from me.* Those who have acted well,

---

* He had just become President.

have nothing to fear; those who have done ill, however, have nothing to hope; nor shall I fail to do justice, lest it should be ascribed to that difference of opinion.

Had the doctrines of Jesus been preached always as pure as they came from his lips, the whole civilized world would now have been Christian. — *June 26, 1822.*

[Letter to S. A. Wells, May 12, 1829.]

SAMUEL ADAMS: I can say that he was truly a great man, wise in council, fertile in resources, immovable in his purposes, and had, I think, a greater share than any other member [of Congress], in advising and directing our measures in the Northern war. As a speaker, he could not be compared with his living colleague and namesake,* whose deep conceptions, nervous style, and undaunted firmness, made him truly our bulwark in debate. But Mr. Samuel Adams, although not of fluent elocution, was so vigorously logical, so clear in his views, abundant in good sense, and master always of his subject, that he commanded the most profound attention whenever he rose in an assembly, by which the froth of declamation was heard with the most sovereign contempt. — *Writings, Vol. I., 99.*

* John Adams.

JAMES MADISON.

BORN, 1751; DIED, 1836, AGED 85.—ENTERED PRINCETON COLLEGE, 1769.—BEGAN PRACTICE OF LAW, 1772.—MEMBER OF VIRGINIA CONVENTION, 1776.—OF THE GENERAL ASSEMBLY, 1776.—OF CONGRESS, 1780.—OF THE GENERAL ASSEMBLY, 1784.—OF THE CONVENTION WHICH FRAMED THE CONSTITUTION OF THE UNITED STATES, 1787.—OF THE VIRGINIA CONVENTION, 1788.—OF CONGRESS, 1789.—PRESIDENT, 1809–1817.

ORANGE Co., VA., November 9, 1722.

"I THINK you make a judicious choice of history and the science of morals for your winter's study. They seem to be of the most universal benefit to men of sense and taste in every post, and must certainly be of great use to youth in settling their principles and refining their judgment, as well as in enlarging knowledge and correcting the imagination. I doubt not but you design to season them with a little divinity now and then, which, like the philosopher's stone, in the hands of a good man, will turn them and every lawful acquirement into the nature of itself, and make them more precious than fine gold. . . . Pray do not suffer those impertinent fops that abound in every city to divert you from your business and philosophical amusements. . . . I am luckily out of the way of such troubles, but I know you are surrounded with them; for they breed in towns and populous places as naturally as flies do in the shambles, because there they get food enough for their vanity and impertinence."

[To William Bradford, Jr., Philadelphia.]

ORANGE CO., VA., 1774.

"If the Church of England had been the established and general religion of all the Northern Colonies, as it has been among us here, and uninterrupted tranquillity had prevailed throughout the continent, it is clear to me that slavery and subjection might and would have been gradually insinuated among us. Union of religious sentiments begets a surprising confidence, and ecclesiastical establishments tend to great ignorance and corruption; all of which facilitates the execution of mischievous projects. . . . . .

"I want again to breathe your free air. I expect it will mend my constitution and confirm my principles. I have indeed as good an atmosphere at home as the climate will allow; but have nothing to brag of as to the state and liberty of my country. Poverty and luxury prevail among all sorts; pride, ignorance, and knavery among the priesthood, and vice and wickedness among the laity. This is bad enough, but it is not the worst I have to tell you. That diabolical, hell-conceived principle of persecution rages among some; and to their eternal infamy, the clergy * can furnish their quota of imps for such business. This vexes me the most of anything whatever. There are at this time in the adjacent county not less than five or six well-meaning men in close jail for publishing their religious sentiments, which in the main are very orthodox. I have neither patience to hear, talk, or think of anything relative to this matter; for I have squabbled and scolded, abused and ridiculed so long about it to little purpose, that I am without common patience. So I must beg you to pity me, and pray for liberty of conscience for all."

[To Mr. Bradford, Philadelphia, 1774.]

"Our Assembly is to meet the first of May, when it is expected something will be done in behalf of the dissenters. Petitions, I hear, are already forming among the persecuted Baptists, and I fancy it is in the thoughts of the Presbyterians also to intercede for greater liberty in matters of religion. . . . The sentiments of our people of fortune and fashion on this subject are vastly different from what you have been used to. That liberal, catholic, and equitable way of thinking, as to the rights of conscience, which is one of

---

* Of the then established church, — the church of England.

the characteristics of a free people, and so strongly marks the people of your Province, is but little known among the zealous adherents of our hierarchy. We have, it is true, some persons in the legislature of generous principles both in Religion and Politics; but number, not merit, you know, is necessary to carry points there. Besides, the clergy [of the church of England] are a numerous and powerful body, have great influence at home by reason of their connection with and dependence on the Bishops and Crown, and will naturally employ all their art and interest to depress their rising adversaries, for such they must consider dissenters, who rob them of the good-will of the people, and may in time endanger their livings and security. You are happy in dwelling in a land where those inestimable privileges are fully enjoyed, and the public has long felt the good effects of this religious as well as civil liberty."

[From an address to the States, April, 1783. Adopted by Congress.]

Let it be remembered that it has ever been the pride and boast of America that the rights for which she contended were the rights of human nature. By the blessing of the Author of these rights on the means exerted for their defence, they have prevailed over all opposition, and form the basis of thirteen independent states. No instance has heretofore occurred, nor can any instance be expected hereafter to occur, in which the unadulterated forms of republican government can pretend to so fair an opportunity of justifying themselves by their fruits. In this view the citizens of the United States are responsible for the greatest trust ever confided to a political society. If justice, good faith, honor, gratitude, and all other qualities which ennoble the character of a nation, and fulfil the ends of government, be the fruits of our establishment, the cause of liberty will acquire a dignity and lustre which it has never yet enjoyed, and an example will be set which cannot but have the most favorable influence on the rights of mankind. If, on the other side, our governments should be unfortunately blotted with the reverse of these cardinal and essential virtues, the great cause which we have engaged to vindicate will be dishonored and betrayed; the last and fairest experiment in favor of the rights of human nature will be turned against them, and their patrons and friends exposed to be insulted and silenced by the votaries of tyranny and usurpation.

. . . . . It were doubtless to be wished that the power of prohibiting the importation of slaves had not been postponed until the year 1808, or rather that it had been suffered to have immediate operation. But it is not difficult to account either for this restriction on the general government, or for the manner in which the whole clause is expressed. It ought to be considered as a great point gained in favor of humanity, that a period of twenty years may terminate forever within these states a traffic which has so long and so loudly upbraided the barbarism of modern policy; that within that period it will receive a considerable discouragement from the federal government, and may be totally abolished by the concurrence of a few states which continue the unnatural traffic, in the prohibitory example which has been given by so great a majority of the Union. Happy would it be for the unfortunate Africans if an equal prospect lay before them of being redeemed from the oppression of their European brethren! — *Federalist*, No. xlii.

..... The British constitution was to Montesquieu what Homer has been to the didactic writers on epic poetry. As the latter have considered the work of the immortal bard as the perfect model from which the principles and rules of the epic art were to be drawn, and by which all similar works were to be judged; so this great political critic appears to have viewed the constitution of England as the standard, or, to use his own expression, as the mirror of political liberty. — *Federalist*, No. xlvii.

A popular government, without popular information, or the means of acquiring it, is but a prologue to a farce or a tragedy, or perhaps to both.

The great security against the gradual concentration of the several powers in the same department, consists in giving to those who administer each department the necessary constitutional means and personal motives to resist encroachments of the others. The provision for defence must in this, as in all other cases, be made commensurate to the danger of attack. Ambition must be made to counteract ambition. The interest of the man must be connected with the constitutional rights of the place. It may be a reflection on human nature that such devices should be necessary to control the abuses of government. But what is government itself but the greatest of all reflections on human nature! If men were angels, no government would be necessary. If angels were to govern men, neither external nor internal controls on government would be necessary. In framing a government which is to be administered by men over men, the great difficulty lies in this: you must first enable the government to control the governed; and in the next place oblige it to control itself. A dependence on the people is no doubt the primary control on the government; but experience has taught mankind

the necessity of auxiliary precautions.—*Federalist,*
No. li.

Justice is the end of government. It is the end of civil society. It ever has been, and ever will be, pursued until it be obtained, or until liberty be lost in the pursuit. In a society under the form of which the stronger faction can unite and oppress the weaker, anarchy may as truly be said to reign as in a state of nature, where the weaker individual is not secured against the violence of the stronger; and as in the latter state, even the stronger individuals are prompted, by the uncertainty of their condition, to submit to a government which may protect the weak as well as themselves, so in the former state, will the more powerful factions or parties be gradually induced, by a like motive, to wish for a government which will protect all parties, the weaker as well as the more powerful. . . . And happily for the republican cause, the practicable sphere may be carried to a very great extent by a judicious modification and mixture of the federal principle.

[To Thomas Jefferson.]

NEW YORK, October 17, 1788.

Wherever the real power in a government resides, there is the danger of oppression. In our government the real power lies in the majority of the community, and the invasion of private rights is chiefly to be apprehended, not from acts of government contrary to the sense of its constituents, but from acts in which the government is the mere instrument of the major number of the constituents. This is a truth of great importance, but not yet sufficiently attended to. . . . Wherever there is an interest and power to do wrong, wrong will generally be done, and not more readily by a powerful and interested party than by a powerful and interested prince. The difference, so far as it relates to the superiority of republics over monarchies, lies in the less degree of probability that interest may prompt abuses of power in the former than in the latter, and in the security of the former against an oppression of more than the smaller part of the society, whereas in the latter, it may be extended in a manner to the whole.

[To Thomas Jefferson.]
NEW YORK, May 23, 1789.

My last enclosed copies of the President's inaugural speech, and the answer of the House of Representatives. I now add the answer of the Senate. It will not have escaped you that the former was addressed with a truly republican simplicity to George Washington, President of the United States. The latter follows the example, with the omission of the personal name, but without any other than the constitutional title. The proceeding on this point was in the House of Representatives spontaneous. The imitation by the Senate was extorted. The question became a serious one between the two houses. John Adams espoused the cause of titles with great earnestness. . . . The projected title was, His Highness the President of the United States and Protector of their liberties. Had the project succeeded, it would have subjected the President to a severe dilemma, and given a deep wound to our infant government.

[To Edmund Randolph, New York, 1789.]

I think it best to give the Senate as little agency as possible in executive matters, and to make the President as responsible as possible in them. Were the heads of departments dependent on the senate, a faction in this branch might support them against the President, distract the executive department, and obstruct the public business. The danger of undue power in the President from such a regulation is not, to me, formidable. I see, and *politically feel* that that will be the weak branch of the government.

[From a message to Congress, 1803.

. . . . . The war* has proved that our free government, like other free governments, though slow in

* The war of 1812–1815, with England.

its early movements, acquires in its progress a force proportioned to its freedom, and that the union of these states, the guardian of the freedom and safety of all and of each, is strengthened by every occasion that puts it to the test.

[Letter to Edward Livingston, 1822.]

..... I observe with particular pleasure the view you have taken of the immunity of religion from civil jurisdiction in every case where it does not trespass on private rights or the public peace. This has always been a favorite principle with me; and it was not with my approbation that the deviation from it took place in Congress when they appointed chaplains to be paid from the national treasury. It would have been a much better proof to their constituents of their pious feeling, if the members had contributed for the purpose a pittance from their own pockets.

There has been another deviation from the strict principle in the executive proclamation of fasts and festivals, so far, at least, as they have spoken the language of injunction, or have lost sight of the equality of all religious sects in the eye of the constitution. Whilst I was honored with the executive trust I found it necessary on more than one occasion to follow the example of predecessors. But I was always careful to make the proclamations absolutely indiscriminate, and merely recommendatory. .....

It was the belief of all sects at one time that the establishment of religion by law was right and necessary ; that the true religion ought to be established in exclusion of every other; and that the only question to be decided was, which was the true religion. . . . We are teaching the world the great truth that governments do better without kings and nobles than with them. The merit will be doubled by the other lesson, that religion flourishes in greater purity without than with the aid of government.

[Letter to Mr. Ringgold, 1831.]

. . . . . I need not to say to you how highly I rated the comprehensiveness and character of his [Monroe's] mind, the purity and nobleness of his principles, the importance of his party services, and the many private virtues of which his whole life was a model.

[Letter to I. C. Caball, 1831.]

. . . . . I know not whence the idea could proceed that I concurred in the doctrine, that although a state could not nullify a law of the Union, it had a right to secede from the Union. Both spring from the same piosonous root, unless the right to secede be limited to cases of intolerable oppression, absolving the party from its constitutional obligations.

I hope that all who now see the absurdity of

nullification will see also the necessity of rejecting the claim to effect it through the state judiciaries, which can only be kept in the constitutional career by the control of the federal jurisdiction. Take the linch-pin from a carriage, and how soon would a wheel be off its axle, — an emblem of the speedy fate of the federal system were the parties to it loosened from the authority which confines them to their sphere.

[James Monroe.] Few men have ever made more of what may be called sacrifices in the service of the public. When he considered the interests or the dignity of his country involved, his own interest was never regarded. Beside this cause, his extreme generosity, not only to the numerous members of his family dependent on him, but to friends not united by blood, has greatly contributed to his impoverishment.

[To J. R. Paulding, 1831.]

[Alexander Hamilton.] That he possessed intellectual powers of the first order, and the moral quality of integrity and honesty in a captivating degree, has been decreed to him by a suffrage now universal. Of his theory of government, deviating from the republican standard, he had the candor to avow it, and the greater merit of co-operating faithfully in maturing and supporting a system which was not his choice.

[Benjamin Franklin.] He has written his own life, and no man had a finer one to write, or a better title to be himself the writer.

[Thomas Jefferson.] It may, on the whole, be truly said of him, that he was greatly eminent for the comprehensiveness and fertility of his genius, for the vast extent and rich variety of his acquisitions, and particularly distinguished by the philosophical impress left on every subject which he touched. Nor was he less distinguished for an early and uniform devotion to the cause of liberty, and systematic preference of a form of government squared with strictest degree to the rights of man. In the social and domestic spheres, he was a model of the virtues and manners which most adorn them.

[John Adams.] That he had a mind rich in ideas of his own, as well as its learned store, with an ardent love of country, and the merit of being a colossal champion of its independence, must be allowed by those most offended by the alloy in his republicanism, and the fervors and flights originating in his moral temperament.

[To N. P. Trist, 1832.]

. . . . . I have received yours of the 19th December, enclosing some of the South Carolina papers. There are in one of them some interesting views of the doctrine of secession — one that had occurred to me, and which for the first time I have seen in print, namely, that if one state can, at will, withdraw from the others, the others can, at will, withdraw from her, and turn her, *nolentem volentem*, out of the Union. . . . It is high time that the claim to secede at will should be put down by the public opinion.

[To Edward Coles, 1834.]

You call my attention, with much emphasis, to the principle that offices and emoluments were the spoils of victory, the personal property of the successful candidate for the presidency, to be given as rewards for electioneering services, and in general to be used as the means of rewarding those who support, and of punishing those who do not support, the dispenser of the fund. I fully agree in all the odium you attach to such a rule of action.

[To Edward Coles, 1834.]

. . . . . Nullification has the effect of putting powder under the Constitution and Union, and a match in the hand of every party to blow them up at pleasure.

[Abolition of the Slave-trade.]

The dictates of humanity, the principles of the people, the national safety and happiness, and prudent policy, require it of us. It is to be hoped that by expressing a national disapprobation of the trade, we may destroy it, and save our country from reproaches, and our posterity from the imbecility ever attendant on a country filled with slaves.

It is wrong to admit into the Constitution the idea that there can be property in man.

We have seen the mere distinction of color made, in the most enlightened period of time, a ground of the most oppressive dominion ever exercised by man over man.

JAMES MONROE.

BORN, 1758; DIED, 1831, AGED 73.—EDUCATED AT WILLIAM AND MARY COLLEGE.—LIEUTENANT IN THE ARMY, 1776.—MAJOR, 1777.—MEMBER OF ASSEMBLY OF VIRGINIA, 1782.—OF THE EXECUTIVE COUNCIL OF VIRGINIA, 1782.—OF CONGRESS, 1783.—RE-ELECTED TO THE GENERAL ASSEMBLY, 1787.—DELEGATE TO THE VIRGINIA CONVENTION FOR DECIDING UPON THE ADOPTION OF THE FEDERAL CONSTITUTION, 1788.—UNITED STATES SENATOR, 1790.—MINISTER TO FRANCE, 1794.—GOVERNOR OF VIRGINIA, 1799.—ENVOY EXTRAORDINARY TO FRANCE, 1802.—MINISTER PLENIPOTENTIARY TO ENGLAND, 1802.—MEMBER OF VIRGINIA GENERAL ASSEMBLY, 1810.—GOVERNOR OF VIRGINIA, 1811.—SECRETARY OF STATE, 1811.—SECRETARY OF WAR, 1814.—PRESIDENT, 1817-1825.

[From a Message, November 17, 1818.]

. . . . . I communicate with great satisfaction the accession of another State, Illinois, to our Union; because I perceive from the proof afforded by the additions already made, the regular progress and sure consummation of a policy, of which history affords no example, and of which the good effect cannot be too highly estimated. By extending our government on the principles of our constitution, over the vast territories within our limits, on the Lakes and the Mississippi and its numerous streams, new life and vigor are infused into every part of our system. By increasing the number of the States, the confidence of the State governments in their own security is increased, and the jealousy of the national government proportionally diminished. The impracticability of one consolidated government for this great and growing nation will be more apparent, and will be universally admitted. Incapable of exercising local authority, except for general purposes, the general government will be no longer dreaded. In those cases of a local nature, and for all the great purposes for which it was instituted, its authority will be cherished. Each government will acquire a new force and a greater freedom of action, within its proper sphere.

[From a Message, 1819.]

..... Due attention has been paid to the suppression of the slave trade, in compliance with the law of the last session. Orders have been given to the commanders of all our public ships to seize all vessels navigated under our flag engaged in the traffic, and to bring them in, to be proceeded against in the manner prescribed by the law. It is hoped that these vigorous measures, supported by the acts of other nations, will soon terminate a commerce so disgraceful to the civilized world.

[From a Message, 1822.]

..... The military academy forms the basis, in regard to science, on which the military establishment rests. It furnishes annually, after due examination, many well-informed youths to fill the vacancies which occur in the several corps of the army, while others, who, retired to private life, carry with them such attainments as, under the right reserved to the several states to appoint the officers and train the militia, will enable them, by affording a wider field for selection, to promote the great object of the power vested in Congress, of providing for the organizing, arming, and disciplining the militia. Thus, by the mutual and harmonious co-operation of the two governments, in the exercise of a power divided between them, an object always to be cherished, the attainment of a great result, on which our liberties may depend, cannot fail to be secured. I have to add, that in proportion as our regular force is small should the instruction and discipline of the militia, the great resource on which we rely, be pushed to the utmost extent that circumstances will admit.

[From a Message, 1824.]

..... Experience has already shown that the difference of climate and of industry proceeding from the cause inseparable from such vast domains, and which, under our system, might have a repulsive tendency, cannot fail to produce, with us, under wise regulations, the opposite effect. What one part wants the other may supply, and this will be most sensibly felt by the parts most distant from each other, forming, thereby, a domestic market and an active intercourse between the extremes, and throughout every part of our Union. Thus, by a happy distribution of power between the National and State governments, governments which rest exclusively on the sovereignty of the people, and are fully adequate to the great purposes for which they were respectively instituted, causes which might otherwise lead to dismemberment, operate powerfully to draw us closer together.

[Message, December, 1823.]

...... The political system of the allied powers* is essentially different from that of America. This difference proceeds from that which exists in their respective governments. As to the defence of our own, which has been achieved by the loss of so much blood and treasure, and matured by the wisdom of their most enlightened citizens, and under

* From 1815 to 1853 the world was substantially preserved from any war of importance by the five great powers who preside over the destinies of Europe, namely, France, Great Britain, Russia, Austria, and Prussia.—*Appleton's Cyclop.*

which we have enjoyed unexampled felicity, this whole nation is devoted. We owe it therefore to candor, and to the amicable relations existing between the United States and those powers to declare, that we should consider any attempt on their part to extend their system to any portion of this hemisphere as dangerous to our peace and safety. . . . . . .

Our policy with regard to Europe, which we adopted at an early stage of the wars which have so long agitated that quarter of the globe, nevertheless remains the same, which is, not to interfere in the internal concerns of any of its powers; to consider the government *de facto* as the legitimate government for us; to cultivate friendly relations with it, and to preserve those relations by a frank, firm, and manly policy; meeting in all cases the just claims of every power; submitting to injuries from none. But in regard to those continents [North and South America], circumstances are eminently and conspicuously different. It is impossible that any allied powers should extend their political system to any portion of either continent without endangering our peace and happiness; nor can any one believe that our Southern brethren, if left to themselves, would adopt it of their own accord. It is equally impossible, therefore, that we should behold such interposition, in any form, with indifference. If we look to the comparative strength and resources of Spain and those new governments, and their distance from each other, it must be obvious that she can never subdue them. It is still the true policy of the United States to leave the parties to themselves, in the hope that other powers will pursue the same course.

[From a speech in the Virginia Convention.]

We have found that this evil (slavery) has preyed upon the very vitals of the Union, and has been prejudicial to all the States in which it has existed.

JOHN QUINCY ADAMS.

BORN, 1767; DIED, 1848, AGED, 81.—AT THE UNIVERSITY OF LEYDEN, 1780.—PRIVATE SECRETARY TO FRANCIS DANA, MINISTER TO RUSSIA, 1782.—ENTERED HARVARD COLLEGE IN ADVANCE, 1786.—BEGAN PRACTICE OF LAW, 1791.—MINISTER TO THE HAGUE, 1794.—MINISTER TO BERLIN, 1797.—MEMBER OF MASSACHUSETTS SENATE, 1802.—OF THE UNITED STATES SENATE, 1803.—PROFESSOR OF RHETORIC AND BELLES LETTRES IN HARVARD COLLEGE, 1806.—MINISTER TO RUSSIA, 1809.—RESIDENT MINISTER IN ENGLAND, 1815.—SECRETARY OF STATE, 1817.—PRESIDENT, 1825-1829.—REPRESENTATIVE TO CONGRESS, 1831.

[From an Oration delivered at Plymouth, 1802.]

THIS theory [a community of good] results, it must be acknowledged, from principles of reasoning most flattering to the human character. If industry, frugality, and disinterested integrity were alike the virtues of all, there would, apparently, be more of the social spirit in making all property a common stock, and giving to each individual a proportional title to the wealth of the whole. Such is the basis upon which Plato forbids in his republic the division of property. Such is the system upon which Rousseau pronounces the first man who enclosed a field with a fence, and said, This is mine, a traitor to the human species. A wiser and more useful philosophy, however, directs us to consider man according to the nature in which he was formed, — subject to infirmities which no wisdom can remedy; to weaknesses which no institution can strengthen; to vices which no legislation can correct. Hence it becomes obvious that separate property is the natural and indisputable right of separate exertion — that community of goods without community of toil is oppressive and unjust; that it counteracts the laws of nature, which prescribe that he only who sows the seed shall reap the harvest; that it discourages all energy by destroying its rewards; and makes the most virtuous and active members of society the slaves and drudges of the worst.

Rhetoric alone can never constitute an orator. No human art can be acquired by the mere knowledge of the principles upon which it is founded. But the artist who understands the principles will exercise his art in the highest perfection.

The profoundest study of the writers upon architecture, the most laborious contemplation of its magnificent monuments, will never make a mason. But the mason thoroughly acquainted with the writers, and familiar with the construction of those monuments, will surely be an abler artist than the mere mechanic, ignorant of the mysteries of his trade, and even of the names of his tools. — *Lectures on Rhetoric and Oratory*, Lect. II.

The art of speaking must be most eagerly sought where it is found to be most useful. It must be most useful where it is capable of producing the greatest effects, and that can be in no other state of things than where the power of persuasion operates upon the will, and prompts the actions of other men. The only birthplace of eloquence, therefore, must be a free state. Under arbitrary governments, where the lot is cast upon one man to command, and upon all the rest to obey; where the despot, like the Roman centurion, has only to say to one man, Go, and he goeth, and to another, Come, and he cometh, persuasion is of no avail. Between authority and obedience there can be no deliberation; and wheresoever submission is the principle of government in a nation, eloquence can never arise. Eloquence is the child of liberty, and can descend from no other stock. . . . Our institutions, from the smallest municipal associations, to the great national bond, which links this continent in union, are republican. Their vital principle is liberty. Persuasion, or the influence of reason and of feeling, is the great if not the only instrument whose operation can effect the acts of all our corporate bodies: of towns, cities, counties, states, and of the whole confederated empire. Here, then, eloquence is recommended by the most elevated usefulness, and encouraged by the promise of the most precious rewards. —*Lect.* II.

When the cause of ages and the fate of nations hang upon the thread of a debate, the orator may fairly consider himself as addressing not only his immediate hearers, but the world at large, and all future times. Then it is, that, looking beyond the moment in which he speaks, and the immediate issue of the deliberation, he makes the question of an hour a question for every age and every region; takes the vote of unborn millions upon the debate of a little senate; and incorporates himself and his discourse with the general history of mankind. On such occasions and at such times, the oration naturally and properly assumes a solemnity of manner and a dignity of language commensurate with the grandeur of the cause. Then it is that deliberative eloquence lays aside the plain attire of her daily occupation, and assumes the port and purple of the queen of the world. Yet even then she remembers that majestic grandeur best comports with simplicity. Her crown and sceptre may blaze with the brightness of the diamond, but she must not, like the kings of the gorgeous cast, be buried under a shower of barbaric pearls and gold. — *Lect.* XI.

[From his Diary, August 19, 1822, when Secretary of State.]

Answered General Dearborn's letter, and received one from my wife, chiefly upon an attack against me in one of the Philadelphia newspapers on account of the negligence of my dress. It says that I wear neither waistcoat nor cravat, and sometimes go to church barefoot. My wife is much concerned at this, and several of my friends at Philadelphia have spoken to her of it as a serious affair. In the *Washington City Gazette*, some person unknown to me has taken the cudgels in my behalf, and answered the accusation gravely as if the charge were true. It is true only as re-regards the cravat, instead of which, in the extremity of the summer heat, I wear round my neck a black silk ribbon. But even in the falsehood of this charge what I may profitably remember is the perpetual and malignant watchfulness with which I am observed in my open day and my secret night, with the deliberate purpose of exposing me to public obloquy or public ridicule. There is nothing so deep and nothing so shallow which political enmity will not turn to account. Let it be a warning to me to take heed to my ways.

[From his Diary, October 13, 1822.]

This ode [Pope's "Dying Christian to his Soul"] is exquisitely beautiful, though most singularly compounded of five half-ludicrous Latin lines, said to have been spoken by the emperor Hadrian at the article of death, of Sappho's fiery lyric ode; and of that triumphant and transporting apostrophe of St. Paul, in the fifty-fifth verse of this fifteenth chapter of Corinthians: "O death, where is thy sting? O grave, where is thy victory?" From these materials, upon a suggestion and at the request of Steele, Pope wrote this truly seraphic song, to be set to music. In comparing it with the lines of Hadrian, I see the effect of the Christian doctrines upon the idea of death. Pope contends that there is nothing trifling, or even gay, in the lines of Hadrian; but his imagination leads his judgment astray. The heathen philosophers taught that death was to be met with indifference, and Hadrian attempted to carry this doctrine into practice by joking at his own death, while in its agonies. Yet the thought of what was to become of his soul was grave and serious, and his idea of its future state was that of darkness and gloom. The character of his lines, therefore, is a singular mixture of levity and sadness, the spirit of which appears to me to be lost in Pope's translation of them, given in a letter to Steele. I set down the lines here, with a translation of them as literal and as much in their spirit as I can make them.

> Animula, vagula, blandula,
> Hospes comesque corporis,
> Quæ nunc abibis in loca?
> Pallidula, rigida, nudula,
> Nec (ut soles) dabis joca!

> Dear, fluttering, flattering little soul,
> Partner and inmate of this clay,

Oh, whither art thou now to stroll?
Pale, shivering, naked, little droll,
No more thy wonted jokes to play!

Pope insists that the diminutives are epithets, not of levity, but of endearment. They are significant of both, and the repetition of them, with the rhyme of "*loca*" and "*joca*," in Latin verses of that age, decisively marks the merriment of affected indifference. In the process of the correspondence, Steele desired Pope to make an ode as of a cheerful, dying spirit; that is to say, the emperor Hadrian's "Animula, vagula," put into two or three stanzas for music. This hint was Pope's inspiration. He made the cheerful, dying spirit a *Christian*, and cheerful death then became the moment of triumphant exultation, and the song is, as it were, the song of an angel.

To a Bereaved Mother.

Sure to the mansions of the blest,
    When infant innocence ascends,
Some angel, brighter than the rest,
    The spotless spirit's flight attends.
On wings of ecstasy they rise,
    Beyond where worlds material roll,
Till some fair sister of the skies
    Receives the unpolluted soul.
That inextinguishable beam,
    With dust united at our birth,
Sheds a more dim, discolored gleam,
    The more it lingers upon earth.

But when the Lord of mortal breath
  Decrees his bounty to resume,
And points the silent shaft of death
  Which speeds an infant to the tomb,
No passion fierce, nor low desire,
  Has quenched the radiance of the flame;
Back to its God the living fire
  Reverts, unclouded as it came.
Fond mourner be that solace thine!
  Let Hope her healing charm impart,
And soothe, with melodies divine,
  The anguish of a mother's heart.

Oh, think! the darlings of thy love,
  Divested of this earthly clod,
Amid unnumbered saints, above,
  Bask in the bosom of their God.
O'er thee, with looks of love they bend;
  For thee the Lord of life implore;
And oft from sainted bliss descend,
  Thy wounded quiet to restore.
Then dry, henceforth, the bitter tear;
  Their part and thine inverted see.
Thou wert their guardian angel here,
  They guardian angels now to thee.

Reading further in Walpole's Memoirs, or Secret History of the British Administrations from 1750 to 1760, I find in them many things that remind me of the present state of things here. The public history of all countries and all ages is but a sort of mask richly colored. The interior working of the machinery must be foul. There is as much mining and countermining for power, as many fluctuations of friendship and enmity, as many attractions and repulsions, bargains, and oppositions, narrated in these Memoirs as might be told of our own times. Walpole witnessed it all as a sharer in the sport, and now tells it to the world as a satirist. And shall not I, too, have a tale to tell?—*Diary*, Nov. 9, 1822.

[From his Inaugural Address, 1825.]

..... Ten years of peace at home and abroad have assuaged the animosities of political contention, and blended into harmony the most discordant elements of public opinion. There still remains one effort of magnanimity, one sacrifice of prejudice and passion, to be made by the individuals throughout the nation who have heretofore followed the standards of political party. It is that of discarding every remnant of rancor against each other, of embracing as countrymen and friends, and of yielding to talents and virtue alone that confidence which in times of contention for principle was bestowed only upon those who bore the badge of party communion.

[From an Address at a public dinner in Faneuil Hall in connection with the annual examination of the public schools.]

It was from schools of public instruction instituted by our forefathers that the light burst forth.

It was in the primary schools, it was by the midnights lamps of Harvard Hall, that were conceived and matured, as it was within these hallowed walls that were first resounded, the accents of that independence which is now canonized in the memory of those by whom it was proclaimed.

[A representation having been made to President Adams, that a certain functionary of the general government was using his influence against his re-election, and therefore ought to be removed, he replied]:

That gentleman is one of the best officers in the public service. I have had occasion to know his diligence, exactness, and punctuality. On public grounds, therefore, there is no cause of complaint against him, and upon no other will I remove him. If I cannot administer the government on these principles, I am content to go back to Quincy.

SUNDAY, November 5, 1826.

Heard Mr. Little from Psalms, cxix. 133. . . . Among his quotations from Scripture was that of the first seven verses of the fifth chapter of Isaiah. — the song of the vineyard that brought forth wild grapes. In this instance, as in numberless others, I was struck with the careless inattention of my own mind when reading the Bible. I had read the chapter of Isaiah containing this parable, I dare say, fifty times, and it was altogether familiar to my memory; but I had never perceived a fiftieth part of its beauty and sublimity. The closing verse of the parable, especially, which points the moral of the allegory, speaks with irresistible energy: "For the vineyard of the Lord of hosts is the house of Israel, and the men of Judah his pleasant plant: and he looked for judgment, but behold oppression; for righteousness, but behold a cry." The parallel is pursued no further. He had said in the parable how the vineyard would be destroyed, and here, after declaring what the vineyard was, and what its fruits had been, he leaves the conclusion of ruin and destruction to the imagination of the reader. This art of selecting ideas to be presented, and of leading the mind to that which is not expressed, is among the greatest secrets of composition — to make the suppressed thoughts, like the statues of Brutus and Cassius at the funeral of Junia, most resplendent because they are not exhibited in the highest effort of skill.—*Diary.* Nov. 5, 1826.

May 6.

..... I heard Mr. Campbell. . . . His text was from Rev. ii. 16: "Repent, or else I will come unto thee quickly." Mr. C. dwelt largely and earnestly upon the universal depravity of mankind. It is a matter of curious speculation to me how men of good understanding and reasoning faculties can be drilled into the sincere belief of these absurdities. The Scripture says that the heart is deceitful and desperately wicked. This is certainly true, and is a profound observation upon the human character. But the language is figurative. By the heart is meant, in this passage, the selfish passions of man. But there is also in man a spirit, and the inspiration of the Almighty giveth him understanding. It is the duty of man to discover the vicious propensities and deceits of his heart, to control them. This, with the grace of God, a large portion of the human race in Christian lands do accomplish. It seems, therefore, to be worse than useless for preachers to declare that mankind are universally depraved. It takes from honest integrity all its honors; it degrades men in their own estimation.

Mr. Campbell read a hymn, which declared that *we* were more base and brutish than the beasts,— a spiritual song of Isaac Watts. What is the meaning of this? If Watts had said this on a week-day to any one of his parishioners, would he not have knocked him down? And how can that be taught as a solemn truth of religion, applicable to all mankind, which, if said at any other time to any one individual, would be punishable as slander?—*Diary*, 1827.

I read also the speech of John Randolph, on retrenchment and reform, published by himself in a pamphlet, with notes. It is, like all his speeches, a farrago of commonplace political declamation, mingled up with a jumble of historical allusions, scraps of Latin from the Dictionary of Quotations, and a continual stream of malignity to others, and of inflated egotism, mixed in proportions like those of the liquor which he now tipples as he speaks in the House, and which he calls toast-water, — about one-third brandy and two-thirds water. This is the speech in which he charges Clay with having condescended to electioneer with him; asserts there was a combination of Webster and Clay against me, which, in a note, he says I defeated by causing the votes which Mr. Crawford got in the New York Legislature to be given to him, and thereby securing his return to the House, and excluding thereby Mr. Clay. This idea of my causing votes of the New York Legislature, which I could not obtain for myself, to be given to Mr. Crawford, is one of the most ingenious in the whole pamphlet, and is a sample of the materials of which his accusations are composed. The rancor of this man's soul against me is that which sustains his life, and so it is of W. B. Giles, now governor of Virginia. The agony of their envy and hatred of me, and the hope of effecting my downfall, are their chief remaining sources of vitality. The issue of the presidential election will kill them by the gratification of their revenge. — *Diary*, March 11, 1828.

[Rev.] Mr. Baker made also some inquiries concerning my religious opinions, and particularly concerning my ideas of the trinity. I spoke to him as freely as I did with the general of the Jesuits at St. Petersburg. I told him, in substance, . . . that I was not either a Trinitarian or a Unitarian; that I believed the nature of Jesus Christ was superhuman; but whether he was God, or only the first of created beings, was not clearly revealed to me in the Scriptures. — *Diary*, March 17, 1828.

I went to the Presbyterian church to hear Mr. Smith, but his place was supplied [by another]. His text was from Luke xv. 17 : " And when he came to himself he said, How many hired servants of my father's have bread enough and to spare, and I perish with hunger ! " A commonplace of Calvinism. The argument was that all unregenerate sinners were insane, or beside themselves, and that conversion was nothing more than a return to reason, or coming to themselves. In the common affairs of the world, an eloquent exhortation to the insane to come to himself would sooner send the preacher to Bedlam than release his hearer from it; but this is orthodox Calvinism, and our pulpit orator urged us all, with great and anxious earnestness, to come to ourselves. — *Diary*, March 20, 1831.

Mr. Munroe is a very remarkable instance of a man whose life has been a continued series of the most extraordinary good fortune, who has never met with any known disaster, has gone through a splendid career of public service, has received more pecuniary reward from the public than any other man since the existence of the nation, and is now dying, at the age of seventy-two, in wretchedness and beggary. I sat with him perhaps half an hour. He spoke of the commotions now disturbing Europe, and of the recent quasi revolution at Washington; but his voice was so feeble that he seemed exhausted by the exertion of speaking. I did not protract my visit, and took leave of him, in all probability, for the last time.—*Diary*, New York, April 27, 1831.

His [President Monroe's] life for the last six years has been one of abject penury and distress, and they have brought him to a premature grave, though in the seventy-third year of his age. His administration, happening precisely at the moment of the breaking up of old party divisions, was the period of the greatest tranquillity which has ever been enjoyed by this country; it was a time of great prosperity, and his personal popularity was unrivalled. Yet no one regretted the termination of his administration, and less of popular veneration followed him into retirement than had accompanied all his predecessors. His last days have been much afflicted, contrasting deeply with the triumphal procession which he made through the Union in 1817 and 1819. — *Diary*, Washington, July 4, 1831.

In the primitive principles of the parties, the Federalists were disposed to consider the first principle of society to be the preservation of order; while their opponents viewed the benefit above all others in the enjoyment of liberty. — *Eulogy of President Monroe*, August 25, 1831.

[From an Oration on the Life and Character of Lafayette, 1834.]

. . . . . Let us observe the influence of political institutions over the destinies and the characters of men. George the Second was a German Prince; he had been made king of the British Islands by the accident of his birth; that is to say, because his great-grandmother had been the daughter of James the First; that great-grandmother had been married to the king of Bohemia, and her youngest daughter had been married to the Elector of Hanover. George the Second's father was her son, and, when James the Second had been expelled from his throne and his country by the indignation of his people, revolted against his tyranny, and when his two daughters, who succeeded him, had died without issue, George the First, the son of the Electress of

Hanover, became king of Great Britain, by the settlement of an act of Parliament, blending together the principle of hereditary succession with that of Reformed Protestant Christianity, and the rites of the Church of England.

The throne of France was occupied by virtue of the same principle of hereditary succession, differently modified, and blended with the Christianity of the Church of Rome. From this line of succession all females were inflexibly excluded. Louis the Fifteenth, at the age of six years, had become the absolute sovereign of France, because he was the great-grandson of his immediate predecessor. He was of the third generation in descent from the preceding king, and, by the law of primogeniture, engrafted upon that of lineal succession, did, by the death of his ancestor, forthwith succeed, though in childhood, to an absolute throne, in preference to numerous descendants from that same ancestor then in the full vigor of manhood.

The first reflection that must occur to a rational being, in contemplating these two results of the principle of hereditary succession, is, that two persons more unfit to occupy the thrones of Britain and of France, at the time of their respective accessions, could scarcely have been found upon the face of the globe. George the Second, a foreigner, the son and grandson of foreigners, born beyond the seas, educated in uncongenial manners, ignorant of the Constitution, of the laws, even of the language of the people over whom he was to rule; and Louis the Fifteenth, an infant, incapable of discerning his right hand from his left. Yet strange as it may sound to the ear of unsophisticated reason, the British nation were wedded to the belief that this act of settlement, fixing their crown upon the heads of this succession of total strangers, was the brightest and most glorious exemplification of their national freedom; and not less strange, if aught in the imperfection of human reason could seem strange, was that deep conviction of the French people, at the same period, that *their* chief glory and happiness consisted in the vehemence of their affection for their king, because he was descended in an unbroken male line of genealogy from Saint Louis.

Among the dark spots in human nature, which in the course of my life I have observed, the devices of rivals to ruin me have been sorry pictures of the heart of man. They first exhibited themselves at college, but in the short time that I was there their operation could not be of much effect. But from the day that I quitted the walls of Harvard, H. G. Otis, Theophilus Parsons, Timothy Pickering, James A. Bayard, Henry Clay, Jonathan Russell, William H. Crawford, John C. Calhoun, Andrew Jackson, Daniel Webster, and John Davis, W. B. Giles, and John Randolph, have used up their faculties in base and dirty tricks to thwart my progress in life, and destroy my character. Others have acted as instruments to these, and among these Russell was the most contemptible, because he was the mere jackal to Clay. He is also the only one of the list whom I have signally punished. To almost all the rest I have returned good for evil. I have never wronged any one of them, and have even neglected too much my self-defence against them. — *Diary*, Washington, Nov. 23, 1835.

There was in the *National Intelligencer*, this morning, an advertisement signed James H. Birch, and Edward Dyer, auctioneer, headed " Sale of Slaves," — a sale at public auction, at four o'clock this afternoon, of Dorcas Allen and her two surviving children, aged about seven and nine years, (the other two having been killed by said Dorcas in a fit of insanity, as found by the jury who lately acquitted her). The advertisement further says that the said slaves were purchased by Birch, on the 22d of August last, of Rezin Orme, warranted sound in body and in mind; that the terms of sale will be cash, as said slaves will be sold on account of said Rezin Orme, who refuses to retake the same and repay the purchase money, and who is notified to attend said sale, and, if he thinks proper, to bid for them, or retake them, as he prefers, upon refunding the money paid and all expenses incurred under the warranty given by him.

I asked Mr. Frye what this advertisement meant. He seemed not to like to speak of it, but said the woman had been sold with her children, to be sent to the South and separated from her husband; that she had killed two of her children by cutting their throats, and cut her own to kill herself, but in that had failed; that she had been tried at Alexandria for the murder of her children, and acquitted on the ground of insanity, and that this sale was now by the purchaser at the expense of the seller, upon the warranty that she was sound in body and mind.

I called at the office of the *National Intelligencer* and saw Mr. Seaton; inquired of him concerning the advertisement. . . . He answered with reluctance, and told me the same story that I had heard from Mr. Frye, adding that there was something very bad about it, but without telling me what it was.

It is a case of conscience with me whether my duty requires or forbids me to pursue the inquiry in this case — to ascertain all the facts, and expose them in all their turpitude to the world. The prohibition of the internal slave-trade is within the constitutional power of Congress, and, in my opinion, is among their incumbent duties. I have gone as far upon this article, the abolition of slavery, as the public opinion of the free portion of the Union will bear, and so far that scarcely a slaveholding member of the House dares to vote with me upon any question. I have, as yet, been throughly sustained in my own State, but one step further and I hazard my own standing and influence there, my own final overthrow, and the cause of liberty itself for indefinite time, certainly for more than my remnant of life. Were there in the House one member capable of taking the lead in this cause of universal emancipation, which is moving onward in the world and in this country, I would withdraw from the contest, which will rage with increasing fury as it draws to its crisis, but for the management of which, my age, infirmities, and approaching end, totally disqualify me. There is no such man in the House. — *Diary*, Oct. 23, 1837.

[To this he added on the 28th.]

There was in the *National Intelligencer* of this morning an advertisement, again, of the sale of a woman and two children, at eleven o'clock. I went between eleven and twelve o'clock to the room. The woman and children, girls of seven and nine years of age, were there, the woman weeping and wailing most piteously. I inquired of Dyer if they were sold. He said, no, that they had been sold last Monday, and bought in by the husband of the woman, who was free, and a waiter at Gadsby's; he had bought them in for four hundred and seventy-five dollars, but was unable to raise the money, which was the reason why they were to be sold again. They were waiting for the man, who was endeavoring to procure, by subscription, upon his own engagement to repay the money, the means of paying for his purchase last Monday. [On the 13th of November Mr. Adams paid fifty dollars towards this object, and General Walter Smith, of Georgetown, undertook, with the other subscriptions, to pay the whole sum and take the bill of sale, by which the emancipation was secured.]

[On presenting what professed to be a petition from some slaves, in the House of Representatives, February 7, 1837, which created intense excitement, Mr. Adams said]:

Sir, it is well known that from the time I entered this House down to the present day, I have felt it a sacred duty to present any petition couched in respectful language, from any citizen of the United States, be its object what it may: be the prayer of it that in which I could concur, or that to which I was utterly opposed. It is for the sacred right of petition that I have adopted this course. . . . .

Where is your law which says that the mean, the low, and the degraded shall be deprived of the right of petition — if their moral character is not good? Where, in the land of freemen, was the right of petition ever placed on the exclusive basis of morality and virtue? Petition is *supplication* — it is *entreaty* — it is *prayer!* And where is the degree of vice or immorality which shall deprive the citizen of the right to *supplicate* for a boon, or to *pray for mercy?* Where is such a law to be found? It does not belong to the most abject despotism. There is no absolute monarch on earth who is not compelled by the Constitution of his country to receive the petitions of his people, whosoever they may be. The Sultan of Constantinople cannot walk the streets and refuse to receive petitions from the meanest and vilest of the land. This is the law even of despotism. And what does your law say? Does it say that before presenting a petition you shall look into it, and see whether it comes from the virtuous, and the great, and the mighty? No, sir, it says no such thing. The right of petition belongs to *all*. And so far from refusing to present a petition because it might come from those low in the estimation of the world, it would be an additional incentive, if such incentive were wanting.

[Speech in the House of Representatives, upon a petition from the women of Plymouth, Mass., remonstrating against the annexation of Texas, as a slaveholding territory.]

June 26, 1838.

..... The honorable gentleman [Mr. Howard] considered it "discreditable" not only to the section of country whence these memorials came, but discreditable to the nation. Sir, was it from a son — was it from a father — was it from a husband, that I heard these words? Does the gentleman consider that women, by petitioning this House in favor of suffering and distress, perform an office "discreditable" to themselves, to the section of country where they reside, and to this nation? I trust to the good nature of that gentleman that he will retract such an assertion. I have a right to make this call upon him. It is to the wives and to the daughters of my constituents that he applies this language. Am I to consider their conduct in petitioning this House as a discredit to that section of the Union and to their country? Sir, if there is anything in which they could do honor to their country, it was in this very act. He says that women have no right to petition Congress on political subjects. Why, sir, what does the gentleman understand by "political subjects?" Everything in which this House has an agency — everything which relates to peace and relates to war, or to any other of the great interests of society, is a political subject. Are women to have no opinions or action on subjects relating to the general welfare? This must be the gentleman's principle. Where did he get it? Did he find it in Sacred history? in the account which is given of the emigration of a whole nation from the land of Egypt, under the guidance of Moses and Aaron? What was the language of Miriam, the prophetess, when, after one of the noblest and most sublime songs of triumph that ever met the human eye or ear, it is said:

"And Miriam, the prophetess, the sister of Aaron, took a timbrel in her hand; and all the *women* went out after her with timbrels and with dances. And Miriam answered them, Sing ye to the Lord, for he hath triumphed gloriously; the horse and his rider hath he thrown into the sea."

Sir, is it in that portion of sacred history that he finds the principle that it is improper for women to take any concern in public affairs? This happened in the infancy of the Jewish nation. But has the gentleman never read or heard read the account which is given, at a later period, of the victory of Deborah?

"And Deborah, a prophetess, the wife of Lapidoth, she *judged* Israel at that time. And she dwelt under the palm-tree of Deborah, between Ramah and Bethel, in Mount Ephraim; and the children of Israel came to her for *judgment*."

Has he never read that inspiring cry:

"Awake, awake, Deborah; awake, awake, utter a song; arise Barak, and lead thy captivity captive, thou son of Abinoam."

Is the principle recognized here that women have nothing to do with political affairs?—no, not so much as even to petition in regard to them? Has he forgotten the deed of Jael, who slew the dreaded enemy of her country, who had so often invaded and ravaged it? Has he forgotten the name of Esther, who, by a PETITION, saved her people and her country? . . . Sir, I might go through the whole of the Sacred history of the Jews, down to the advent of our Saviour, and find innumerable examples of women who not only took an active part in the politics of their times, but who are held up with honor to posterity because they did so. I might point him to the names of Abigail, of Huldah, of Judith, the beautiful widow of Bethulia, who, in the days of the captivity, slew Holofernes, the commanding-general of the King of Babylon. But let me come down to a happier age under the dispensation of the new covenant. . . . But now, to leave sacred history and go to profane history. Does the chairman of the Committee find there that it is "discreditable" for women to take any interest or any part in political affairs? Let him read the history of Greece. Let him examine the character of Aspasia, and this in a country where the conduct and freedom of women were more severely restricted than in any modern nation, save among the Turks. It was in Athens, where female character had not that full development which is permitted to it in our state of society. . . . Can he have forgotten the innumerable instances recorded by the profane historians, where women distinguished, nay, immortalized their names, by the part they took in the affairs of their country?

. . . . . Why does it follow that women are fitted for nothing but the cares of domestic life? for bearing children and cooking the food of a family? devoting all their time to the domestic circle, to promoting the immediate personal comfort of their husbands, brothers, and sons? Observe, sir, the point of departure between the chairman of the committee and myself. I admit that it is their duty to attend to these things. I subscribe fully to the elegant compliment passed by him upon those members of the female sex who devote their time to these duties. But I say that the correct principle is, that women are not only justified, but exhibit the most exalted virtue when they do depart from the domestic circle, and enter on the concerns of their country, of humanity, and of their God. The mere departure of woman from the duties of the domestic circle, far from being a reproach to her, is a virtue of the highest order, when it is done from purity of motive, by appropriate means, and towards a virtuous purpose. There is the true distinction. The motive must be pure, the means appropriate, and the purpose good. And I say that woman, by the discharge of such duties, has manifested a virtue which is even above the virtues of mankind, and approaches to a superior nature.

[Speech in the House of Representatives, 1838.]

I am well aware of the change which is taking place in the moral and political philosophy of the South. I know well that the doctrine of the Declaration of Independence, that "all men are born free and equal," is there held as incendiary doctrine, and deserves Lynching; that the Declaration itself is a farrago of abstractions. I know all this perfectly; and that is the very reason that I want to put my foot upon such doctrine; that I want to drive it back to its fountain, — its corrupt fountain, — and pursue it till it is made to disappear from this land and from the world. Sir, this philosophy of the South has done more to blacken the character of this country in Europe than all other causes put together. They point to us as a nation of liars and hypocrites, who publish to the world that all men are born free and equal, and then hold a large portion of our own population in bondage.

But I have been drawn into observations which

are, here, very much out of place; and which I probably should not have made, and certainly not with the force I have endeavored to give them, had it not been for the interruption of the gentleman from South Carolina.* If he will put such questions he must expect to receive answers corresponding to them; and he will receive not only my answer, but those of others, who are far deeper thinkers than I, not only in this country but abroad; for this debate will go on the wings of the wind. The account of the gentleman's principles will come back from all parts of Europe and of the civilized world in hisses and execrations that a man should have been found, in the highest legislative body of this free republic, to avow opinions such as we have just heard from the lips of that gentleman. I shall dismiss that branch of the subject now. If the gentleman is desirous of more; if he wishes to enter into a full and strict scrutiny of the question of slavery in all its bearings, either at this session or the next, and God shall give me life, and breath, and the faculty of speech, he shall have it to his heart's content.

* Mr. Campbell had said, among other remarks, that "many worthy men, who were formerly somewhat uneasy at the existence of this institution, now feel themselves called upon by every motive, personal and private, by every consideration, public and patriotic, to guard it with the most jealous watchfulness, — to defend it at every hazard."

[From the same Speech.]

The Declaration of Independence, which united the people of thirteen separate and independent states into one, speaks from the beginning to the end in the name of the people.... I pass on to the Constitution of the United States.... The very first words were such as put the People in action; they declare that it is the act of one People who have separated themselves from another, and have agreed to frame for themselves this Constitution of Government.

I shall not enter on the captious quibbling whether the People voted man by man, throughout the Union, or whether they voted by their representatives in special conventions assembled in each of the states separately. It is not necessary to settle any such questions. These are the cobweb threads of justification, all spun from the bowels of slavery. The language of the whole instrument is, "We, the People." It has, from the beginning, been the government of "us, the People," and will, I trust, be that of posterity.

The conflict between the principle of liberty and the fact of slavery is coming gradually to an issue. Slavery has now the power, and falls into convulsions at the approach of freedom. That the fall of slavery is predetermined in the counsels of Omnipotence, I cannot doubt; it is a part of the great moral improvement in the condition of man, attested by all the records of history. But the conflict will be terrible, and the progress of improvement perhaps retrograde before its final progress to consummation. — *Diary*, December 13, 1838.

On December 20th, 1838, in the House of Representatives, Mr. Adams presented a petition for the establishment of international relations with the Republic of Hayti, and said : . . . Then, sir, I come back to my position, that every man in this country has a right to be an abolitionist, and that in being so he offends no law, but, in my opinion, obeys the most sacred of all laws.

[In 1832, South Carolina passed an ordinance declaring the tariff laws "null and void," and that the State would secede from the Union if force should be employed to collect any revenue at Charleston; upon which President Jackson issued a Proclamation denouncing "nullification," and declaring his purpose to execute the laws. It was in December of this year, that Mr. Adams wrote in his Diary] : "I told Hoffman that the real question now convulsing this Union was, whether a population spread over an immense territory, consisting of one great division, all freemen, and another, of masters and slaves, could exist permanently together as members of one community or not; tnat, to go a step further back, the question at issue was slavery."

I do believe slavery to be a sin before God. — *Speech in the House of Representatives*, 1838.

It is among the evils of slavery, that it taints the very sources of moral principle. It establishes false estimates of virtue and vice; for what can be more false and more heartless than this doctrine, which makes the first and holiest rights of humanity to depend upon the color of the skin? It perverts human reason, and induces men endowed with logical powers to maintain that slavery is sanctioned by the Christian religion; that slaves are happy and contented in their condition; that between master and slave there are ties of mutual attachment and affection; that the virtues of the master are refined and exalted by the degradation of the slave, while, at the same time, they vent execrations upon the slave-trade, curse Britain for having given them slaves, burn at the stake negroes convicted of crimes, for the terror of the example, and writhe in agonies of fear at the very mention of human rights as applicable to men of color. — *Diary*.

[From the Introduction to the Memoir of Elijah P. Lovejoy, 1838.]

In the biographical narratives of the Founder of the Christian religion, and of his primitive disciples, there is an internal evidence of truth, not less conclusive than that of the miracles which they performed. The miracles were the evidence necessary to prove the authenticity of his mission to his contemporaries, to whom he was accredited, to whom he revealed the hidden mystery of their own immortality, and to whom he proclaimed the laws of their own nature, the obligations of mutual benevolence and charity : — *love* upon earth and *life* hereafter were the everlasting pillars of his system of religion and of morals. . . . . .

In the progressive revolutions effected by the Christian system of religion and morals, it was in the order of Providence that its operations should be slow and gradual, embracing a period of many thousand years. . . . In these doctrines [of universal love and eternal life], however, there was a principle of vitality destined to survive all persecution, and to triumph over all human power. The moral precepts of the Levitical law, purified and refined, shone with undying lustre in the new dispensation, — its rites and ceremonies, its priests and Levites, its sacrifices of blood, its visions, and its dreams, gave way to a simple and spiritual form of worship ; the working of miracles, no longer necessary for the authentication of faith, was withdrawn from the disciples of the cross, and the new system of religion and morals was left to make its way in the world by the perpetual miracle of its celestial origin, self-evident by the internal demonstration of its irresistible power and its superhuman perfection.

[On the opening of the 26th Congress, December, 1839, there being a twofold delegation from New Jersey, the clerk, on reaching that State, refused to proceed with calling the roll, and the members could effect no organization. It was so for three days. On the fourth day, when the State of New Jersey was reached,* Mr. Adams rose and said] : "I rise to interrupt the clerk," — which created an intense excitement. "It was not my intention to take any part in these extraordinary proceedings. I had hoped that this House would succeed in organizing itself; that a Speaker

On December 2, 1839, at the opening of the 26th Congress, the clerk commenced calling the roll of members. When he came to New Jersey, (whose members were then elected by general ticket,) he stated that the seats of five of the six members from that state were contested: that he did not feel authorized to decide the question of their right to their seats, and that he should therefore pass over their names, and proceed with the call. The election of these members was certified to by the governor of New Jersey. It so happened that these five members were all whigs. Parties were so evenly balanced in the House, that if these five members were admitted at once, it would give the whigs control of its organization, including the election of Speaker. — *Appleton's New Amer. Cyclop.,* Art. Fillmore.

and Clerk would be elected, and the ordinary business of legislation would go on. This is not the time or place to discuss the merits of the conflicting claimants for seats from New Jersey; the subject belongs to the House of Representatives, which, by the Constitution, is made the ultimate arbiter of the qualifications of its members. But what a spectacle we here present! We degrade and disgrace ourselves; we degrade and disgrace our constituents and the country. We do not, and cannot organize; and why? Because the clerk of this house, the mere clerk, whom we create, whom we employ, and whose existence depends upon our will, usurps the throne, and sets us, the Representatives, the vicegerents of the whole American people, at defiance, and holds us in contempt. And what is this clerk of yours? Is he to control the destinies of sixteen millions of freemen? Is he to suspend, by his mere negative, the functions of government, and put an end to this Congress? He refuses to call the roll! It is in your power to compel him to call it, if he will not do it voluntarily. [A member here said that he was authorized to say that the clerk would resign rather than call the roll of New Jersey.] Well, sir, then let him resign, and we may possibly discover some way by which we can get along without the aid of his all-powerful talent, learning, and genius. If we cannot organize in any other way — if this clerk of yours will not consent to our discharging the trusts confided to us by our constituents, then let us imitate the example of the Virginia House of Burgesses, which, when the colonial governor, Dinwiddie, ordered it to disperse, refused to obey the imperious and insulting mandate, and, like *men* — [here followed a burst of enthusiasm, when Mr. Adams submitted a motion requiring the acting clerk to proceed in calling the roll. Many members inquiring, " How shall the question be put?" "Who will put the question?" Mr. Adams replied, "*I intend to put the question myself!*" Whereupon Mr. Rhett, of South Carolina, exclaimed, "I move that the Hon. John Quincy Adams take the chair of the Speaker of this House, and officiate as presiding officer till the House be organized by the election of its constitutional officers. As many as agree to this will say, Aye; those — " which was followed by an universal shout of Aye. And order came out of confusion.]

[A "gag-law," forbidding the presentation of petitions on the subject of slavery, having passed the House of Representatives, Mr. Adams, at the commencement of each subsequent session, demanded its abolition, and continued to hand in petitions as before. He was threatened with expulsion, assassination, and indictment before the grand jury of the District of Columbia. On one occasion he said]:

Do the gentlemen from the South think they can frighten me by their threats? If that be their object, let me tell them, sir, they have mistaken their man. I am not to be frightened from the discharge of a sacred duty by their indignation, by their violence, nor, sir, by all the grand juries in the universe. I have done only my duty; and I shall do it again under the same circumstances, even though they recur to-morrow.

[When, in the year 1845, the "gag-law" was rescinded, Mr. Adams exclaimed]: "God be praised; the seals are broken, the door is open."

[In an address at Pittsfield, Mass, in 1843, he said]: In 1775 the minute-men from a hundred towns in the province were marching at a moment's warning to the scene of opening war. Many of them called at my father's house in Quincy, and received the hospitality of John Adams. All were lodged in the house whom the house would contain; others in the barns, and wherever they could find a place. There were then in my father's kitchen some dozen or two of pewter spoons; and I well recall going into the kitchen and seeing some of the men engaged in running those spoons into bullets for the use of the troops! Do you wonder that a boy of seven years of age, who witnessed this scene, should be a patriot?

. . . . . The influence of Mr. Jefferson over the mind of Mr. Madison was composed of all that genius, talent, experience, splendid public services, exalted reputation, added to congenial temper, undivided friendship, and habitual sympathies of interest and of feeling could inspire. Among the numerous blessings which it was the rare good fortune of Mr. Jefferson's life to enjoy, was that of the uninterrupted, disinterested, and efficient friendship of Madison. But it was the friendship of a mind not inferior in capacity, and tempered with a calmer sensibility and a cooler judgment than his own. — *Eulogy on President Madison.*

A confederation is not a country. There is no magnet of attraction in any league of sovereign and independent states which causes the heartstrings of the individual man to vibrate in unison with those of his neighbor. Confederates are not countrymen. — *Eulogy on President Madison.*

The Declaration of Independence annulled the national character of the American people. That character had been common to them all as subjects of one and the same sovereign, and that sovereign was a king. The dissolution of that tie was pronounced by one act common to them all, and it left them as members of distinct communities in the relation towards each other, bound only by the obligations of the law of nature and of the Union, by which they had renounced their connection with the mother country.

But what was to be the character of their national existence? This was the problem of difficult solution for them; and this was the opening of the new era in the science of government, and in the history of mankind. — *Eulogy on President Madison.*

[From the same.]

..... The principle that religious opinions are altogether beyond the sphere of legislative control is but one modification of a more extensive axiom, which includes the unlimited freedom of the press, of speech, and of the communication of thought in all its forms.

[From the same.]

In most of the inspirations of genius there is a simplicity which, when they are familiarized to the general understanding of men by their effects, detracts from the opinion of their greatness. That the people of the British colonies, who, by their united counsels and energies, had achieved their independence, should continue to be one people, and constitute a nation under the form of one organized government, was an idea in itself so simple, and addressed itself at once so forcibly to the reason, to the imagination, and to the benevolent feelings of all, that it can scarcely be supposed to have escaped the mind of any reflecting man from Maine to Georgia. It was the dictate of nature. But no sooner was it conceived than it was met by obstacles innumerable and insuperable to the general mass of mankind. They resulted from the existing social institutions, diversified among the parties to the projected national union, and seeming to render it impracticable. There were chartered rights, for the maintenance of which the war of the revolution itself had first been waged. There were state sovereignties, corporate feudal baronies, tenacious of their own liberty, impatient of a superior, and jealous and disdainful of a paramount sovereign, even in the whole democracy of the nation. There were collisions of boundary and of proprietary right westward in the soil; southward, in its cultivator. In fine, the diversities of interests, of opinions, of manners, of habits, and even of extraction, were so great, that the plan of constituting them one people appears not even to have occurred to any of the members of the convention * before they were

* For forming new Constitution.

assembled together. . . . Nearly four months of anxious deliberation were employed by an assembly composed of the men who had been the most distinguished for their services, civil and military, in conducting the country through the arduous struggles of the revolution; of men who, to the fire of genius, added all the lights of experience, and were stimulated by the impulses at once of ardent patriotism and of individual ambition aspiring to that last and most arduous labor of constituting a nation destined in after times to present a model of government for all the civilized nations of the earth. . . . . .

[From the same.]

Government, in the first and most obvious aspect which it assumes, is a restraint upon human action, and, as such, a restraint upon liberty. The constitution of the United States was intended to be a government of great energy, and, of course, of extensive restriction, not only upon individual liberty, but upon the corporate action of states claiming to be sovereign and independent. The convention had been aware that such restraints upon the people could be imposed by no earthly power other than the people themselves. They were aware that to induce the people to impose upon themselves such binding ligaments, motives not less cogent than those which form the basis of human association were indispensably necessary; that the first principles of politics must be indissolubly linked with the first principles of morals. They assumed, therefore, the existence of a People of the United States, and made them declare the constitution to be their own work, speaking in the first person, and saying, *We, the People* of the United States, do ordain and establish this constitution for the United States of America; and then the allegation of motives, to form a more perfect union, to establish justice, insure domestic tranquillity, provide for the common defence, promote the general welfare, and secure the blessings of liberty to ourselves and our posterity. These are precisely the purposes for which it has pleased the Author of nature to make man a social being, and has blended into one his happiness with that of his kind.

How much of the South Carolina character originated in Locke's Constitution? How much in the sub-tropical climate? How much in the cultivation of indigo, rice, and cotton? How much (more than all the rest) in negro slavery? How much in the Christian religion? And how much in Anglo-Saxon descent? These elements, mixed with the casual diversities of individual men in the progress of population, have produced an average associate character different from that of any other state in the Union — from none more than from that of its next-door neighbour, North Carolina. This character shows itself everywhere — in the city, in the field, by the family fireside, in the social circle, at the bar, in the legislative hall, and finally in the pulpit. — *Diary*, May, 1840.

ANDREW JACKSON.

BORN, 1767; DIED, 1845, AGED 78.—BEGAN PRACTICE OF LAW, 1786.—SOLICITOR OF THE WESTERN DISTRICT OF N. CAROLINA, 1788.—DISTRICT ATTORNEY OF TENNESSEE, 1796.—MEMBER OF CONVENTION TO FRAME A CONSTITUTION FOR TENNESSEE, 1796.—REPRESENTATIVE IN CONGRESS, 1796.—UNITED STATES SENATOR, 1797.—JUSTICE IN THE SUPREME COURT OF TENNESSEE, 1798.—ENGAGED IN THE CREEK WAR, 1813, 1814.—MAJOR-GENERAL IN THE UNITED STATES ARMY, 1814.—COMMANDER AT NEW ORLEANS, 1815.—COMMANDER-IN-CHIEF OF THE SOUTHERN DIVISION OF THE U. S., 1815—ENGAGED IN THE SEMINOLE WAR, 1817.—GOVERNOR OF FLORIDA, 1829.—UNITED STATES SENATOR, 1823.—PRESIDENT, 1829-1837.

[From a Message to Congress, December, 1831.]

[AFTER a review of our foreign relations, the President said] : "I have great satisfaction in making this statement of our affairs, because the course of our national policy enables me to do it without any indiscreet exposure of what in other governments is usually concealed from the people. Having none but a straightforward, open course to pursue, — guided by a single principle that will bear the strongest light, — we have happily no political combinations to form, no alliance to entangle us, no complicated interests to consult; and in subjecting all that we have done to the consideration of our citizens, and to the inspection of the world, we give no advantage to other nations, and lay ourselves open to no injury.

[From a Message to Congress, July 10, 1832.]

The Congress, the Executive, and the [Supreme] Court must each for itself be guided by its own opinion of the Constitution. Each public officer, who takes an oath to support the Constitution, swears that he will support it as as he understands it, and not as it is understood by others. It is as much the duty of the House of Representatives, of the Senate, and of the President to decide upon the constitutionality of any bill or resolution which may be presented to them for passage or approval, as it is of the Supreme Judges, when it may be brought before them for judicial decision. The opinion of the judges has no more authority over Congress, than the opinion of Congress has over the judges, and on that point the President is independent of both.

It is to be regretted that the rich and powerful too often bend the acts of government to their selfish purposes. Distinctions in society will always exist under every just government. Equality of talents, of education, or of wealth, cannot be produced by human institutions. In the full enjoyment of the gifts of Heaven and the fruits of superior industry, economy, and virtue, every man is equally entitled to protection by law. But when the laws undertake to add to these natural and just advantages artificial distinctions, to grant titles, gratuities, and exclusive privileges — to make the rich richer and the potent more powerful — the humble members of society — the farmers, mechanics, and laborers, who have neither the time nor the means of securing like favors to themselves, have a right to complain of the injustice of their government. There are no necessary evils in government. Its evils exist only in its abuses. If it would confine itself to equal protection, and, as Heaven does its rains, shower its favors alike on the high and the low, the rich and the poor, it would be an unqualified blessing.

[Letter to Col. A. J. Hamilton.]

WASHINGTON, November 2, 1832.

MY DEAR SIR: I have just received your letter of the 31st ult., with the enclosure, for which I thank you.

I am well advised of the views and proceedings of the great leading nullifiers of the South in my native State (South Carolina), and weep for its fate, and over the delusion into which the people are led by the wickedness, ambition, and folly of their leaders. I have no doubt of the intention of their leaders to alarm the other States to submit to their views rather than a dissolution of the Union should take place. If they fail in this, to cover their own disgrace and wickedness, to nullify the tariff, and secede from the Union.

We are wide awake here. The Union will be preserved, rest assured of this. There has been too much blood and treasure shed to obtain it, to let it be surrendered without a struggle. Our liberty and that of the whole world rests upon it, as well as the peace, prosperity, and happiness of these United States. It must be perpetuated.

[Letter to Col. J. A. Hamilton.]

WASHINGTON, December 6, 1832.

Yours of the 3d inst. is just received. I accord with you fully in the propriety of the people giving fully and freely their sentiments and opinions on nullification, and the course pursued by South Carolina in her late proceedings.

The ordinance passed, when taken in connection with the Governor's message, is rebellion and war against the Union. The raising of troops under them to resist the laws of the United States is absolute treason. The crisis must be, and as far as my constitutional and legal powers go, will be met with energy and firmness. Therefore the propriety of the public voice being heard, and it ought now to be spoken in a voice of thunder that will make the leaders of the nullifiers tremble, and which will cause the good citizens of South Carolina to retrace their steps and adhere to that constitution of perpetual union they have sworn to support. This treasonable procedure against the Union is a blow against not only our liberties but the liberties of the world.

This nullifying movement in the South has done no great injury abroad, and must not only be promptly met and put down, but frowned down by public opinion. It is therefore highly proper for the people to speak all over the Union. I am preparing a proclamation to the people of the South, and as soon as officially advised of these rebellious proceedings, will make a communication to Congress.

[From a Message to Congress, January 16, 1833.]

..... A recent proclamation of the present Governor of South Carolina has openly defied the authority of the Executive of the Union, and general orders from the head-quarters of the State announced his determination to accept the services of volunteers, and his belief that, should their country need their services, they will be found at the post of honor and duty, ready to lay down their lives in her defence. Under these orders, the forces referred to are directed to " hold themselves in readiness to take the field at a moment's warning; and in the city of Charleston, within a collection district and a port of entry, a rendezvous has been opened for the purpose of enlisting men for the magazine and municipal guard. Thus South Carolina presents herself in the attitude of hostile preparation, and ready even for military violence, if need be, to enforce her laws for preventing the collection of the duties within her limits. . . . . .

It therefore becomes my duty to bring the subject to the serious consideration of Congress, in order that such measures as they, in their wisdom, may deem fit, shall be seasonably provided; and that it may be thereby understood that, while the government is disposed to remove all just cause of complaint, so far as may be practicably consistent with a proper regard to the interests of the community at large, it is nevertheless determined that the supremacy of the laws shall be maintained. . . .

By these various proceedings the State of South Carolina has forced the general government, unavoidably, to decide the new and dangerous alternative of permitting a State to obstruct the execution of the laws within its limits, or seeing it able to execute a threat of withdrawing from the Union. That portion of the people at present exercising the authority of the State solemnly assert their right to do either, and as solemnly announce their determination to do one or the other.

In my opinion both purposes are to be regarded as revolutionary in their character and tendency, and subversive of the supremacy of the Constitution and of the integrity of the Union. The result of each is the same; since a State, in which, by an usurpation of power, the constitutional authority of the Federal government is openly defied and set aside, wants only the form to be independent of the Union.

The right of the people of a single State to absolve themselves at will, and without the consent of other States, from their most solemn obligations, and hazard the liberties and happiness of the millions composing the Union, cannot be acknowledged. Such authority is believed to be utterly repugnant both to the principles upon which the General Government is constructed, and to the objects which it is expressly formed to attain.

Against all acts which may be alleged to transcend the constitutional power of the government, or which may be inconvenient and oppressive in their operation, the Constitution itself has prescribed the modes of redress. It is the acknowledged attribute of free institutions that, under them, the empire of reason and law is substituted for the power of the sword. To no other source can appeals from supposed wrongs be made consistently with the obligations of South Carolina; to no other can such appeals be made with safety at any time; and to their decisions, when constitutionally pronounced, it becomes the duty, no less of the public authorities than of the people, in every case to yield to a patriotic submission. . . .

Independently of these considerations, it will not escape observation that South Carolina still claims to be a component part of the Union, to participate in the national councils, and to share in the public benefits, without contributing to the public burdens — thus asserting the dangerous anomaly of continuing in an association without acknowledging any other obligation to its laws than what depends upon her own will.

In this posture of affairs the duty of the Government seems to be plain. It inculcates the recognition of that State as a member of the Union, and subject to its authority; a vindication of the just power of the Constitution; the preservation of the integrity of the Union, and the execution of the laws by all consistent means. . . . . .

While a forbearing spirit may, and, I trust, will, be exercised towardsth e errors of our brethren in a particular quarter, duty to the rest of the Union demands that open and organized resistance to the laws should not be executed with impunity. . . . .

For myself, fellow-citizens, devoutly relying upon that kind Providence which has hitherto watched over our destiny, and actuated by a profound reverence for those institutions I have so much cause to love, and for the American people, whose partiality honored me with this high trust,

I have determined to spare no effort to discharge the duty which, in this conjuncture, is devolved upon me. That a similar spirit will actuate the Representatives of the American people is not to be questioned; and I fervently pray that the Great Ruler of nations may so guide your deliberations, and our joint measures, as that they may prove salutary examples, not only to the present, but to future times; and solemnly proclaim that the Constitution and the laws are supreme, and the Union indissoluble.

[From a letter to Rev. A. J. Crawford, May 1, 1833.]

. . . . . The tariff was only a pretext [for nullification], and Disunion and a Southern Confederacy the real object. The next pretext will be the negro or slavery question.

[From a Message, December 6, 1836.]

. . . . . Variableness must ever be the character of a currency of which the precious metals are not the chief ingredient, or which can be expanded or contracted without regard to the principles that regulate the value of those metals as a standard in the general trade of the world. . . . The progress of an expansion, or rather a depreciation of the currency, by excessive bank issues, is always attended by a loss to the laboring classes. This part of the community has neither time nor opportunity to watch the ebbs and flows of the money market. Engaged from day to day in their useful toils, they do not perceive that although their wages are nominally the same, or even somewhat higher, they are greatly reduced in fact by the rapid increase of a spurious currency, which, as it appears to make money abound, they are at first inclined to consider a blessing.

To a Major Lewis, of Kentucky, who rather pompously said to General Jackson, " Well, General, I have all my life been voting against you," he replied, " Well, Major, I have all my life been fighting the battles of my country in order that you might enjoy that privilege."—*Nashville Banner*, 1880.

MARTIN VAN BUREN.

BORN, 1782; DIED, 1862, AGED 80.—SURROGATE OF COLUMBIA COUNTY, N. Y., 1808.—STATE SENATOR, 1812.—MEMBER OF THE CONVENTION TO REVISE THE NEW YORK STATE CONSTITUTION, 1821.—UNITED STATES SENATOR, 1827.—GOVERNOR OF NEW YORK, 1828.—SECRETARY OF STATE, 1829.—MINISTER TO ENGLAND, 1831.—VICE-PRESIDENT, 1832-1836.—PRESIDENT, 1837-1841.

[From an Address, 1819.]

THE struggle which gave birth to our nation must ever be regarded as one of the most important and interesting eras the world has ever witnessed. History records no event which called into action a race of statesmen equal in all the splendid virtues which adorn and give celebrity to the human character. And it is a fact honorable to our nation, that of the long·list of patriots and sages who, at the hazard of all that was dear to man, signed the Declaration of Independence, and of those who framed the grand charter of our liberties, there has not been one who, in after life, has fallen from the eminence to which, by his connection with those events, he was raised, or has in the least impaired the character he thus acquired. Those whom the ravages of time have yet spared to their country are everywhere honored and respected; and those whose deaths we deplore, who are now numbered with "the spirits of just men made perfect," have descended to the tomb accompanied by a nation's tears, and blessed with a nation's gratitude.

[From a Speech in the Convention for revising the Constitution of New York, 1821, in favor of a proposition to vest in the Governor a revisory power upon the acts of the legislature.]

. . . . . . Distinct branches are not only necessary to the existence of government, but when you have prescribed them, it is necessary that you should make them, in a great degree, independent of each other. No government can be so favored as to make them entirely separate; but it has been the study of the wisest and best men to invent a plan by which they might be rendered as independent of each other as the nature of government would admit. The legislative department is by far the strongest, and is constantly inclined to encroach upon the weaker branches of government, and upon individual rights. This arises from a variety of causes. In the first place, the powers of that department are more extended and indefinable than those of any other, which gives its members an exalted idea of their superiority. They are the representatives of the people, from which circumstance they think they possess, and of right ought to possess, all the power of the people. This is natural, and it is easy to imagine the consequences that necessarily follow.

This is not all. They hold the purse-strings of the state; and every member of all the branches of the government is dependent on them for his subsistence. You have been told, and correctly told, that those who feed men, and enjoy the privilege of dispensing the public bounty, will, in a greater or less degree, influence and control them. Is it unreasonable or improbable to suppose that power, thus constituted, should have a tendency to exert itself for purposes not congenial with the true interests of the other branches of government? . . . Such is the superior force and influence of legislative power; such is the reverence and regard with which it is looked up to, that no man in the community will have the temerity, on ordinary occasions, to resist its acts or check its proceedings. I cannot illustrate this position more strongly than by a reference to the constitution of England. There the executive is a branch of the legislature, and has an absolute negative. Surrounded as he is with prerogative, and placed far beyond the reach of the people, yet since the year 1692 no objection has been made by the king of Great Britain to any bill presented for his approval. Rather than produce the excitement and irritation which, even there, would result from the rejection of a bill passed by the Parliament, he has resorted to means which have degraded the government and dishonored the nation, to prevent the passage of bills which he should feel it his duty to reject. In the Declaration of Independence, in the category of wrongs under which our fathers had been suffering, one of the most prominent was, that the king had exercised his prerogative, and had refused his sanction to salutary laws. Gentlemen may, therefore, rest satisfied that very little danger is to be apprehended on this subject.

[From "Political Parties in the United States."]

John Adams was in every sense a remarkable man. Nature seems to have employed in his construction intellectual materials sufficient to have furnished many minds respectably. It would not be easy to name men either of his day or of any period, whose character presents a deeper or a stronger soil, one which during his long and somewhat boisterous public life was thoroughly probed by his enemies without disclosing any variation in its depths from the qualities and indications of its surface. Still more deeply was it turned up and exposed to light by himself with the same result. His writings, which have been more extensive and more varied than those of any of his contemporaries, have been given to the world apparently without reserve. These, with his diaries and autobiography have turned his character inside out, and shown us, without disguise of any sort, the kind of man he was; and the representation is invariably that of the same "always honest man" that he was three quarters of a century ago when that high praise was accorded to him by his not too particular friend Benjamin Franklin, in a communication not designed to be over civil. . . . Mr. Jefferson, but two years before the death of both of them, on referring to that [the revolutionary] period, and to Mr. Adams' great services, in my presence, was warmed by the subject, and spoke of him as having been the mainmast of the ship—the orator of the Revolution, etc.

[From the Same.]

. . . . . Mr. Jefferson commenced the discharge of his official duties by an act which, though one of form, involved matter of the highest moment. I allude to the decision and facility with which, in his intercourse with other branches of the government, he suppressed the observance of empty ceremonies which had been borrowed from foreign courts by officials who took an interest in such matters, and were reluctantly tolerated by Washington, who was himself above them. Instead of proceeding in state to the capitol to deliver a speech to the legislature, according to the custom of monarchs, he performed his constitutional duty by means of a message in writing, sent to each House by the hands of his private secretary, and they performed theirs by a reference of its contents to appropriate committees. The executive procession, instead of marking the intercourse between the different branches of the government, was reserved for the Inauguration, when the President appeared before the people themselves, and in their presence took the oath of office.

[From his Reply to the Committee of the Convention which nominated him for the Presidency.]

..... We hold an immense stake for the weal or woe of mankind, to the importance of which we should not be insensible. The intense interest manifested abroad in every movement here that threatens the stability of our system, shows the deep conviction which pervades the world that upon its fate depends the cause of republican government. The advocates of monarchical systems have not been slow in perceiving danger to such institutions in the permanency of our Constitution, nor backward in seizing upon every passing event by which their predictions of its speedy destruction could be in any degree justified. Thus far they have been disappointed in their expectations, and the circumstances by which they were encouraged, however alarming at the time, have in the end only tended to show forth the depth of that devotion to the Union which is yet, thank God, the master passion of the American bosom.

[From a Message to Congress, September 5, 1837.]

..... It has since appeared that evils similar to those suffered by ourselves, have been experienced in Great Britain, on the Continent, and indeed throughout the commercial world, and that in other countries as well as in our own, they have been uniformly preceded by an undue enlargement of the boundaries of trade, prompted, as with us, by unprecedented expansions of the systems of credit. A reference to the amount of banking capacity and the issues of paper credits put in circulation in Great Britain by banks and in other ways, during the years 1834, 1835, and 1836, will show an augmentation of the paper currency there, as much disproportioned to the real wants of trade as in the United States. With this redundance in the paper currency, there arose in that country also a spirit of adventurous speculation embracing the whole range of human enterprise. Aid was profusely given to projected improvements; large investments made in foreign stocks and loans; credits for goods were granted with unbounded liberality to merchants in foreign countries; and all the means of acquiring and employing credit were put in active operation, and extended, in their effects, to every department of business, and to every quarter of the globe. The reaction was proportioned in its violence to the extensive character of the events which preceded it.

. . . . In view of these facts, it would seem impossible for sincere inquirers after truth to resist the conviction, that the causes of the revulsion in both countries have been substantially the same. Two nations, the most commercial in the world, enjoying but recently the highest degree of apparent prosperity, and maintaining with each other the closest relations, are suddenly, in a time of profound peace, and without any great national disaster, arrested in their career, and plunged into a state of embarrassment and distress. In both countries we have witnessed the same redundancy of paper money, and other facilities of credit; the same spirit of speculation, the same partial successes; the same difficulties and reverses; and at length nearly the same overwhelming catastrophe. . . . .

All communities are apt to look to government for too much. Even in our own country, where its powers and duties are so strictly limited, we are prone to do so, especially at periods of sudden embarrassment and distress. But this ought not to be. The framers of our excellent Constitution, and the people who approved it, with calm and sagacious deliberation, acted at the time on a sounder principle. They wisely judged that the less government interferes with private pursuits, the better for the general prosperity. It is not its legitimate object to make men rich, or to repair, by direct grants of money or legislation in favor of particular pursuits, losses not incurred in the public service. This would be substantially, to use the property of some for the benefit of others. But its real duty, that duty, the performance of which makes a good government the most precious of human blessings, is to enact and enforce a system of general taxes commensurate with, but not exceeding, the objects of its establishment, and to leave every citizen and every interest to reap, under its benign protection, the rewards of virtue, industry, and prudence. . . . . . .

The great agricultural interest has, in many parts of the country, suffered comparatively little; and, as if Providence intended to display the munificence of its goodness at the moment of our greatest need, and in direct contrast to the evils occasioned by the waywardness of man, we have been blessed, throughout our extended territory, with a season of general health and of uncommon fruitfulness. . . . . . .

It is a high gratification to know that we act for a people to whom the truth, however unpromising, can always be spoken with safety, for the trial of whose patience no emergency is too severe, and who are sure never to despise a public functionary honestly laboring for the public good.

WILLIAM HENRY HARRISON.

BORN, 1773; DIED, 1841, AGED 68.—CAPTAIN IN THE ARMY, 1795.—SECRETARY OF THE TERRITORY NORTH-WEST OF THE OHIO, 1797.—DELEGATE TO CONGRESS, 1790.—GOVERNOR OF THE TERRITORY OF INDIANA, 1801.—ENGAGED IN THE BATTLE OF TIPPECANOE, 1811.—BRIGADIER-GENERAL AND COMMANDER OF THE NORTH-WEST FRONTIER, 1812.—MAJOR-GENERAL, 1813.—COMMANDER IN THE BATTLE OF THE THAMES, 1813.—REPRESENTATIVE TO CONGRESS, 1816.—IN THE STATE SENATE OF OHIO, 1819.—IN THE UNITED STATES SENATE, 1824.—MINISTER TO COLOMBIA, 1828.—PRESIDENT, 1841.

[From an Address, when Governor and Commander-in-chief of the territory of Indiana, to the Legislative Council and House of Representatives, 1805.]

..... An enlightened and generous policy has forever removed all cause of contention with our western neighbors [by the acquisition of Louisiana in 1803]. The mighty river which separates us from the Louisianians will never be stained with the blood of contending nations, but will prove the bond of our Union, and will convey upon its bosom, in a course of many thousand miles, the produce of our great and united empire. . . . . .

The interests of your constituents, the interests of the miserable Indians, and your own feelings, will sufficiently urge to take it into your most serious consideration, and provide the remedy which is to save thousands of our fellow-creatures. . . . So destructive has the progress of intemperance been among them, that whole villages have been swept away. A miserable remnant is all that remains to mark the names and situation of many numerous and warlike tribes. In the energetic language of one of their orators, it is a dreadful conflagration, which spreads misery and desolation through their country, and threatens the annihilation of the whole race.

Is it then to be admitted as a political axiom, that the neighborhood of a civilized nation is incompatible with the existence of savages? Are the blessings of our republican government only to be felt by ourselves? And are the nations of North America to experience the same fate with their brethren of the Southern Continent? It is with you, gentlemen, to divert from those children of nature the ruin which hangs over them. Nor can I believe that the time will be considered as misspent which is devoted to an object so consistent with the spirit of Christianity and with the principles of republicanism.

[To the Legislature of the territory of Indiana, 1807.]

..... The propriety and policy of a law of this kind [authorizing the general and circuit courts to grant divorces] has been strongly contested in many parts of the United States; and it is believed that the principle has been everywhere condemned, save in one or two States only. It cannot be denied that the success of one applicant for a divorce has always the effect of producing others, and that the advantages which a few individuals may derive from a dissolution of this solemn contract, are too dearly purchased by its injurious effects upon the morals of the community. The scenes which are frequently exhibited in trials of this kind are shocking to humanity. The ties of consanguinity and nature are loosened — the child is brought to give testimony against his parent — confidence and affection are destroyed — family secrets disclosed — and human nature is exhibited in the worst colors.

[From a letter dated Headquarters, Detroit, 9 October, 1813, giving an account of the victory of the American troops over the combined Indian and British forces under General Proctor.]

..... Whilst I was engaged in forming the infantry, I had directed Colonel Johnson's * regiment,

* Richard M. Johnson.

which was still in front, to be formed in two lines, opposite to the enemy, and, upon the advance of the infantry, to take ground to the left, and forming upon that flank, to endeavor to turn the right of the Indians. A moment's reflection, however, convinced me that from the thickness of the woods and swampiness of the ground, they would be unable to do anything on horseback; and there was no time to dismount them and place their horses in security; I therefore determined to refuse my left to the Indians, and to break the British lines at once by a charge of the mounted infantry. The measure was not sanctioned by anything I had seen or heard of, but I was fully convinced that it would succeed. The American backwoodsmen ride better in the woods than any other people. A musket or rifle is no impediment to them, being accustomed to carry them on horseback from their earliest youth. I was persuaded, too, that the enemy would be quite unprepared for the shock, and that they could not resist it. Conformably to this idea, I directed the regiment to be drawn up in close column, with its right at the distance of fifty yards from the road (that it might be in some measure protected by the trees from the artillery), its left upon the swamp, and to charge at full speed as soon as the enemy delivered their fire. The few regular troops of the 27th regiment, under their colonel (Paul), occupied, in column of sections of four, the small space between the road and the river, for the purpose of seizing the enemy's artillery, and some ten or twelve friendly Indians were directed to move under the bank. The *crotchet* formed by the front line and General Desha's division was an important point. At that place the venerable governor of Kentucky (Shelby) was posted, who, at the age of sixty-six, preserved all the vigor of youth, the ardent zeal which distinguished him in the Revolutionary war, and the undaunted bravery which he manifested at King's Mountain.* With my aid-de-camp, the acting assistant adjutant-general, Captain Butler, my gallant friend, Commodore Perry, who did me the honor to serve as my volunteer aid-de-camp, and Brigadier-General Cass,† who, having no command, tendered me his assistance, I placed myself at the head of the front line of infantry, to direct the movements of the cavalry, and give them the necessary support. The army had moved on in this manner but a short distance, when the mounted men received the fire of the British line, and were ordered to charge; the horses in the front of the column recoiled from the fire; another was given by the enemy, and our column at length getting in motion, broke through the enemy with irresistible force. In one minute the contest

* In North Carolina, October 9, 1780.
† Lewis Cass.

in front was over; the British officers, seeing no hopes of reducing their disordered ranks to order, and our mounted men wheeling upon them, and pouring in a destructive fire, immediately surrendered. It is certain that three only of our troops were wounded in this charge. Upon the left, however, the contest was more severe with the Indians. Colonel Johnson, who commanded on the flank of his regiment, received a most galling fire from them, which was returned with great effect. The Indians still farther to the right advanced, and fell in with our front line of infantry, near its junction with Desha's division, and for a moment made an impression upon it. His excellency Governor Shelby, however, brought up a regiment to its support, and the enemy, receiving a severe fire in front, and a part of Johnson's regiment having gained their rear, retreated with precipitation. The loss was very considerable in the action, and many were killed in the retreat.*

[From his Inaugural Address, 1841.]

..... The spirit of liberty is the sovereign balm for every injury which our institutions may receive. On the contrary, no care that can be used in the construction of our government, no division of powers, no distribution of checks in its several

---

* Tecumseh was killed in this battle.

departments, will prove effectual to keep us a free people, if this spirit is suffered to decay, and decay it will without constant nurture. . . . And although there is at times much difficulty in distinguishing the false from the true spirit, a calm and dispassionate investigation will detect the counterfeit, as well by the character of its operations as the results that are produced. The true spirit of liberty, although devoted, persevering, bold, and uncompromising in principle; *that* secured, is mild, and tolerant, and scrupulous as to the means it employs; whilst the spirit of party, assuming to be that of liberty, is harsh, vindictive, and intolerant, and totally reckless as to the character of the allies which it brings to the aid of its cause.

JOHN TYLER.

BORN, 1790; DIED, 1862, AGED 72.—GRADUATED AT WILLIAM AND MARY COLLEGE, 1807.—BEGAN PRACTICE OF LAW, 1809.—IN LEGISLATURE OF VIRGINIA, 1811.—CONGRESS, 1816.—STATE LEGISLATURE, 1823.—GOVERNOR OF VIRGINIA, 1825.—UNITED STATES SENATOR, 1827.—IN THE STATE LEGISLATURE, 1838.—VICE-PRESIDENT, 1841.—PRESIDENT, 1841.

[From an Address as President of the Senate, March, 1841.]

..... HERE are to be found the immediate Representatives of the States, by whose sovereign will the government has been spoken into existence. Here exists that perfect equality among the members of this confederacy, which gives to the smallest State in the Union a voice as potential as that of the largest. To this body is committed, in an eminent degree, the trust of guarding and protecting the institutions handed down to us from our fathers, as well against the waves of popular and rash impulses on the one hand, as against attempts at executive encroachment on the other. It may properly be regarded as holding the balance in which is weighed the powers conceded to this government, and the rights reserved to the States and to the people. It is its province to concede what has been granted — to withhold what has been denied; thus, in all its features, exhibiting a true type of the glorious confederacy under which it is our happiness to live. Should the spirit of faction, that destructive spirit which recklessly walks over prostrate rights, and tramples laws and constitutions in the dust, ever find an abiding place within this hall, then, indeed, will a sentence of condemnation be issued against the peace and happiness of this people, and their political institutions be made to topple to their foundations. But while this body shall continue to be what by its framers it was designed to be, deliberative in its character, unbiassed in its counsel, and independent in its action, then may liberty be regarded as intrenched in safety behind the sacred ramparts of the Constitution.

[From a Message to Congress, June 1, 1841.]

..... I must be permitted to add, that no scheme of governmental policy, unaided by individual exertions, can be available for ameliorating the present condition of things. Commercial modes of exchange, and a good currency are but the necessary means of commerce and intercourse, not the direct productive sources of wealth. Wealth can only be accumulated by the earnings of industry and the savings of frugality, and nothing can be more ill-judged than to look to facilities in borrowing, or to a redundant currency, for the power of discharging pecuniary obligations. The country is full of resources, and the people full of energy; and the great and permanent remedy for present embarrassments must be sought in industry, economy, the observance of good faith, and the favorable influence of time.

JAMES K. POLK.

BORN, 1795; DIED, 1849, AGED 54.—GRADUATED AT THE UNIVERSITY OF NORTH CAROLINA, 1818.—ADMITTED TO THE BAR, 1820.—IN THE TENNESSEE STATE LEGISLATURE, 1823.—ELECTED TO CONGRESS, 1825.—SPEAKER OF THE HOUSE OF REPRESENTATIVES, 1835.—GOVERNOR OF TENNESSEE, 1839.—PRESIDENT, 1845-1849.

[From his Inaugural Address, March, 1845.]

..... "Who shall assign limits to the achievements of free minds and free hands, under the protection of the glorious Union? No treason to mankind, since the organization of society, would be equal in atrocity to that of him who would lift his hand to destroy it. He would overthrow the noblest structure of human wisdom, which protects himself and his fellow-men. He would stop the progress of free government, and involve his country either in anarchy or destruction.

Has the sword of despots proved to be a safer or surer instrument of reform in government than enlightened reason? Does he expect to find among the ruins of this Union a happier abode for our swarming millions than they now have under it? Every lover of his country must shudder at the thought of the possibility of its dissolution, and will be ready to adopt the political sentiment: Our Federal Union; it must be preserved.

. . . . . .

Nor will it become in a less degree my duty to assert and maintain, by all consistent means, the right of the United States to that part of our territory which lies beyond the Rocky Mountains. Our title to the country of the Oregon is clear and unquestionable, and already are our people preparing to perfect that title, by occupying it with their wives and children. But eighty years ago our population was confined on the west by the ridge of the Alleghanies. Within that period — within the lifetime, I may say, of some of my hearers — our people, increasing to many millions, have filled the eastern valley of the Mississippi, adventurously ascended the Mississippi to its head springs, and are already engaged in establishing the blessings of self-government in valleys of which the rivers flow to the Pacific. The world beholds the peaceful triumphs of the industry of our emigrants. To us belongs the duty of protecting them adequately, wherever they may be upon our soil. The jurisdiction of our laws, and the benefits of our republican institutions, should be extended over them in the distant regions which they have selected for their homes.

[From his first annual Message, December, 1845.]

..... It is well known to the American people, and to all nations, that this government has never interfered with the relations subsisting between other governments. We have never made ourselves parties to their wars or their alliances; we have not sought their territories by conquest; we have not mingled with parties in their domestic struggles; and believing our own form of government to be the best, we have never attempted to propagate it by intrigues, by diplomacy, or by force. We may claim on this continent a like exemption from European interference. The nations of America are equally sovereign and independent with those of Europe. They possess the same rights, independent of all foreign interposition, to make war, to conclude peace, and to regulate their internal affairs. The people of the United States cannot, therefore, view with indifference attempts of European powers to interfere with the independent action of the nations on this continent. The American system of government is entirely different from the European. Jealousy among the different sovereigns of Europe lest any one of them might become too powerful for the rest has caused them anxiously to desire the establishment of what they term the "balance of power." It cannot be permitted to have any application on the North American Continent, and especially to the United States. We must ever maintain the principle, that the people of this continent alone have the right to decide their own destiny. Should any portion of them, constituting an independent state, propose to unite themselves with our confederacy, this will be a question for them and us to determine, without any foreign interposition.

. . . .

Nearly a quarter of a century ago the principle was distinctly announced to the world in the annual message of one of my predecessors, that " the American continents, by the free and independent condition which they have assumed and maintained, are henceforth not to be considered as subjects for future colonization by any European powers." This principle will apply with greatly increased force should any European power attempt any new colony in North America.

[From a Message, December, 1848.]

. . . . . Any attempt to coerce the President to yield his sanction to measures which he cannot approve would be a violation of the spirit of the constitution, palpable and flagrant; and if successful would break down the independence of the executive department, and make the President, elected by the people, and clothed by the constitution with power to defend their rights, the mere instrument of a majority of Congress. A surrender on his part of the powers with which the constitution has invested his office would effect a practical alteration of that instrument, without resorting to the prescribed form of amendment.

ZACHARY TAYLOR.

BORN, 1784; DIED, 1850, AGED 66.—CAPTAIN IN THE UNITED STATES ARMY, 1810.—COLONEL, 1832.—IN THE BLACK HAWK WAR, 1832.—BRIGADIER-GENERAL, 1837.—COMMANDER-IN-CHIEF IN FLORIDA, 1838.—IN THE MEXICAN WAR, 1846, 1847.—PRESIDENT, 1849.

[From a Message to Congress, December 27, 1849.]

. . . . . As indispensable to the preservation of our system of self-government, the independence of the representatives of the states and the people is guaranteed by the constitution, and they owe no responsibility to any human power but their constituents. By holding the representative responsible only to the people, and exempting him from all other influences, we elevate the character of the constituents, and quicken his sense of responsibility to his country. It is under these circumstances only that the elector can feel that, in the choice of a lawmaker, he is himself truly a component part of the sovereign power of the nation.

With equal care we should study to defend the rights of the executive and judicial departments; our government can only be preserved in its purity by the suppression and entire elimination of every claim or tendency of one co-ordinate branch to encroachment upon another. With the strict observance of this rule, and the other injunctions of the constitution; with a sedulous inculcation of the respect and love of the union of the states, which our fathers cherished and enjoined upon their children; and with the aid of the overruling Providence which has so long and so kindly guarded our liberties and institutions, we may reasonably expect to transmit them, with their innumerable blessings, to the remotest posterity.

But attachment to the union of the states should be habitually fostered in every American heart. For more than half a century, during which kingdoms and empires have fallen, this Union has stood unshaken. . . . In my judgment, its dissolution would be the greatest of calamities, and to avert that should be the study of every American. Upon its preservation must depend our own happiness and that of countless generations to come. Whatever dangers may threaten it, I shall stand by it and maintain it in its integrity to the full extent of the obligations and the power conferred upon me by the constitution.

MILLARD FILLMORE.

BORN, 1800; DIED, 1874, AGED 74.—BEGAN PRACTICE OF LAW 1823.—ELECTED TO THE NEW YORK LEGISLATURE, 1828.— TO CONGRESS, 1832.—RE-ELECTED, 1836.—AGAIN, 1838 AND 1840.—CHAIRMAN OF COMMITTEE ON WAYS AND MEANS. —NEW YORK STATE COMPTROLLER, 1847.—VICE-PRESIDENT, 1849.—PRESIDENT, JULY 10, 1850-1853.

..... No individuals have a right to hazard the peace of the country, or to violate its laws, upon vague notions of altering or reforming governments in other states. . . . Friendly relations with all, but entangling alliances with none, has been a maxim with us. Our true mission is not to propagate our opinions, or impose upon other countries our form of government, by artifice or force, but to teach by example, and show by our success, moderation, and justice, the blessings of self-government and the advantages of free institutions. Let every people choose for itself, and make and alter its political institutions to suit its own condition and convenience. But while we avow and maintain this neutral policy ourselves, we are anxious to see the same forbearance on the part of other nations, whose forms of government are different from our own. The deep interest which we feel in the spread of liberal principles and the establishment of free governments, and the sympathy with which we witness every struggle against oppression, forbid that we should be indifferent to a case in which the strong arm of a foreign power is involved to stifle public sentiment and repress the spirit of freedom in any country.

[From a Message, December, 1850.]

. . . . . The great law of morality ought to have a national as well as a personal and individual application. We should act toward other nations as we wish them to act toward us; and justice and conscience should form the rule of conduct between governments instead of mere power, self-interest, and the desire of aggrandizement. To maintain a strict neutrality in foreign wars, to cultivate friendly relations, to reciprocate every noble and generous act, and to perform punctually and scrupulously every treaty obligation; these are the duties which we owe to other states, and by the performance of which we best entitle ourselves to like treatment from them; or if, in any case that be refused, we can enforce our own rights with a just and clear conscience.

[From a Message, December, 1852.]

..... It has been the uniform policy of this government, from its foundation to the present day, to abstain from all interference in the domestic affairs of other nations. The consequence has been that while the nations of Europe have been engaged in desolating wars, our country has pursued its peaceful course to unexampled prosperity and happiness. . . . During the terrible contest of nation against nation which succeeded the French revolution, we were enabled, by the wisdom and firmness of President Washington, to maintain our neutrality. While the nations were drawn into this wide-spreading whirlpool, we sat quiet and unmoved upon our own shores. While the flower of their numerous armies was wasted by disease, or perished by hundreds of thousands upon the battle-field, the youth of this favored land were permitted to enjoy the blessings of peace beneath the paternal roof. While the states of Europe incurred enormous debts, under the burden of which their subjects still groan, and which must absorb no small part of the produce of the honest industries of those countries for generations to come, the United States have once been enabled to exhibit the proud spectacle of a nation free from public debt; and if permitted to pursue our prosperous way for a few years longer in peace, we may do the same again.

But it is now said that this policy must be changed. Europe is no longer separated from us by a voyage of months, but steam navigation has brought her within a few days' sail of our shores. We see more of her movements, and take a deep interest in her controversies. Although no one proposes that we should join the fraternity of potentates who have for ages lavished the blood and treasure of their subjects in maintaining "the balance of power," yet it is said that we ought to interfere between contending governments and their subjects, for the purpose of overthrowing the monarchies of Europe, and establishing in their place republican institutions. It is alleged that we have hitherto pursued a different course from a sense of our weakness, but that now our conscious strength dictates a change of policy, and that it is consequently our duty to mingle in these controversies, and aid those who are struggling for liberty.

This is a most seductive but dangerous appeal to the generous sympathies of freemen. Enjoying, as we do, the blessings of a free government, there is no man who has an American heart that would not rejoice to see these blessings extended to all other nations. . . . Nevertheless, is it prudence, or is it wisdom to involve ourselves in these foreign wars? Is it indeed true that we have heretofore refrained from doing so merely from the degrading motive of a conscious weakness? For the honor of the patriots who have gone before, I cannot admit it. . . . The truth is, that the course which they pursued was dictated by a stern sense of international justice, by a statesman-like prudence, and a far-seeing wisdom, looking not merely to the present necessities, but to the permanent safety and interest of the country. They knew that the world is governed less by sympathy than by reason and force; that it was not possible for this nation to become a "propagandist" of free principles without arraying against itself the combined powers of Europe; and that the result was more likely to be the overthrow of republican liberty here than its establishment there.

FRANKLIN PIERCE.

BORN, 1804; DIED, 1869, AGED 65.—GRADUATED AT BOWDOIN COLLEGE (ME.), 1824. — ADMITTED TO THE BAR, 1827. — ELECTED TO THE NEW HAMPSHIRE STATE LEGISLATURE, 1829. — SPEAKER, 1832.—ELECTED TO CONGRESS, 1833. — TO THE UNITED STATES SENATE, 1837.—GENERAL IN THE MEXICAN WAR.—PRESIDENT OF THE CONSTITUTIONAL STATE CONVENTION, 1850.—PRESIDENT, 1853-1857.

[From a Message, December 6, 1854.]

. . . . . Our forefathers of the thirteen United Colonies, in acquiring their independence, and in founding this republic of the United States of America, have devolved upon us their descendants the greatest and most noble trust ever committed to the hands of men, imposing upon all, and especially such as the public will may have invested, for the time being, with political functions, the most solemn obligations. We have to maintain inviolate the great doctrine of the inherent right of popular self-government; to reconcile the largest liberty of the individual citizen with complete security of the public order; to render cheerful obedience to the laws of the land, to unite in enforcing their execution, and to frown indignantly on all combinations to resist them; to harmonize a sincere and ardent devotion to the institutions of religious faith with the most universal religious toleration; to preserve the rights of all by causing each to respect those of the other; to carry forward every social improvement to the utmost limit of human perfectibility by the free action of mind upon mind, not by obtrusive intervention of misplaced force; to uphold the integrity and guard the limitations of our organic law; to preserve sacred from all touch of usurpation, as the very palladium of our political salvation, the reserved rights and powers of the several States and of the people; to cherish, with loyal fealty and devoted affection, this Union, as the only sure foundation on which the hopes of civil liberty rest; to administer government with vigor, integrity, and rigid economy; to cultivate peace and friendship with foreign nations, and to demand and exact equal justice from all, but to do wrong to none; to eschew intermeddling with the national policy and the domestic repose of other governments, and to repel it from our own; never to shrink from war when the rights and the honor of our country call us to arms, but to cultivate in preference the arts of peace, seek enlargement of the rights of neutrality, and elevate and liberalize the intercourse of nations; and by such just and honorable means, and such only, while exalting the condition of the republic, to assure to it the legitimate influence and the benign authority of a great example amongst all the powers of Christendom.

JAMES BUCHANAN.

BORN, 1791; DIED, 1868, AGED 77.—GRADUATED AT DICKINSON COLLEGE (PENN.), 1809.—ADMITTED TO THE BAR, 1812.—ELECTED TO PENNSYLVANIA LEGISLATURE, 1814.—TO CONGRESS, 1821.—MINISTER TO RUSSIA, 1831.—UNITED STATES SENATOR, 1833.—SECRETARY OF STATE, 1845-1849. MINISTER TO ENGLAND, 1853.—PRESIDENT, 1857-1861.

[From his Message to Congress, December, 1860.]

..... In order to justify secession as a constitutional remedy, it must be on the principle that the Federal Government is a mere voluntary association of States, to be dissolved at pleasure by any one of the contracting parties. If this be so, the confederacy is a rope of sand, to be penetrated and dissolved by the first adverse wave of public opinion in any of the States. In this manner our thirty-three States may resolve themselves into as many petty, jarring, and hostile republics, each one retiring from the Union, without responsibility, whenever any sudden excitement might impel them to such a course. By this process, a union might be entirely broken into fragments in a few weeks, which cost our forefathers many years of toil, privation, and blood to establish.

Such a principle is wholly inconsistent with the

history as well as the character of the Federal Constitution. After it was framed with the greatest deliberation and care, it was submitted to conventions of the people of the several States for ratification. Its provisions were discussed at length in these bodies, composed of the first men of the country. Its opponents contended that it conferred powers upon the Federal Government dangerous to the rights of the States; while its advocates maintained that, under a fair construction of the instrument, there was no foundation for such apprehension. In that mighty struggle between the first intellects of this or any other country, it never occurred to any individual, either among its opponents or advocates, to assert, or even to intimate, that their efforts were all vain labor, because the moment that any State felt herself aggrieved she might secede from the Union. What a crushing argument would this have proved against those who dreaded that the rights of the States would be endangered by the Constitution! The truth is, that it was not till many years after the origin of the Federal Government that such a proposition was first advanced. It was then met and refuted by the conclusive arguments of General Jackson, who, in his Message of the 16th of January, 1833, transmitting the nullifying ordinance of South Carolina to Congress, employs the following language: "The right of the people of a single State to absolve themselves at will, and without the consent of the other States, from their most solemn obligations, and hazard the liberty and happiness of the millions composing this Union, cannot be acknowledged. Such authority is believed to be entirely repugnant both to the principle upon which the General Government is constituted, and to the objects which it was expressly formed to attain."

. . . . . "This government, therefore, is a great and powerful government, invested with all the attributes of sovereignty over the special subjects to which its authority extends. Its framers never intended to implant in its bosom the seeds of its own destruction, nor were they at its creation guilty of the absurdity of providing for its own dissolution. It was not intended by its framers to be the baseless fabric of a vision, which, at the touch of the enchanter, would vanish into thin air; but a substantial and mighty fabric, capable of resisting the slow decay of time, and of defying the storms of ages."

[Proclamation for a National Fast, on January 4, 1861.]

. . . . . The Union of the States is at the present moment threatened with alarming and immediate danger — panic and distress of a fearful character prevail throughout the land — our laboring population are without employment, and consequently deprived of the means of earning their bread — indeed, hope seems to have deserted the minds of men. All classes are in a state of confusion and dismay; and the wisest counsels of our best and purest men are wholly disregarded.

ABRAHAM LINCOLN.

BORN, 1809; DIED, 1865, AGED 56.—CAPTAIN IN THE BLACK HAWK WAR.—ELECTED TO THE ILLINOIS STATE LEGISLATURE, 1834.—AGAIN, 1836.—ADMITTED TO THE BAR, 1837.—ELECTED TO CONGRESS, 1846.—MEMBER OF THE COMMITTEE ON POST-OFFICES AND POST-ROADS AND WAR-DEPARTMENT EXPENSES.—MADE HIS FIRST SPEECH IN CONGRESS, JAN. 12, 1848, IN OPPOSITION TO THE MEXICAN WAR.—SPEECH IN COOPER'S INSTITUTE, NEW YORK CITY, 1860.—PRESIDENT, 1860–1865.

["He is the author of a multitude of good sayings, so disguised as pleasantries that it is certain they had no reputation at first but as jests; and only later by the very acceptance and adoption they find in the mouths of millions, turn out to be the wisdom of the hour. I am sure if this man had ruled in a period of less facility of printing, he would have become mythological in a very few years, like Æsop or Pilpay, or one of the Seven Wise Masters, by his fables and proverbs.

"But the weight and penetration of many passages in his letters, messages, and speeches, hidden now by the very closeness of their application to the moment, are destined hereafter to a wide fame. What pregnant definitions! what unerring common-sense! what foresight! and, on great occasions, what lofty, and, more than national, what humane tone."—*Ralph Waldo Emerson.*

..... How his quaint wit made home-truth seem more true. — *London Punch.*]

[From a Lecture before the Springfield Lyceum, on the Perpetuation of our Free Institutions, January, 1837.]

..... At what point, then, is the approach of danger to be expected? I answer, if it ever reach us, it must spring up amongst us. It cannot come from abroad. If destruction be our lot, we must ourselves be its author and finisher. As a nation of freemen, we must live through all time, or die by suicide.

[Letter to Mr. Herndon.]*

WASHINGTON, February 1, 1848.

..... That vote affirms that the [Mexican] war was unnecessarily and unconstitutionally commenced by the President; and I will stake my life, that, if you had been in my place, you would have voted just as I did. Would you have voted what you felt and knew to be a lie? I know you would not. Would you have gone out of the House, — skulked the vote? I expect not. If you had skulked one vote, you would have to

* Mr. Lincoln voted for Mr. Ashmun's amendment.

skulk many more before the end of the session. Richardson's resolutions, introduced before I made any move, or gave any vote upon the subject, make the direct question of the justice of the war; so that no man can be silent if he would. You are compelled to speak; and your only alternative is to tell the *truth* or tell a *lie.*

[To the Same.]

WASHINGTON, July 10, 1848.

..... The way for a young man to rise is to improve himself every way he can, never suspecting that anybody wishes to hinder him. Allow me to assure you that suspicion and jealousy never did help any man in any situation. There may sometimes be ungenerous attempts to keep a young man down; and they will succeed, too, if he allows his mind to be diverted from its true channel, to brood over the attempted injury. Cast about, and see if this feeling has not injured every person you have ever known to fall into it.

[From a Speech in Congress, July 27, 1848.]

..... The other day one of the gentlemen from Georgia, an eloquent man, and a man of learning, so far as I could judge, not being learned myself, came down upon us astonishingly. He spoke in what the *Baltimore American* calls the "scathing and withering style." At the end of his second severe flash I was struck blind, and found myself feeling with my fingers for an assurance of my continued physical existence. A little of the bone was left, and I gradually revived.

I say that no man is good enough to govern another man without that other's consent. — Oct. 1854.

[From a Speech in 1856.]

Twenty-two years ago, Judge Douglas and I became first acquainted; we were both young men — he a trifle younger than I. Even then we were both ambitious, I perhaps quite as much as he. With me the race of ambition has been a failure — a flat failure. With him it has been one of splendid success. His name fills the nation, and it is not unknown in foreign lands. I affect no contempt for the high eminence he has reached, so reached that the oppressed of my species might have shared with me in the elevation. I would rather stand on that eminence than wear the richest crown that ever pressed a monarch's brow.

[From a Speech delivered in 1857. Describing the helpless state of the American slave, he said]:

They have him in his prison-house. They have searched his person and left no prying instrument with him. One after another they have closed the heavy iron doors upon him, and now they have him, as it were, bolted in with a lock of a hundred keys, which can never be unlocked without the concurrence of every key; the keys in the hands of a hundred different men, and they scattered to a hundred different and distant places; and they stand musing as to what invention, in all the dominions of mind and matter, can be produced to make the impossibility of his escape more complete than it is.

[From a Speech,* delivered at Springfield, Illinois, June 17, 1858, before the Republican State Convention.]

If we could first know where we are, and whither we are tending, we could better judge what to do, and how to do it. We are now far into the fifth year since a policy was initiated with the avowed object and confident promise of putting an end to slavery agitation. Under the operation of that policy, that agitation has not only not ceased,

---

* Mr. Lincoln read this speech, before its public delivery, to Mr. Herndon. When he had finished the first paragraph, he asked his auditor, "How do you like that? What do you think of it?" "I think," returned Mr. Herndon, "it is true; but is it entirely *politic* to read or speak it as it is written?" "What makes the difference?" Mr. Lincoln said. "That expression is a truth of all human experience, 'A house divided against itself cannot stand;' and 'he that runs may read.' The proposition is indisputably true, and has been true for more than six thousand years; and —— I will deliver it as written. I want to use some universally known figure, expressed in simple language as universally

but has constantly augmented. In my opinion, it will not cease until a crisis shall have been reached and passed. "A house divided against itself cannot stand." I believe this government cannot endure permanently half slave and half free. I do not expect the Union to be dissolved. I do not expect the house to fall; but I do expect it will cease to be divided. It will become all one thing, or all the other. Either the opponents of slavery will arrest the further spread of it, and place it where the public mind shall rest in the belief that it is in the course of ultimate extinction, or its advocates will push it forward till it shall become alike lawful in all the states, old as well as new, north as well as south.

[In the same speech, Mr. Lincoln said that the doctrine of "Squatter Sovereignty," otherwise

known, that may strike home to the minds of men, in order to rouse them to the peril of the times. I would rather *be defeated with this expression in* the speech, and it held up and discussed before the people, than *to be victorious without it.*"

Mr. Lincoln was not elected senator. In the summer of 1859, at a party of friends, the subject of this speech was discussed. "We all insisted," says Mr. Swett, who was one of the company, "that it was a great mistake," losing him his election. "Well, gentlemen," replied Mr. Lincoln, "you may think that speech was a mistake; but I never have believed it was, and you will see the day when you will consider it was the nicest thing I ever said."— See LAMON'S *Life of Lincoln.*

called "sacred right of self-government," as expressed in the "Nebraska Bill," by which the right of a slaveholder to hold slaves in any territory or state, was affirmed, amounted to this :] —" That if any *one* man chose to enslave *another*, no *third* man shall be allowed to object."

[From a Speech in reply to Mr. Douglas, July 10, 1858.]

We are now a mighty nation; we are thirty, or about thirty millions of people, and we own and inhabit about one-fifteenth part of the dry land of the whole earth. We run our memory back over the pages of history for about eighty-two years, and we discover that we were then a very small people in point of numbers, vastly inferior to what we are now, with a vastly less extent of country, with vastly less of everything we deem desirable among men,—we look upon the change as extremely advantageous to us, and to our posterity, and we fix upon something that happened away back, as in some way or other being connected with this rise of prosperity. We find a race of men living in that day whom we claim as our fathers and grandfathers; they were iron men; they fought for the principle that they were contending for; and we understood that by what they then did it has followed that the degree of prosperity which we now enjoy has come to us. We hold this annual celebration to remind ourselves of all the good done in this process of time, of how it was done, and who did it, and how we are historically connected with it; and we go from these meetings in better humor with ourselves; we feel more attached the one to the other, and more firmly bound to the country we inhabit. In every way we are better men in the age, and race, and country in which we live, for these celebrations.

But after we have done all this we have not yet reached the whole. . . . We have besides these descended by blood from our ancestors, men among us, perhaps half our people, who are not descendants at all of these men; they are men who have come from Europe, — German, Irish, French, and Scandinavian, — men that have come from Europe themselves, or whose ancestors have come hither and settled here, finding themselves our equals in all things. If they look back through their history to trace their connection with those days by blood, they find they have none; they cannot carry themselves back into that glorious epoch, and make themselves feel that they are part of us; but when they look through that old Declaration of Independence, they find that those old men say that " We hold these truths to be self-evident, that all men are created equal," etc., and then they feel that that moral sentiment taught in that day evidences their relation to those men, that it is the father of all moral principle in them, and that they have a right to claim it as though they were blood of the blood and flesh of the flesh of the men who wrote that declaration; and so they are. That is the electric cord in that declaration that links the hearts of patriotic and liberty-loving men together, that will link those patriotic hearts as long as the love of freedom exists in the minds of men throughout the world. . . . . .

Those arguments that are made, that the inferior race are to be treated with as much allowance as they are capable of enjoying; that as much is to be done for them as their condition will allow. What are these arguments? They are the arguments that kings have made for enslaving the people in all ages of the world. You will find that all the arguments in favor of king-craft were of this class; they always bestrode the necks of the people, not that they wanted to do it, but because the people were better off for being ridden. That is their argument, and this argument of the judge is the same old serpent that says, You work, and I eat; you toil, and I will enjoy the fruits of it. Turn it whatever way you will, whether it come from the mouth of a king, an excuse for enslaving the people of his country, or from the mouth of men of one race as a reason for enslaving the men of another race, it is all the same old serpent, and I hold if that course of argumentation that is made for the purpose of convincing the public mind that we should not care about this, should be granted, it does not stop with the negro. I should like to know, taking this old Declaration of Independence, which declares that all men are equal upon principle, and making exceptions to it, where will it stop? If one man says it does not mean the negro, why not another say it does not mean some other man? If that declaration is not the truth, let us get the statute book in which we find it and tear it out! Who is so bold as to do it! If it is not true, let us tear it out! [Cries of " No, no! "] Let us stick to it, then; let us stand firmly by it, then.

[From a letter to Mr. Speed, August 24, 1858.]

Our progress in degeneracy appears to me to be pretty rapid. As a nation, we began by declaring that "all men are created equal." We now practically read it, " All men are created equal, except negroes." When the Know-nothings get control it will read, " All men are created equal, except negroes, and foreigners, and Catholics." When it comes to this I should prefer emigrating to some country where they make no pretence of loving liberty; to Russia, for instance, where despotism can be taken pure, and without the base alloy of hypocrisy.

[From a speech delivered October, 1858.]

The judge has alluded to the Declaration of Independence, and insisted that negroes are not included in that declaration; and that it is a slander upon the framers of that instrument to suppose that negroes were meant therein; and he asks you, Is it possible to believe that Mr. Jefferson, who penned the immortal paper, could have supposed himself applying the language of that instrument to the negro race, and yet held a portion of that race in slavery? Would he not at once have freed them? I only have to remark, . . . that I believe the entire records of the world, from the date of the Declaration of Independence up to within three years ago, may be searched in vain for one single affirmation, from one single man, that the negro was not included in the Declaration of Independence; . . . that Washington ever said so, that any President ever said so, that any member of Congress ever said so, or that any living man upon the whole earth ever said so, until the necessities of the present policy of the Democratic party, in regard to slavery, had to invent that affirmation. And I will remind Judge Douglas and this audience, that while Mr. Jefferson was the owner of slaves, in speaking upon this very subject, he used the strong language, that "he trembled for his country when he remembered that God was just."

... He supposed there was a question of God's eternal justice wrapped up in the enslaving of any race of men, or any man, and that those who did so braved the arm of Jehovah; that when a nation thus dared the Almighty, every friend of that nation had cause to dread His wrath.

[From a Speech delivered in 1858.]

Judge Douglas declares that, if any community want slavery, they have a right to have it. He can say that logically, if he says that there is no wrong in slavery; but if you admit that there is a wrong in it, he cannot logically say that anybody has a right to do wrong. He insists that, upon the score of equality, the owners of slaves and owners of property, — of horse, and every other sort of property, — should be alike, and hold them alike, in a new territory. That is perfectly logical if the species of property are alike, and are equally founded in right. But if you admit that one of them is wrong, you cannot institute any equality between right and wrong. And from this difference of sentiment, — the belief on the part of one that the institution is wrong, and a policy springing from that belief which looks to the arrest of the enlargement of that wrong; and this other sentiment, that it is no wrong, and a policy sprung from that sentiment which will tolerate no idea of preventing that wrong from growing larger, and looks to there never being an end of it through all the existence of things, — arises the real difference between Judge Douglas and his friends on the one hand, and the Republicans on the other. Now I confess myself as belonging to that class in the country who contemplate slavery as a moral, social, and political evil, having due regard for its actual existence amongst us, and the difficulties of getting rid of it in any satisfactory way, and to all the constitutional obligations which have been thrown about it; but, nevertheless, desire a policy that looks to the prevention of it as a wrong, and looks hopefully to the time when, as a wrong, it may come to an end.

[From a Speech at Alton, Illinois. To the question, "Is slavery wrong?" Mr. Lincoln said]:

That is the real issue. That is the issue that will continue in this country when these poor tongues of Judge Douglas and myself shall be silent. It is the eternal struggle between these two principles — right and wrong — throughout the world. They are two principles that have stood face to face from the beginning of time, and will ever continue to struggle. The one is the common right of humanity, and the other the divine right of kings.

[From a Speech at Springfield, Illinois.]

Judge Douglas is going back to the era of the Revolution, and, to the extent of his ability, muzzling the cannon which thunders its * annual joyous return. When he invites any people willing to have slavery to establish it, he is blowing out the moral lights around us. When he says he "cares not whether slavery is voted down or voted up,"—that it is a sacred right of self-government,—he is, in my judgment, penetrating the human soul, and eradicating the light of reason and the love of liberty in this American people.

[From a Speech in New York, at the Cooper Institute, February 27, 1860.]

. . . . . Wrong as we think slavery is, we can yet afford to let it alone where it is, because that much is due to the necessity arising from its actual presence in the nation; but can we, while our votes will prevent it, allow it to spread into the national Territories, and to overrun here in these Free States?

If our sense of duty forbids this, then let us stand by our duty fearlessly and effectively. Let us be diverted by none of these sophistical contrivances wherewith we are so industriously plied

---

* The celebration of Independence, on the 4th of July.

and belabored — contrivances such as groping for some middle ground between the right and the wrong, vain as the search for a man who should be neither a living man nor a dead man — such a policy of "don't care" on a question about which all true men do care, — such as Union appeals beseeching true Union men to yield to Disunionists, reversing the divine rule, and calling, not the sinners, but the righteous, to repentance — such as invocations to Washington, imploring men to unsay what Washington said, and undo what Washington did.

Neither let us be slandered from our duty by false accusations against us, nor frightened from it by menaces of destruction to the government, nor of dungeons to ourselves. Let us have faith that right makes might; and in that faith, let us, to the end, dare to do our duty as we understand it.

[Farewell Speech to his neighbors, from the platform of the car, as he was leaving Springfield for Washington, February 11, 1861.]

Friends, — No one who has never been placed in a like position can understand my feelings at this hour, nor the oppressive sadness I feel at this parting. For more than a quarter of a century I have lived among you, and during that time I have received nothing but kindness at your hands. Here I have lived from my youth, until now I am an old man. Here the most sacred ties of earth were assumed. Here all my children were born; and here one of them lies buried. To you, dear friends, I owe all that I have, all that I am. All the strange, checkered past seems to crowd now upon my mind. To-day I leave you. I go to assume a task more difficult than that which devolved upon Washington. Unless the great God, who assisted him, shall be with and aid me, I must fail; but if the same omniscient mind and almighty arm that directed and protected him, shall guide and support me, I shall not fail, — I shall succeed. Let us all pray that the God of our fathers may not forsake us now. To Him I commend you all. Permit me to ask that, with equal sincerity and faith, you will invoke His wisdom and guidance for me. With these few words I must leave you; for how long I know not. Friends, one and all, I must now bid you an affectionate farewell.

[In an Address to the Legislature of New Jersey, on his way to Washington, February, 1861, Mr. Lincoln said]:

I shall endeavor to take the ground I deem most just to the North, the East, the West, the South, and the whole country. I take it, I hope, in good temper, — certainly with no malice toward any section. I shall do all that may be in my power to promote a peaceful settlement of all our difficulties.

The man does not live who is more devoted to peace than I am — none who would do more to preserve it. But it may be necessary to put the foot down firmly. And if I do my duty, and do right, you will sustain me, will you not? Received as I am by the members of a Legislature, the majority of whom do not agree with me in political sentiments, I trust that I may have their assistance in piloting the ship of State through this voyage, surrounded by perils as it is; for if it should suffer shipwreck now, there will be no pilot ever needed for another voyage.

[At Philadelphia, in "Independence Hall," from which was issued the Declaration of Independence, in 1776, Mr. Lincoln said]:

I am filled with deep emotion at finding myself standing here, in this place, where were collected the wisdom, the patriotism, the devotion to principle, from which sprang the institutions under which we live. You have kindly suggested to me that in my hands is the task of restoring peace to the present distracted condition of the country. I can say in return, sir, that all the political sentiments I entertain have been drawn, so far as I have been able to draw them, from the sentiments which originated and were given to the world from this hall. I have never had a feeling politically that did not spring from the sentiments embodied in the Declaration of Independence. I have often pondered over the dangers which were incurred by the men who assembled here, and framed and adopted the Declaration of Independence. I have pondered over the toils that were endured by the officers and soldiers of the army who achieved that independence. I have often inquired of myself what great principle or idea it was that kept this confederacy so long together. It was not the mere matter of the separation of the colonies from the mother-land, but that sentiment in the Declaration of Independence which gave liberty, not alone to the people of this country, but, I hope, to the world for all future time. It was that which gave promise that in due time the weight would be lifted from the shoulders of all men. This is a sentiment embodied in the Declaration of Independence. Now, my friends, can this country be saved upon this basis? If it can, I will consider myself one of the happiest men in the world if I can help to save it. If it cannot be saved upon that principle, it will be truly awful. But if this country cannot be saved without giving up that principle, I was about to say, I would rather be assassinated on this spot than surrender it. Now, in my view of the present aspect of affairs, there need be no bloodshed or war. There is no necessity for it. I am not in favor of such a course, and I may say, in advance, that there will be no bloodshed unless it be forced upon the Government, and then it will be compelled to act in self-defence.

My friends, this is wholly an unexpected speech. ... I may, therefore, have said something indiscreet. I have said nothing but what I am willing to live by, and, if it be the pleasure of Almighty God, to die by.

[From his Inaugural Address, March 4, 1861.]

..... Why should there not be a patient confidence in the ultimate justice of the people? Is there any better or equal hope in the world? In our present differences, is either party without faith of being in the right? If the Almighty Ruler of nations, with his eternal truth and justice, be on your side of the North, or on yours of the South, that truth and that justice will surely prevail, by the judgment of the great tribunal of the American people. .....

You can have no conflict without being yourselves the aggressors. You have no oath registered in heaven to destroy the government, while I shall have the most solemn one to "preserve, protect, and defend" it.

I am loath to close. We are not enemies, but friends. We must not be enemies. Though passion may have strained, it must not break our bonds of affection. The mystic chord of memory, stretching from every battle-field and patriot grave to every living heart and hearthstone all over this broad land, will yet swell the chorus of the Union, when again touched, as surely it will be, by the better angels of our nature.

[From a Message to Congress, July 4, 1861:]

..... It might seem, at first thought, to be of little difference whether the present movement at the South be called "secession," or "rebellion." The movers, however, will understand the difference. At the beginning they knew they could never raise their treason to any respectable magnitude by any name which implies violation of law. They knew their people possessed as much of moral sense, as much of devotion to law and order, and as much pride in, and reverence for, the history and government of their common country, as any other civilized and patriotic people. They knew they could make no advancement directly in the teeth of these strong and noble sentiments. Accordingly they commenced by an insidious debauching of the public mind. They invented an ingenious sophism, which, if conceded, was followed by perfectly logical steps, through all the incidents, to the complete destruction of the Union. The sophism itself is, that any State of the Union may, consistently with the National Constitution, and therefore lawfully and peacefully, withdraw from the Union without the consent of the Union, or of any other State. The little disguise that the supposed right is to be exercised only for just cause, themselves to be the sole judge of its justice, is too thin to want any notice.

With rebellion thus sugar-coated, they have been drugging the public mind of their section for more than thirty years, and until at length they have brought many good men to a willingness to take up arms against the government the day after some assemblage of men have enacted that farcical pretense of taking their State out of the Union, who could have been brought to no such thing the day before.

[Speaking of what was called the right of peaceful secession, that is, secession in accordance with the National Constitution, he said]:

This sophism derives much, perhaps the whole, of its currency from the assumption that there is some omnipotent and sacred supremacy pertaining to a *State* — to each State of our Federal Union. Our States have neither more nor less power than that reserved to them in the Union by the Constitution, no one of them ever having been a State *out* of the Union. The original ones passed into the Union even *before* they cast off their British colonial dependence, and the new ones each came into the Union directly from a condition of dependence, excepting Texas. And even Texas, in its temporary independence, was never designated a State. The new ones only took the designation of States on coming into the Union, while that name was first adopted for the old ones in and by the Declaration of Independence. Therein the "United Colonies" were declared to be "free and independent States;" but, even then, the object plainly was not to declare their independence of *one another*, or of the *Union*, but directly the contrary, as their mutual pledge, and their mutual action, before, at the time, and afterward, abundantly show. The express plighting of faith by each and all of the original thirteen, in the articles of Confederation, two years later, that the Union shall be perpetual, is most conclusive. Having never been States, either in substance or in name, *outside* of the Union, whence this magical omnipotence of "State rights," asserting a claim of power to lawfully destroy the Union itself? Much is said about the "sovereignty" of the States; but the word even is not in the National Constitution, nor, as is believed, in any of the State Constitutions. What is a "sovereignty" in the political sense of the term? Would it be far wrong to define it a "political community, without a political superior?" Tested by this, no one of our States, except Texas, ever was a sovereignty; and even Texas gave up the character on coming into the Union; by which act she acknowledged the Constitution of the United States, and the laws and treaties of the United States made in pursuance of the Constitution, to be, for her, the supreme laws of the land. The States have their *status* IN the Union, and they have no other legal *status*. If they break from this, they can only do so against law, and by revolution. The Union, and not themselves separately, procured their independence and their liberty. By conquest, or purchase, the Union gave each of them whatever of independence and liberty it has. The Union is older than any of the States; and, in fact, it created them as States. Originally, some dependent colonies made the Union, and, in turn, the Union threw off their old dependence for them, and made them States, such as they are. Not one of them ever had a State constitution independent of the Union. Of course, it is not forgotten that all the new States framed their constitutions before they entered the Union; nevertheless dependent upon, and preparatory to, coming into the Union.

. . . . . .

This relative matter of National power and State rights, as a principle, is no other than the principle of *generality*, and *locality*. Whatever concerns the whole should be confided to the whole —

to the general government; while whatever concerns *only* the State should be left exclusively to the State. This is all there is of original principle about it.

. . . . . .

Our adversaries have adopted some declarations of independence, in which, unlike the good old one penned by Jefferson, they omit the words, "All men are created equal." Why? They have adopted a temporary national constitution, in the preamble of which, unlike our good old one signed by Washington, they omit "We, the people," and substitute "We, the deputies of the sovereign and independent States." Why? Why this deliberate pressing out of view the rights of men and the authority of the people? This is essentially a people's contest. On the side of the Union, it is a struggle for maintaining in the world that form and substance of government whose leading object is to elevate the condition of men; to lift artificial weights from all shoulders; to clear the paths of laudable pursuit to all; to afford all an unfettered start, and a fair chance in the race of life. Yielding to partial and temporary departures, from necessity, this is the leading object of the government, for whose existence we contend. I am most happy to believe that the plain people understand and appreciate this.

[Reply to a Letter of Horace Greeley, entitled, "The Prayer of Twenty Millions," to President Lincoln.]
August 22, 1862.

I have just read yours of the nineteenth, addressed to myself through the *New York Tribune*. If there be in it any statement, or assumptions of fact, which I may know to be erroneous, I do not now and here controvert them. If there be in it any inference, which I may believe to be falsely drawn, I do not now and here argue against them. If there be perceptible in it an impatient and dictatorial tone, I waive it in deference to an old friend, whose heart I have always supposed to be right.

As to the policy I "seem to be pursuing," as you say, I have not meant to leave any one in doubt.

I would save the Union. I would save it the shortest way under the Constitution. The sooner the National authority can be restored, the nearer the Union will be "the Union as it was." If there be those who would not save the Union unless they could at the same time save Slavery, I do not agree with them. If there be those who would not save the Union unless they could at the same time *destroy* slavery, I do not agree with them. My paramount object in this struggle *is* to save the Union, and is not either to save or destroy slavery. If I could save the Union without freeing *any* slave, I would do it; and if I could save it by freeing *all* the slaves, I would do it; and if I could do it by freeing some and leaving others alone, I would also do that. What I do about slavery and the colored race, I do because I believe it helps to save this Union; and what I forbear, I forbear because I do *not* believe it would help to save the Union. I shall do *less* whenever I shall believe what I am doing hurts the cause, and I shall do *more* whenever I shall believe doing more will help the cause. I shall try to correct errors when shown to be errors; and I shall adopt new views so fast as they shall appear to be true views.

I have here stated my purpose according to my view of *official* duty, and I intend no modification of my oft-expressed *personal* wish, that all men, everywhere, could be free.

[To a delegation of clergymen from Chicago, who urged him to issue a proclamation of emancipation, September 13, 1862.]

. . . . . I do not want to issue a document that the whole world will see must necessarily be inoperative, like the pope's bull against the comet. . . . Do not misunderstand me, because I have mentioned these objections. They indicate the difficulties which have thus far prevented my action in some such way as you desire. I have not decided against a proclamation of liberty to the slaves, but hold the matter under advisement. And I can assure you that the subject is on my mind, by day and night, more than any other. Whatever shall appear to be God's will, I will do.

[To strictures upon his conduct of the war by some Western gentlemen, he replied]:

Gentlemen, suppose all the property you were worth was in gold, and you had put it in the hands of Blondin to carry across Niagara Falls on a tight-rope, would you shake the rope while he was passing over it, or keep shouting to him, "Blondin, stoop a little more;" "Go a little faster?" No, I am sure you would not. You would hold your breath as well as your tongue, and keep your hands off until he was safely over. Now the government is in the same situation, and is carrying across a stormy ocean an immense weight; untold treasures are in its hands; it is doing the best it can; don't badger it; keep silence, and it will get you safely over.

[General Order respecting the observance of the Sabbath in the army and navy.]
November 16, 1862.

The President, Commander-in-Chief of the Army and Navy, desires and enjoins the orderly observance of the Sabbath by the officers and men in the military and naval service. The importance for man and beast of the prescribed weekly rest, the sacred rights of Christian soldiers and sailors, a becoming deference to the best sentiment of a Christian people, and a due regard for the Divine will, demand that Sunday labor in the army and navy be reduced to the measure of strict necessity.

The discipline and character of the national forces should not suffer, nor the cause they defend be imperilled, by the profanation of the day or the name of the Most High. "At this time of public distress," adopting the words of Washington in 1776, "men may find enough to do in the service of God and their country without abandoning themselves to vice and immorality." The first general order issued by the Father of his Country after the Declaration of Independence, indicates the spirit in which our institutions were founded and should ever be defended : " The General hopes and trusts that every officer and man will endeavor to live and act as becomes a Christian soldier defending the dearest rights and liberties of his country."

[To Mr. Colfax, on the evening of the day on which Mr. Lincoln signed the Emancipation Proclamation, January 1, 1863.]

The South had fair warning, that if they did not return to their duty, I should strike at this pillar of their strength. The promise must now be kept, and I shall never recall one word.

[Reply to an Address by the citizens of Manchester, England, after the issuing of the Proclamation of Emancipation.]

January 19, 1863.

To the Workingmen of Manchester: . . . When I came, on the fourth of March, 1861, through a free and constitutional election, to preside in the Government of the United States, the country was found at the verge of civil war. Whatever might have been the cause, or whosesoever the fault, one duty, paramount to all others, was before me, namely, to maintain and preserve at once the Constitution and the integrity of the Federal Republic. A conscientious purpose to perform this duty is the key to all the measures of administration which have been, and to all which will hereafter be pursued. Under our frame of government and my official oath, I could not depart from this purpose if I would. It is not always in the power of governments to enlarge or restrict the scope of moral results which follow the policies that they may deem it necessary, for the public safety, from time to time to adopt. . . . . .

I know, and deeply deplore, the sufferings which the workingmen at Manchester, and in all Europe, are called to endure in this crisis. It has been often studiously represented that the attempt to overthrow this Government, which was built upon the foundation of human rights, and to substitute for it one which should rest exclusively on the basis of human slavery, was likely to obtain the favor of Europe. Through the action of our disloyal citizens, the workingmen of Europe have been subjected to severe trial, for the purpose of forcing their sanction to that attempt. Under these circumstances I cannot but regard your decisive utterances upon the question as an instance of sublime Christian heroism which has not been surpassed in any age or in any country. It is indeed an energetic and re-inspiring assurance of the inherent power of truth, and of the ultimate and universal triumph of justice, humanity, and freedom. I do not doubt that the sentiments you have expressed will be sustained by your great nation; and, on the other hand, I have no hesitation in assuring you that they will excite admiration, esteem, and the most reciprocal feelings of friendship among the American people.

I hail this interchange of sentiment, therefore, as an augury that, whatever else may happen, whatever misfortune may befall your country or my own, the peace and friendship which now exist between the two nations will be, as it shall be my desire to make them, perpetual.

[From his Reply to Resolutions of the New York Democrats, May 19, 1863, protesting against his suspension of the writ of *habeas corpus*, and arrest of Mr. Vallandingham for the crime of seeking to prevent the enlistment of troops.]

. . . . . Prior to my installation here it had been inculcated that any State had a lawful right to secede from the National Union, and that it would be expedient to exercise the right whenever the devotees of the doctrine should fail to elect a president to their own liking. I was elected contrary to their liking; and accordingly, so far as it was legally possible, they had taken seven States out of the Union, had seized many of the United States forts, and had fired upon the United States flag, all before I was inaugurated, and of course before I had done any official act whatever. The rebellion thus begun soon ran into the present civil war; and, in certain respects, it began on very unequal terms between the parties. The insurgents had been preparing for it more than thirty years, while the government had taken no steps to resist them. The former had carefully considered all the means which could be turned to their account. It undoubtedly was a well-pondered reliance with them that in their own unrestricted efforts to destroy Union, Constitution, and law, all together, the government would, in great degree, be restrained by the same Constitution and law from arresting their progress. Their sympathizers pervaded all departments of the government and nearly all communities of the people. From this material, under cover of "liberty of speech," "liberty of the press," and *habeas corpus*, they hoped to keep on foot amongst us a most efficient corps of spies, informers, suppliers, and aiders and abettors of their cause in a thousand ways. They knew that in times such as they were inaugurating, by the constitution itself, the *habeas corpus* might be suspended; but they also knew they had friends who would make a question as to who was to suspend it; meanwhile their spies and others might remain at large to help on their cause. Or if, as has happened, the executive should suspend the writ, without ruinous waste of time, instances of arresting innocent persons might occur, as are always likely to occur in such cases, and then a clamor could be raised in regard to this, which might be, at least, of some service to the insurgent cause. It needed no very keen perception to discover this part of the enemy's programme so soon as by open hostilities their machinery was fairly put in motion. Yet, thoroughly imbued with a reverence for the guaranteed rights of individuals, I was slow to adopt the strong measures which by degrees I have been forced to regard as being within the exceptions of the Constitution, and as indispensable to the public safety. . . . . .

I understand the meeting, whose resolutions I am considering, to be in favor of suppressing the rebellion by military force — by armies. Long experience has shown that armies cannot be maintained unless desertion shall be punished by the severe penalty of death. The case requires, and the law and the Constitution sanction this punishment. Must I shoot a simple-minded soldier-boy who deserts, while I must not touch a hair of a wily agitator who induces him to desert? This is none the less injurious when effected by getting a father, or brother, or friend, into a public meeting, and there working upon his feelings till he is persuaded to write the soldier-boy that he is fighting in a bad cause, for a wicked administration of a contemptible government, too weak to arrest and punish him if he shall desert. I think that in such a case to silence the agitator and save the boy, is not only constitutional, but withal a great mercy.

. . . .

Nor am I able to appreciate the danger apprehended by the meeting, that the American people will, by means of military arrests during the rebellion, lose the right of public discussion, the liberty of speech and the press, the law of evidence, trial by jury, and *habeas corpus* throughout the indefinite peaceful future which, I trust, lies before them, any more than I am able to believe that a man could contract so strong an appetite for emetics during temporary illness as to persist in feeding upon them during the remainder of his healthful life.

In giving the resolutions the earnest consideration which you request of me, I cannot overlook the fact that the meeting speak as "Democrats." Nor can I with full respect for their known intelligence, and the fairly presumed deliberation with which they prepared these resolutions, be permitted to suppose that this occurs by accident, or in any way other than that they prefer to designate themselves Democrats rather than American citizens. In this time of national peril I would have preferred to meet you on a level one step higher than any party platform, because I am sure that from such more elevated position we could do better battle for the country we all love than we possibly can from those lower ones where, from the force of habit, the prejudices of the past, and selfish hopes of the future, we are sure to expend much of our ingenuity and strength in finding fault with, and aiming blows at, each other. But, since you have denied me this, I will yet be thankful, for the country's sake, that not all Democrats have done so.

[Letter to James C. Conkling.]

August 16, 1863.

. . . . . There are those who are dissatisfied with me. To such I would say, You desire peace, and you blame me that we do not have it. But how can we obtain it? There are but three conceivable ways. First, to suppress the rebellion by force of arms. This I am trying to do. Are you for it? If you are so, we are agreed. If you are not for it, a second way is to give up the Union. I am against this. If you are, you should say so plainly. If you are not for force, nor yet for dissolution, there only remains some imaginary compromise. I do not believe that any compromise embracing the maintenance of the Union is now possible. All that I learn leads to a directly opposite belief. The strength of the rebellion is its military, its army. The army dominate all the country, and all the people within its range. Any offer of terms made by any man or men within that range in opposition to that army is simply nothing for the present; because such man or men have no power whatever to enforce their side of a compromise, if one were made with them.

. . . . . .

You dislike the Emancipation Proclamation, and perhaps would have it retracted. You say it is unconstitutional. I think differently. I think the Constitution invests its Commander-in-chief with the law of war in the time of war. The most that can be said, if so much, is that slaves are property. Is there, has there ever been, any question that by the law of war property, both of enemies and friends, may be taken when needed? And is it not needed whenever taking it helps us and hurts the enemy! Armies the world over destroy enemy's property when they cannot use it; and even destroy their own to keep it from the enemy. Civilized belligerents do all in their power to help themselves and hurt the enemy, except a few things regarded as barbarous or cruel. Among the exceptions are the massacre of vanquished foes and non-combatants, male and female.

But the Proclamation, as law, is valid, or is not valid. If it is valid, it cannot be retracted any more than the dead can be brought to life. Some of you profess to think that its retraction would operate favorably for the Union. Why better after the retraction than before the issue? There was more than a year and a half of trial to suppress the rebellion before the Proclamation was issued, the last one hundred days of which passed under an explicit notice that it was coming, unless averted by those in revolt returning to their allegiance. The war has certainly progressed as favorably for us since the issue of the Proclamation as before. . . . . .

You say you will not fight to free negroes. Some of them seem to be willing to fight for you. But no matter. Fight you then exclusively to save the Union. I issued the Proclamation on purpose to aid you in saving the Union.

Whenever we shall have conquered all resistance to the Union, if I shall urge you to continue fighting, it will be an apt time then for you to declare that you will not fight to free negroes.

I thought that in your struggle for the Union, to whatever extent the negroes should cease helping the enemy, to that extent it weakened the enemy in his resistance to you. Do you think differently? I thought that whatever negroes can be got to do as soldiers leaves just so much less for white soldiers to do in saving the Union. Does it appear otherwise to you? But negroes, like other people, act upon motives. Why should they do anything for us if we will do nothing for them? If they stake their lives for us they must be prompted by the strongest motive, even the promise of their freedom. And the promise, being made, must be kept.

The signs look better. The Father of Waters again goes unvexed to the sea. Thanks to the great North-west for it. Nor yet wholly to them. Three hundred miles up they met New England, Empire, Keystone, and Jersey hewing their way right and left. The sunny South, too, in more colors than one, also lent a hand. On the spot their part of the history was jotted down in black and white. The job was a great national one, and let none be banned who bore an honorable part in it. And while those who have cleared the great river may well be proud, even that is not all. It is hard to say that anything has been more bravely or better done than at Antietam, Murfreesboro, Gettysburg, and on many fields of lesser note.

Nor must Uncle Sam's web-foot be forgotten. At all the waters' margins they have been present, not only on the deep sea, the broad bay, and the rapid river, but also up the narrow, muddy bayou, and wherever the ground was a little damp, they have been and made their tracks.

Thanks to all. For the great Republic, — for the principles by which it lives and keeps alive for man's vast future, — thanks to all.

Peace does not appear so distant as it did. I hope it will soon come, and come to stay, and so come as to be worth keeping in all future time. It will then have been proved that among freemen there can be no successful appeal from the ballot to the bullet, and that they who take such appeal are sure to lose their case, and pay the cost.

And then there will be some black men who can remember that, with silent tongue, and clenched teeth, and steady eye, and well-poised bayonet, they have helped mankind on to this great consummation, while I fear there will be some white men unable to forget that, with malignant heart and deceitful speech, they have striven to hinder it.

Still, let us not be over sanguine of a speedy

final triumph. Let us be quite sober. Let us diligently apply the means, never doubting that a just God, in his own good time, will give us the rightful result.

[To Mr. Colfax, in the winter of 1863, the morning after unfavorable news from the army.]

How willingly would I exchange places to-day with the soldier who sleeps on the ground in the Army of the Potomac.

[From his third Annual Message to Congress, December 8, 1863.]

..... When Congress assembled a year ago, the war had already lasted nearly twenty months, and there had been many conflicts on both land and sea with varying results. The rebellion had been pressed back into reduced limits; yet the tone of public feeling and opinion, at home and abroad, was not satisfactory. With other signs, the popular election, then just passed, indicated uneasiness among ourselves, while amid much that was cold and menacing, the kindest words coming from Europe were uttered in accents of pity that we were too blind to surrender a hopeless cause.

[From a Speech after his re-election, November 10, 1864.]

So long as I have been here I have not willingly planted a thorn in any man's bosom. While I am deeply sensible of the high compliment of a reëlection, and duly grateful, I trust, to Almighty God for having directed my countrymen to a right conclusion, as I think, for their own good, it adds nothing to my satisfaction that any other man may be disappointed or pained by the result.

[To a Committee of the New York Workingmen's Republican Association, March 21, 1864.]

..... The strongest bond of human sympathy, outside of the family relation, should be one uniting all working people, of all nations, tongues, and kindreds. Nor should this lead to a war upon property or the owners of property. Property is the fruit of labor; property is desirable, is a positive good in the world. That some should be rich shows that others may become rich, and hence is just encouragement to independence and enterprise. Let not him who is houseless pull down the house of another, but let him labor diligently and build one for himself; thus by example assuring that his own shall be safe from violence when built.

[From a letter to Colonel Hodges, of Kentucky.]

WASHINGTON, April 4, 1864.

You ask me to put in writing the substance of what I verbally said the other day in your presence to Governor Bramlette and Senator Dixon.

It was about as follows: "I am naturally anti-slavery. If slavery is not wrong, nothing is wrong. I cannot remember when I did not so think and feel, and yet I have never understood that the Presidency conferred upon me an unrestricted right to act officially upon this judgment and feeling. It was in the oath I took that I would to the best of my ability preserve, protect, and defend the Constitution of the United States. I could not take the office without taking the oath. Nor was it in my view that I might take an oath to get power, and break the oath in using the power. I understand, too, that in ordinary and civil administration this oath even forbids me to practically indulge my primary abstract judgment on the moral question of slavery. I had publicly declared this at many times and in many ways. And I aver that, to this day, I have done no official act in mere deference to my abstract judgment and feeling on slavery. I did understand, however, that my oath to preserve the Constitution to the best of my ability imposed upon me the duty of preserving, by every indispensable means, that Government — that nation — of which the Constitution was the organic law. Was it possible to lose the nation, and yet preserve the Constitution? By general law, life *and* limb must be protected; yet often a limb must be amputated, to save a life;

but a life is never wisely given to save a limb. I felt that measures, otherwise unconstitutional, might become lawful by becoming indispensable to the preservation of the Constitution, through the preservation of the nation. Right or wrong, I assumed this ground; and now avow it. I could not feel that, to the best of my ability, I had even tried to preserve the Constitution, if, to save slavery, or any minor matter, I should permit the wreck of government, country, and constitution all together. . . . I add a word which was not in the verbal conversation. In telling this tale, I attempt no compliments to my own sagacity. I claim not to have controlled events, but confess plainly that events have controlled me. Now at the end of three years' struggle the nation's condition is not what either party or any man devised or expected. God alone can claim it. Whither it is tending seems plain. If God now wills the removal of a great wrong, and wills also that we of the North, as well as you of the South, shall pay fairly for our complicity in that wrong, impartial history will find therein new causes to attest and revere the justice and goodness of God."

[From Carpenter's "Six Months at the White House," 1865.]

I put the draft of the Emancipation Proclamation* aside, waiting for a victory. Well, the next news we had was of Pope's disaster at Bull Run. Things looked darker than ever. Finally came the week of the battle of Antietam [September 17, 1862]. I determined to wait no longer. The news came, I think, on Monday, that the advantage was on our side. I was then staying at the Soldiers' Home. Here I finished writing the second draft of the proclamation; came up on Saturday; called the cabinet together to hear it, and it was published the following Monday. I made a solemn vow before God, that if General Lee was driven back from Maryland, I would crown the result by the declaration of freedom to the slaves.

As affairs have turned, it is the central act of my administration, and the great event of the nineteenth century.

[From Noah Brooks's "Reminiscences."]

I should be the most presumptuous blockhead upon this footstool, if I, for one day, thought that I could discharge the duties which have come upon

* The original draft was prepared in the July preceding when the Federal forces were in the midst of reverses.

me since I came into this place, without the aid and enlightenment of One, who is stronger and wiser than all others.

[From "Six Months," &c.]

I have never united myself to any church, because I have found difficulty in giving my assent, without mental reservation, to the long, complicated statements of Christian doctrine which characterize their Articles of Belief and Confessions of Faith. When any church will inscribe over its altar, as its sole qualification for membership, the Saviour's condensed statement of the substance of both law and gospel, "Thou shalt love the Lord thy God with all thy heart, and with all thy soul, and with all thy mind, and thy neighbor as thyself," that church will I join with all my heart and all my soul.*

You say your husband is a religious man; tell him, when you meet him, that I say I am not much of a judge of religion, but that, in my opinion, the religion which sets men to rebel and fight against their government, because, as they think, that government does not sufficiently help *some* men to eat their bread in the sweat of *other* men's

* Said to Hon. H. C. Deming.

faces, is not the sort of religion upon which people can get to heaven.*

Here are twenty-three ministers, [of Springfield, Illinois,] of different denominations, and all of them are against me † but three; and here are a great many prominent members of the churches, a very large majority are against me. Mr. Bateman, I am not a Christian, — God knows I would be one, — but I have carefully read the Bible, and I do not so understand this book.‡ These men well know that I am for freedom in the Territories, freedom everywhere as free as the constitution and the laws will permit, and that my opponents are for slavery. They *know* this, and yet, with this book in their hands, in the light of which human bondage cannot live a moment, they are going to vote against me; I do not understand it at all. . . . . .

Doesn't it appear strange that men can ignore the moral aspect of this contest? A revelation could not make it plainer to me that slavery or the government must be destroyed. The future would be something awful, as I look at it, but for this rock on which I stand, [alluding to the Testa-

---

* Said to a lady from Tennessee, who asked the release of her husband, N. Brook, held as prisoner of war.

† In the canvass for United States senator.

‡ He had in his hand a copy of the New Testament.

ment, which he still held in his hand,] especially with the knowledge of how these ministers are going to vote. It seems as if God had borne with this thing [slavery] until the very teachers of religion had come to defend it from the Bible, and to claim for it a divine character and sanction; and now the cup of iniquity is full, and the vials of wrath will be poured out.*

[With reference to a remark made by a lady: "Some men seem able to do what they wish in any position, being equal to them all," Mr. Lincoln replied]:

Versatility is an injurious possession, since it can never be greatness. It misleads you in your calculations from its very agreeability, and it inevitably disappoints you in any great trust from its want of depth. A versatile man, to be safe from execration, should never soar; mediocrity is sure of detection.   C.

There is no more dangerous or expensive analysis than that of trying a man.   C.

[From an article in the *New York Citizen*, by Colonel Charles G. Halpine, containing an account of an interview with President Lincoln. The reference is to presidential receptions.]

..... But the office of President is essentially a civil one. For myself, I feel — though the tax

---

* Said privately to Mr. Newton Bateman, Superintendent for Public Institutions for the State of Illinois, residing at Springfield. — Holland's *Life of Abraham Lincoln.*

on my time is heavy — that no hours of my day are better employed than those which thus bring me again within the direct contact and atmosphere of the average of our whole people. Men moving only in an official circle are apt to become merely official — not to say arbitrary — in their ideas, and are apter and apter, with each passing day, to forget that they only hold power in a representative capacity. Now this is all wrong. I go into these promiscuous receptions of all who claim to have business with me twice each week, and every applicant for audience has to take his turn, as if waiting to be shaved in a barber's shop. Many of the matters brought to my notice are utterly frivolous, but others are of more or less importance, and all seem to renew in me a clearer and more vivid image of that great popular assemblage out of which I sprung, and to which, at the end of two years, I must return. I tell you that I call these receptions my *public-opinion baths;* for I have but little time to read the papers, and gather public opinion that way; and though they may not be pleasant, in all their particulars, the effect, as a whole, is renovating and invigorating to my perceptions of responsibility and duty.

[In reply to the remark of a clergyman that he "hoped the Lord was on our side," Mr. Lincoln said]:

I am not at all concerned about that, for I know that the Lord is always on the side of the right.

But it is my constant anxiety and prayer that I and this nation should be on the Lord's side.   c.

[After the repeal of the Fugitive-slave law, in June, 1864, Mr. Lincoln said]:

"There have been men base enough to propose to me to return to slavery our black warriors of Port Hudson and Olustee, and thus win the respect of the masters they fought. Should I do so, I should deserve to be damned in time and eternity. Come what will, I will keep my faith with friend and foe. My enemies pretend I am now carrying on this war for the sole purpose of abolition. So long as I am President it shall be carried on for the sole purpose of restoring the Union; but no human power can subdue this rebellion without the use of the emancipation policy, and every other policy calculated to weaken the moral and physical forces of the rebellion."

[In the Annual Message to Congress, December 6, 1864, Mr. Lincoln said]:

"In presenting the abandonment of armed resistance to the national authority on the part of the insurgents as the only indispensable condition to ending the war on the part of the government, I retract nothing heretofore said as to slavery.

"I repeat the declaration made a year ago, that while I remain in my present position I shall not attempt to retract or modify the Emancipation

Proclamation. Nor shall I return to slavery any person who is free by the terms of that proclamation or by any of the acts of Congress. If the people should, by whatever mode or means, make it an executive duty to re-enslave such persons, another, and not I, must be their instrument to perform it. In stating a single condition of peace, I mean simply to say that the war will cease on the part of the government whenever it shall have ceased on the part of those who began it."

[Of his second inaugural address, the London *Spectator* said: "We cannot read it without a renewed conviction that it is the noblest political document known to history, and should have for the nation and the statesmen he left behind him something of a sacred and almost prophetic character. Surely, none was ever written under a stronger sense of the reality of God's government. And certainly none written in a period of passionate conflict ever so completely excluded the partiality of victorious faction, and breathed so pure a strain of mingled justice and mercy."

"No statement of the true objects of the war more complete than this has ever been made. It includes them all — Nationality, Liberty, Equal Rights, and Self-Government. These are the principles for which the Union soldier fought, and which it was his aim to maintain and to perpetuate." — *President Hayes*, September, 1878.

Of Mr. Lincoln's second inaugural, M. Edouard Laboulaye said: "His inaugural address shows us what progress had been made in his soul. This piece of familiar eloquence is a masterpiece; it is the testament of a patriot. . . . I do not believe that any eulogy of the President would equal this page, in which he has depicted himself in all his greatness and in all his simplicity."]

[Second Inaugural Address, March 4, 1865.]

Fellow Countrymen: At this second appearing to take the oath of the Presidential office, there is less occasion for an extended address than there was at the first. Then a statement somewhat in detail of a course to be pursued seemed very fitting and proper. Now, at the expiration of four years, during which public declarations have been constantly called forth on every point and phase of the great contest which still absorbs the attention and engrosses the energies of the nation, little that is new could be presented.

The progress of our arms, upon which all else chiefly depends, is as well known to the public as to myself; and it is, I trust, reasonably satisfactory and encouraging to all. With high hope for the future, no prediction in regard to it is ventured.

On the occasion corresponding to this, four years ago, all thoughts were anxiously directed to an impending civil war. All dreaded it; all sought to avoid it. While the inaugural address was being delivered from this place, devoted altogether to saving the Union without war, insurgent agents were in the city, seeking to destroy it without war, — seeking to dissolve the Union and divide the effects by negotiation. Both parties deprecated war; but one of them would make war rather than let the nation survive, and the other would accept war rather than let it perish; and the war came.

One eighth of the whole population were colored slaves, not distributed generally over the Union, but localized in the Southern part of it. These slaves constituted a peculiar and powerful interest. All knew that this interest was somehow the cause of the war. To strengthen, perpetuate, and extend this interest, was the object for which the insurgents would rend the Union, even by war, while the government claimed no right to do more than to restrict the territorial enlargement of it.

Neither party expected for the war the magnitude or the duration which it has already attained. Neither anticipated that the cause of the conflict might cease with, or even before the conflict itself should cease. Each looked for an easier triumph, and a result less fundamental and astounding.

Both read the same Bible, and pray to the same God, and each invokes his aid against the other. It may seem strange that any men should dare to ask a just God's assistance in wringing their bread from the sweat of other men's faces; but let us judge not, that we be not judged. The prayer of both could not be answered. That of neither has been answered fully. The Almighty has his own purposes. "Woe unto the world because of offences, for it must needs be that offences come; but woe to that man by whom the offence cometh." If we shall suppose that American slavery is one of these offences which, in the providence of God, must needs come, but which, having continued through his appointed time, he now wills to remove, and that he gives to both North and South this terrible war as the woe due to those by whom the offence came, shall we discern therein any departure from those divine attributes which the believers in a living God always ascribe to him?

Fondly do we hope, fervently do we pray, that this mighty scourge of war may soon pass away. Yet if God wills that it continue until all the wealth piled by the bondman's two hundred and fifty years of unrequited toil shall be sunk, and until every drop of blood drawn with the lash shall be paid with another drawn with the sword; as was said three thousand years ago, so still it must be said, "The judgments of the Lord are true and righteous altogether."

With malice toward none, with charity for all, with firmness in the right, as God gives us to see the right, let us strive on to finish the work we are in, to bind up the nation's wounds, to care for him who shall have borne the battle, and for his widow and orphans, to do all which may achieve and cherish a just and a lasting peace among ourselves and with all nations.

[From an Address, March 7, 1865.]

I have always thought that all men should be free; but if any should be slaves, it should be first those who desire it for themselves, and secondly, those who desire it for others.

I have been driven many times to my knees by the overwhelming conviction that I had nowhere else to go. My own wisdom, and that of all about me, seemed insufficient for that day.*

I should be the most presumptuous blockhead upon this footstool, if I for one day thought that I could discharge the duties which have come upon me since I came into this place, without the aid and enlightenment of One who is wiser and stronger than all others.†

[The Emancipation Proclamation in the Cabinet. From the Diary of Secretary Salmon P. Chase, September 22, 1862.]

Gentlemen,—I have, as you are aware, thought a great deal about the relation of this war to slavery, and you all remember that, several weeks ago, I read to you an order I had prepared upon the subject, which, on account of objections made by some of you, was not issued. Ever since then

* From Holland's "Life of Lincoln."
† The Proclamation was issued January 1, 1863.

my mind has been occupied with this subject, and I have thought all along that the time for acting on it might probably come. I think the time has come now. I wish it was a better time. I wish that we were in a better condition. The action of the army against the rebels has not been quite what I should have best liked. But they have been driven out of Maryland, and Pennsylvania is no longer in danger of invasion. When the rebel army was at Frederick, I determined, as soon as it should be driven out of Maryland, to issue a proclamation of emancipation, such as I thought most likely to be useful. I said nothing to any one, but I made a promise to myself and [hesitating a little] to my Maker. • The rebel army is now driven out, and I am going to fulfil that promise. I have got you together to hear what I have written down. I do not wish your advice about the main matter, for that I have determined for myself. This I say without intending anything but respect for any one of you. But I already know the views of each on this question. They have been heretofore expressed, and I have considered them as thoroughly and carefully as I can. What I have written is that which my reflections have determined me to say. If there is anything in the expressions I use, or in any minor matter, which any one of you thinks had best be changed, I shall be glad to receive your suggestions. One other observation I will make. I know very well that many others might, in this matter as in others, do better than I can; and if I was satisfied that the public confidence was more fully possessed by any one of them than by me, and knew of any constitutional way in which he could be put in my place, he should have it. I would gladly yield it to him. But though I believe that I have not so much of the confidence of the people as I had sometime since, I do not know that, all things considered, any other person has more; and, however this may be, there is no way in which I can have any other man put where I am. I am here. I must do the best I can, I bear the responsibility of taking the course which I feel I ought to take.

[From "Six Months," etc.]

Many of my strongest supporters urged emancipation before I thought it indispensable, and, I may say, before I thought the country ready for it. It is my conviction, that, had the proclamation been issued even six months earlier than it was, public sentiment would not have sustained it. Just so as to the subsequent action in reference to enlisting blacks in the Border States. The step, taken sooner, could not, in my judgment, have been carried out. A man watches his pear-tree day after day, impatient for the ripening of the fruit. Let him attempt to force the process, and he may spoil both fruit and tree. But let him patiently wait, and the ripe pear at length falls into his lap! We have seen this great revolution in public sentiment slowly but surely progressing, so that, when final action came, the opposition was not strong enough to defeat the purpose. I can now solemnly assert that I have a clear conscience in regard to my action on this momentous question. I have done what no man could have helped doing, standing in my place.

[Dedicatory Address at Gettysburg.*]

Four score and seven years ago our fathers brought forth upon this continent a new nation, conceived in liberty, and dedicated to the proposition that all men are created equal.

Now we are engaged in a great civil war, testing whether that nation, or any nation so conceived and so dedicated, can long endure. We are met on a great battle-field of that war. We are met to dedicate a portion of it as the final resting-place of those who here gave their lives that that nation might live. It is altogether fitting and proper that we should do this.

* "His brief speech at Gettysburg will not easily be surpassed by words on any recorded occasion. This, and one American speech, — that of John Brown to the court that tried him, — and part of Kossuth's speech at Birmingham, can only be compared with each other, and with no fourth." — *R. W. Emerson.*

But in a larger sense we cannot dedicate, we cannot consecrate, we cannot hallow this ground. The brave men, living and dead, who struggled here, have consecrated it far above our power to add or detract. The world will little note nor long remember what we say here, but it can never forget what they did here. It is for us the living rather to be dedicated here to the unfinished work that they have thus far so nobly carried on. It is rather for us to be here dedicated to the great task remaining before us — that from these honored dead we take increased devotion to the cause for which they here gave the last full measure of devotion — that we here highly resolve that the dead shall not have died in vain; that the nation shall, under God, have a new birth of freedom, and that the government of the people, by the people, and for the people, shall not perish from the earth.

[When Mr. Lincoln had ended his speech, which had been preceded by a long and eloquent one by Edward Everett, he turned and congratulated the latter on having succeeded so well. "Ah, Mr. Lincoln," was the reply, "how gladly would I exchange all my one hundred pages, to have been the author of your twenty lines."]

EXECUTIVE MANSION, WASHINGTON, July 13, 1863.*

To MAJOR GENERAL GRANT.

My Dear General: I do not remember that you and I ever met personally. I write this now as a grateful acknowledgment for the almost inestimable service you have done the country. I wish to say a word further. When you first reached the vicinity of Vicksburg, I thought you should do what you finally did, march the troops across the Neck, run the batteries, with the transports, and thus go below. I never had any faith, except a general hope, that you knew better than I did; that the Yazoo Pass Expedition, and the like, could succeed. When you got below, and took Port Gibson, Grand Gulf and vicinity, I thought you should go down the river and join Gen. Banks; and when you turned northward, east of the Big Black, I feared it was a mistake. I now wish to make a personal acknowledgment that you were right and I was wrong.

Yours very truly, A. LINCOLN.

[Written after the Battle of Chattanooga, 1863.]

To GENERAL GRANT: ... Understanding that your lodgment at Chattanooga and at Knoxville is now secure, I wish to tender you and all under your command my more than thanks, my pro-

* After the capture of Vicksburg.

foundest gratitude for the skill, courage, and perseverance with which you and they, over so great difficulties, have effected the important object. God bless you all.

[To General Grant, April 30, 1864.]

LIEUTENANT-GENERAL GRANT: Not expecting to see you before the Spring campaign opens, I wish to express, in this way, my entire satisfaction with what you have done up to this time, so far as I understand it. The particulars of your plans I neither know nor seek to know.

You are vigilant and self-reliant, and, pleased with this, I wish not to obtrude any restraints or constraints upon you. While I am very anxious that any great disaster or capture of our men in great numbers shall be avoided, I know that these points are less likely to escape your attention than they would be mine. If there be anything wanting which is within my power to give, do not fail to let me know it. And now, with a brave army and a just cause, may God sustain you.

[In reply to a deputation from the National Union League, June 8, 1864, who congratulated him upon his re-nomination for the Presidency, Mr. Lincoln said:] . . . "I have not permitted myself, gentlemen, to conclude that I am the best man in the country; but I am reminded in this connection of a story of an old Dutch farmer, who remarked to a companion once, that 'it was not best to swop horses when crossing streams.'"

[From a letter written December 11, 1864]:

"You say you are praying for the war to end. So am I, but I want it to end right. God alone knows how anxious I am to see these rivers of blood cease to flow; but they must flow until treason hides its head."

It matters not to me whether Shakespeare be well or ill acted; with him the thought suffices.

There is one passage of the play of "Hamlet" which is very apt to be slurred over by the actor, or omitted altogether, which seems to me the choicest part of the play. It is the soliloquy of the king after the murder. It always struck me as one of the finest touches of nature in this world.

The opening of the play of "King Richard the Third" seems to me often entirely misapprehended. It is quite common for an actor to come upon the stage, and, in a sophomoric style, to begin with a flourish:

> "Now is the winter of our discontent
> Made glorious summer by this sun of York,
> And all the clouds that lowered upon our house,
> In the deep bosom of the ocean buried."

Now this is all wrong. Richard, remember, had been, and was then, plotting the destruction of his brothers, to make room for himself. Outwardly, the most loyal to the newly-crowned king, secretly, he could scarcely contain his impatience at the obstacles still in the way of his own elevation. He appears upon the stage, just after the crowning of Edward, burning with repressed hate and jealousy. The prologue is the utterance of the most intense bitterness and satire.

[From a letter written just before the assassination.]

I assure you that as soon as the business of this war is settled, the Indians shall have my first attention; and I will not rest until they shall have justice with which both you and they will be satisfied.

There are some quaint, queer, verses, written, I think, by Oliver Wendell Holmes, entitled, "The Last Leaf," one of which is to me inexpressibly touching:

"The mossy marbles rest
On the lips that he has pressed
In their bloom;
And the names he loved to hear
Have been carved for many a year
On the tomb."

For pure pathos, in my judgment, there is nothing finer than those six lines in the English language.

ANDREW JOHNSON.

BORN, 1808; DIED, 1875, AGED 67. — ALDERMAN AT GREENVILLE, TENN., 1828. — MAYOR, 1830. — IN THE STATE LEGISLATURE, 1835. — AGAIN, 1839. — STATE SENATOR, 1841. — REPRESENTATIVE TO CONGRESS, 1843. — GOVERNOR OF TENNESSEE, 1853. — RE-ELECTED, 1855. — UNITED STATES SENATOR, 1857. — MILITARY GOVERNOR OF TENNESSEE, 1862. — VICE-PRESIDENT, 1865. — PRESIDENT, 1865-1869.

[From a Speech in the United States Senate, March 2, 1861.]

..... SIR, have we reached a point of time at which we dare not speak of treason? Our forefathers talked about it; they spoke of it in the Constitution of the country; they defined what treason is. Is it an offence, is it a crime, is it an insult, to recite the Constitution that was made by Washington and his compatriots?

What does the Constitution define treason to be? "Treason against the United States shall consist only in levying war against them, or in adhering to their enemies, giving them aid and comfort." There it is defined clearly. . . . Who is it that has been engaged in conspiracies? Who is it that has been engaged in making war upon the United States? Who is it that has fired upon our flag? Who is it that has given instructions to take your arsenals, to take your forts, to take your dock-yards, to seize your custom-houses, and rob your treasuries? Who is it that has been engaged in secret conclaves, and issuing orders for the seizure of public property in violation of the Constitution they were sworn to support? In the language of the Constitution of the United States, are not these who have been engaged in this nefarious work guilty of treason? I will now present a fair issue, and I hope it will be fairly met. Show me the man who has been engaged in these conspiracies; show me the man who has been sitting in these nightly and secret conclaves, plotting the overthrow of the government; show me who has fired upon our flag, has given instructions to take our forts, our custom-houses, our arsenals, and our dock-yards, and I will show you a traitor! [Applause in the galleries, followed by a demand to have them cleared.]

Mr. President, when I was interrupted . . . I was making a general allusion to treason as defined in the Constitution of the United States, and to those who were traitors and guilty of treason within the scope and meaning of the law and the Constitution. My proposition was, that if they would show me who were guilty of the offences I have enumerated, I would show them who were the traitors. That being done, were I the President of the United States, I would do as Thomas Jefferson did in 1806 with Aaron Burr, who was charged with treason : I would have them arrested and tried for treason; and, if convicted, by the Eternal God, they should suffer the penalty of the law at the hands of the executioner. Sir, treason must be punished.

[From a Speech at Nashville, 1864.]

Slavery is dead, and you must pardon me if I do not mourn over its dead body; you can bury it out of sight. . . . I desire that all men shall have a fair start and an equal chance in the race of life, and let him succeed who has the most merit. I am for emancipation, for two reasons: first, because it is right in itself; and second, because in the emancipation of the slaves we break down an odious and dangerous aristocracy. I think that we are freeing more whites than blacks in Tennessee.

In the support and practice of correct principles, we can never reach wrong results.

[Speech, when Governor of Tennessee, Nashville, 1864.]

Colored Men of Nashville : you have all heard of the President's Proclamation, by which he announced to the world, that the slaves in a large portion of the seceded states were thenceforth and forever free. For certain reasons, which seemed wise to the President, the benefits of that Proclamation did not extend to you and to your native state. Many of you, consequently, were left in bondage. The taskmaster's scourge was not yet broken, and the fetters still galled your limbs. Gradually this iniquity has been passing away; but the hour has come when the last vestiges of it must be removed. Consequently I, too, without reference to the President, or any other person, have a proclamation to make; and, standing here upon the steps of the Capitol, with the past history of the state to witness, the present condition to guide, and its future to encourage me, I, Andrew Johnson, do hereby proclaim freedom, full, broad, and unconditional, to every man in Tennessee. . . . I speak now as one who feels the world his country, and all who love equal rights his friends., I speak, too, as a citizen of Tennessee. I am here on my own soil; and here I mean to stay, and fight this great battle of truth and justice to the triumphant end. Rebellion and slavery shall, by God's good help, no longer pollute our state. Loyal men, whether white or black, shall alone control her destinies; and when this strife, in which we are all engaged, is past, I know we shall have a better state of things, and shall all rejoice that honest labor shall have the fruit of its own industry, and that every man has a fair chance in the race of life.

[To a delegation of citizens of New Hampshire, after the death of Mr. Lincoln.]

I have now, as always, an abiding faith in the ultimate triumph of justice and right, and I shall seek the inspiration and guidance of this faith in the assured belief that the present struggle will result in the permanent establishment of our government, and in making us a free, united and happy people. This government is now passing through a fiery, and, let us hope, its last ordeal, — one that will test its powers of endurance, and will determine whether it can do what its enemies have denied, — suppress and punish treason. . . . . .

I know it is easy, gentlemen, for any one who is so disposed, to acquire a reputation for clemency and mercy. But the public good imperatively requires a just discrimination in the exercise of these qualities. What is clemency? What is mercy? It may be considered merciful to relieve an individual from pain and suffering; but to relieve one from the penalty of crime may be promotive of national disaster. The American people must be taught to know and understand that treason is a crime. Arson and murder are crimes, the punishment of which is the loss of liberty and life. If, then, it is right in the sight of God to take away human life for such crimes, what punishment, let me ask you, should be inflicted upon him who is guilty of the atrocious crime of assassinating the Chief Magistrate of a great people? I am sure there is no one present who has not the answer ready upon his lips! Him, whom we loved, has been removed from our midst, by the hand of a ruthless assassin, and his blessed spirit has gone to that bourn whence no traveller returns. If his murderer should suffer the severest penalty known to the law, what punishment should be inflicted upon the assassins who have raised their daggers against the life of a nation, against the happiness and lives of thirty millions of people? Treason is a crime, and must be punished as a crime. It must not be regarded as a mere difference of political opinion. It must not be excused as an unsuccessful rebellion, to be overlooked and forgiven. It is a crime before which all other crimes sink into insignificance; and in saying this, it must not be considered that I am influenced by angry or revengeful feelings.

Of course, a careful discrimination must be observed, for thousands have been involved in this rebellion who are only technically guilty of the crime of treason. They have been deluded and deceived, and have been made the victims of the more intelligent, artful, and designing men, the instigators of this monstrous rebellion. The number of this latter class is comparatively small. The former may stand acquitted of the crime of treason — the latter never; the full penalty of their crimes should be visited upon them. To the others I would accord amnesty, leniency, and mercy.

[To the 1st Colored Regiment of the District of Columbia, October 10, 1865.]

. . . . . Liberty is not a mere idea, a mere vagary. . . . Liberty does not consist in doing all things as we please; and there can be no liberty without law. In a government of freedom and of liberty, there must be law, and there must be obedience and submission to the law without regard to color. Liberty (and may I not call you my countrymen?) consists in the glorious privilege of work; of pursuing the ordinary avocations of peace with industry and with economy; and, that being done, all those who have been industrious and economical are permitted to appropriate and enjoy the products of their own labor. This is one of the great blessings of freedom. . . . . .

Henceforth each and all of you must be measured according to your merit. If one man is more meritorious than another, they cannot be equals; and he is the most exalted that is the most meritorious, without regard to color. And the idea of having a law passed in the morning that would make a white man a black man before night, and a black man a white man before day, is absurd. That is not the standard. It is your own conduct; it is your own merit; it is the development of your own talents and of your own intellectuality and moral qualities.

ULYSSES S. GRANT.

BORN, 1822.—ENTERED WEST POINT MILITARY ACADEMY, 1839.—LIEUTENANT IN THE ARMY, 1845.—IN THE MEXICAN WAR, 1846-1847.—CAPTAIN, 1847.—ENGAGED IN BUSINESS, 1854.—CAPTAIN OF VOLUNTEERS, 1861.—COLONEL, JUNE 17, 1861.—BRIGADIER-GENERAL, AUGUST 23, 1861.—COMMANDER OF THE MILITARY DISTRICT OF CAIRO, DECEMBER, 1861.—TOOK FORT DONELSON, FEBRUARY 15, 1862.—COMMANDER OF THE DEPARTMENT OF WESTERN TENNESSEE, JULY, 1862.—TOOK VICKSBURG, JULY 4, 1863.—MAJOR-GENERAL, 1863.—COMMANDER OF THE MILITARY DISTRICT OF THE MISSISSIPPI, OCTOBER, 1863.—LIEUTENANT-GENERAL, MARCH 1, 1864.—ASSUMED COMMAND OF THE ARMIES OF THE UNITED STATES, MARCH 17, 1864.—CAPTAIN-GENERAL, APRIL, 1865.—SECRETARY OF WAR "AD INTERIM," AUGUST 12, 1867.—PRESIDENT, 1869-1877.

[At the outbreak of the rebellion, 1861, he said to a friend]:

THE government has educated me for the army. What I am, I owe to my country. I have served her through one war, and, live or die, will serve her through this. — *Phelps.*

[To the citizens of Paducah, Kentucky, September 6, 1861.]

I have come among you not as an enemy, but as your fellow-citizen; not to maltreat or annoy you, but to respect and enforce the rights of all loyal citizens. An enemy in rebellion against our constitutional government has taken possession of, and planted its guns on the soil of Kentucky, and fired upon you. Columbus and Hickman are in his hands. He is moving upon your city. I am here to defend you against this enemy, to assert the authority and sovereignty of your government. I have nothing to do with opinions. I shall deal only with armed rebellion and its aiders and abettors. You can pursue your usual avocations without fear. The strong arm of the government is here to protect its friends, and punish its enemies. Whenever it is manifest that you are able to defend yourselves, and to maintain the authority of the government, and protect the rights of loyal citizens, I shall withdraw the forces under my command.

[General Buckner, of the Confederate army at Fort Donelson, having sent a letter to General Grant, February 16, 1862, proposing "the appointment of Commissioners, to agree upon terms of capitulation," General Grant replied the same day.]

Yours of this date proposing an armistice and the appointment of commissioners to settle on the terms of capitulation, is just received.

No terms, except unconditional and immediate surrender, can be accepted.

I propose to move immediately on your works.

I am, very respectfully,
Your obedient servant.

[After Mr. Lincoln's Emancipation Proclamation, General Grant issued the following order]:

MILLIKEN'S BEND, LOUISIANA.

..... Corps, division, and post commanders will afford all facilities for the completion of the negro regiments now organizing in this department. Commissioners will issue supplies, and quarter-masters will furnish stores, on the same requisitions and returns as are required for other troops. It is expected that all commanders will especially exert themselves in carrying out the policy of the Administration, not only in organizing colored regiments and rendering them efficient, but also in removing prejudices against them.

[From a letter to General Banks, with reference to Vicksburg, May 25, 1863.]

..... I feel that my force is abundantly strong to hold the enemy where he is, or to whip him should he come out. The place is so strongly fortified, however, that it cannot be taken without either a great sacrifice of life or by a regular siege. I have determined to adopt the latter course, and save my men.

[To a proposition of General Pemberton, July 3, 1863, for "an armistice for — hours, with a view to arranging terms for the capitulation of Vicksburg, . . . to save the further effusion of blood," General Grant replied the same day]:

GENERAL: Your note of this date [July 3] just received proposes an armistice of several hours for the purpose of arranging terms of capitulation through commissioners to be appointed, etc. The effusion of blood you propose stopping by this course can be ended at any time you may choose, by an unconditional surrender of the city and garrison. Men who have shown so much endurance and courage as those now in Vicksburg will also challenge the respect of an adversary, and, I can assure you, will be treated with all the respect due to them as prisoners of war. I do not favor the proposition of appointing commissioners to arrange terms of capitulation, because I have no other terms than those indicated above.

I am, General, very respectfully, your obedient servant.

On the afternoon of the same day (July 3) Gen. Pemberton sought an interview with Gen. Grant, and said: "General Grant, I meet you in order to arrange terms for the capitulation. What terms do you demand?"

"Unconditional surrender," was General Grant's reply.

Pemberton rejoined: "Unconditional surrender! Never, so long as I have a man left me. I will fight rather."

General Grant replied, "Very well."

On July 4, came the following from Pemberton: "General, I have the honor to acknowledge the receipt of your communication of this date, and, in reply, to say that the terms proposed by you are accepted."

[When recommending (1863) Sherman and McPherson for promotion to the rank of Brigadier-General in the regular army, General Grant wrote]:

"The first reason for this is their great fitness for any command that it may ever become necessary to intrust to them. Second, their great purity of character and disinterestedness in anything except the faithful performance of their duty and the success of every one engaged in the great battle for the preservation of the Union. Third, they have honorably won this distinction upon many well-fought battle-fields. The promotion of such men as Sherman and McPherson always adds strength to our army."

[To a letter from Secretary Chase (July 4, 1863), in which he says: "I find that a rigorous line within districts occupied by our military forces, from beyond which no cotton or other produce can be brought, and within which no trade can be carried on, gives rise to serious and to some apparently well-founded complaints." Gen. Grant replied] :

..... My experience in West Tennessee has convinced me that any trade whatever with the rebel states is weakening to us of at least thirty-three per cent. of our force. No matter what the restrictions thrown around trade, if any whatever is allowed, it will be made the means of supplying the enemy with what they want. Restrictions, if lived up to, make trade unprofitable, and hence none but dishonorable men go into it. I will venture to say that no honorable man has made money in Western Tennessee in the last year, while many fortunes have been made there during that time.

The people in the Mississippi valley are now nearly subjugated. Keep trade out for a few months, and I doubt not that the work of subjugation will be so complete, that trade can be opened freely with the States of Arkansas, Louisiana, and Mississippi; that the people of these States will be more anxious for the enforcement and protection of our laws than the people of the loyal States. They have experienced the misfortune of being without them, and are now in a most happy condition to appreciate their blessings.

No theory of my own will ever stand in the way of my executing, in good faith, any order I may receive from those in authority over me; but my position has given me an opportunity of seeing what would not be known by persons away from the scene of war; and, I venture, therefore, to suggest great caution in opening trade with rebels.

VICKSBURG, July 11, 1863.

"I am anxious to get as many of these negro regiments as possible, and to have them full, and completely equipped. . . . I am particularly desirous of organizing a regiment of heavy artillery from the negroes, to garrison this place, and shall do so as soon as possible."

VICKSBURG, July 24.

The negro troops are easier to preserve discipline among than our white troops, and I doubt not will prove equally good for garrison duty. All that have been tried have fought bravely.

[In 1863, hearing that some negro troops in the service of the United States had been hung at Milliken's Bend, General Grant wrote to General Richard Taylor]:

I feel no inclination to retaliate for the offences of irresponsible persons; but if it is the policy of any General intrusted with the command of troops to show no quarter, or to punish with death prisoners taken in battle, I will accept the issue. It may be you propose a different line of policy towards black troops, and officers commanding them, to that practiced towards white troops. If so, I can assure you that these colored troops are regularly mustered into the service of the United States. The Government, and all officers under the Government, are bound to give the same protection to these troops that they do to any other troops.

GENERAL ORDERS, No. 50, VICKSBURG, August 1, 1863.

. . . . . 2. The citizens of Mississippi within the limits above described, are called upon to pursue their peaceful avocations, in obedience to the laws of the United States. Whilst doing so in good faith, all the United States forces are prohibited from molesting them in any way. It is earnestly recommended that the freedom of negroes be acknowledged, and that, instead of compulsory labor, contracts on fair terms be entered into between the former masters and servants, or between the latter and other persons who may be willing to give them employment. Such a system as this, honestly followed, will result in substantial advantages to all parties.

All private property will be respected, except when the use of it is necessary for the government, in which case it must be taken under the direction of a commissioned officer, with specific instructions to seize certain property, and no other. A staff officer of the Quartermaster of Subsistence Department will, in each instance, be designated to receipt for such property as may be seized, the property to be paid for at the end of the war on proof of loyalty, or on proper adjustment of the claim, under such regulations and laws as may hereafter be established.

..... 4. Within the county of Warren, laid waste by the long presence of contending armies, the following rules, to prevent suffering, will be observed: Major-General Sherman and Major-General McPherson will each nominate a Commissary of Subsistence who will issue articles of prime necessity to all destitute families calling for them, under such restrictions for the protection of the government as they may deem necessary. Families who are able to pay for the provisions drawn, will in all cases be required to do so.

[On August 25, 1863, General Grant visited Memphis, Tennessee. A committee of loyal citizens having tendered him the hospitality of the city, he sent a letter of acceptance, in which he said]:

In accepting this testimonial, which I do at a great sacrifice of my personal feelings, I simply desire to pay a tribute to the first public exhibition in Memphis of loyalty to the government which I represent in the Department of the Tennessee. I should dislike to refuse, for considerations of personal convenience, to acknowledge anywhere, or in any form, the existence of sentiments I have so long and so ardently desired to see manifested in this department. The stability of this government and the unity of this nation depend solely on the cordial support and the earnest loyalty of the people. While, therefore, I thank you sincerely for the kind expressions you have used toward myself, I am profoundly gratified at this public recognition, in the city of Memphis, of the power and authority of the government of the United States.

[IN THE FIELD, CHATTANOOGA, TENN., December 10, 1863.—Congratulatory Order.]

The General commanding takes this opportunity of returning his sincere thanks and congratulations to the brave armies of the Cumberland, the Ohio, and the Tennessee, and their comrades from the Potomac, for their recent splendid and decisive successes achieved over the enemy. In a short time you have recovered from him the control of the Tennessee River, from Bridgeport to Knoxville. You dislodged him from his great stronghold upon Lookout Mountain, drove him from Chattanooga Valley, wrested from his determined grasp the possession of Missionary Ridge, repelled, with heavy loss to him, his repeated assaults upon Knoxville, forcing him to raise the siege there; driving him at all points, utterly routed and discomfited, beyond the limits of the State. By your noble heroism and determined courage you have most effectually defeated the plans of the enemy for regaining possession of the States of Kentucky and Tennessee. You have secured positions from which no rebellious power can drive or dislodge you. For all this, the General commanding thanks you, collectively and individually. The loyal people of the United States thank and bless you. Their hopes and prayers for your success against this unholy rebellion are with you daily. Their faith in you will not be in vain. Their hopes will not be blasted. Their prayers to Almighty God will be answered. You will yet go to other fields of strife, and with the invincible bravery and unflinching loyalty to justice and right which have characterized you in the past; you will prove that no enemy can withstand you, and that no defence, however formidable, can check your onward march.

IN THE WILDERNESS, HEAD-QUARTERS IN THE FIELD,
May 11, 1864, 8 A. M.

We have now ended the sixth day of very heavy fighting. The result, to this time, is very much in our favor. Our losses have been heavy, as have been those of the enemy. I think the losses of the enemy must be greater.

We have taken over five thousand prisoners by battle, while he has taken from us but few, except stragglers.

I propose to fight it out on this line if it takes all summer.

City Point, Virginia, August 16, 1864.

To Hon. E. B. Washburne.

Dear Sir: I state to all citizens who visit me, that all we want now to insure an early restoration of the Union is a determined unity of sentiment North. The rebels have now in their ranks their last man. The little boys and old men are guarding prisoners, grading railroad bridges, and forming a good part of their garrisons for entrenched positions. A man lost by them cannot be replaced. They have robbed the cradle and the grave equally to get their present force. Besides what they lose in frequent skirmishes and battles, they are now losing from desertion and other causes at least one regiment per day.

With this drain upon them the end is not far distant, if we will only be true to ourselves. Their only hope now is in a divided North. This might give them re-enforcements from Tennessee, Kentucky, Maryland, and Missouri, while it would weaken us. With the draft quickly enforced the enemy would become despondent, and would make but little resistance. I have no doubt but the enemy are exceedingly anxious to hold out until after the presidential election. They have many hopes from its effects.

They hope a counter revolution; they hope the election of the Peace candidate. In fact, like

"Micawber," they hope for something to "turn up." Our Peace friends, if they expect peace from separation, are much mistaken. . It would be but the beginning of war with thousands of Northern men joining the South because of our disgrace in allowing separation. To have "peace on any terms," the South would demand the restoration of their slaves already freed; they would demand indemnity for losses sustained; and they would demand a treaty which would make the North slave-hunters for the South. They would demand pay for the restoration of every slave escaping to the North.

[Address to all the armies.]

WASHINGTON, June 2, 1865.

SOLDIERS OF THE ARMIES OF THE UNITED STATES: By your patriotic devotion to your country in the hour of danger and alarm, your magnificent fighting, bravery, and endurance, you have maintained the supremacy of the Union and the Constitution, overthrown all armed opposition to the enforcement of the law, and of the proclamation forever abolishing slavery, — the cause and precept of the rebellion, — and opened the way to the rightful authorities to restore order and inaugurate peace on a permanent and enduring basis on every foot of American soil. Your marches, sieges, and battles, in distance, duration, resolution, and brilliancy of results, dim the lustre of the world's past military achievements, and will be the patriot's precedent in defence of liberty and right in all time to come. In obedience to your country's call you left your homes and families, and volunteered in its defence. Victory has crowned your valor, and secured the purpose of your patriotic hearts; and with the gratitude of your countrymen, and the highest honors a great and free nation can accord, you will soon be permitted to return to your homes and families conscious of having discharged the highest duty of American citizens. To achieve these glorious triumphs, and secure to yourselves, your fellow-countrymen, and posterity, the blessings of free institutions, tens of thousands of your gallant comrades have fallen and sealed the priceless legacy with their lives. The graves of these a grateful nation bedews with tears, honors their memories, and will ever cherish and support their stricken families.

[From the Report of the Operations of the Armies of the United States, 1864-'65.]

WASHINGTON, July 22, 1865.

..... From an early period of the rebellion I had been impressed with the idea that active and continuous operations of all the troops that could be brought into the field, regardless of season and weather, were necessary to a speedy termination of the war. The resources of the enemy and his numerical strength were far inferior to ours; but, as an offset to this, we had a vast territory with a population hostile to the government to garrison, and long lines of river and railroad communications to protect, to enable us to supply the operating armies.

The armies in the East and West acted independently and without concert, like a balky team, no two ever pulling together, enabling the enemy to use to great advantage his interior lines of communication for transporting troops from East to West, re-enforcing the army most vigorously pressed, and to furlough large numbers, during seasons of inactivity on our part, to go to their homes and do the work of producing for the support of their armies. It was a question whether our numerical strength and resources were not more than balanced by these disadvantages and the enemy's superior position.

From the first I was firm in the conviction that no peace could be had that would be stable and conducive to the happiness of the people, both North and South, until the military power of the rebellion was entirely broken.

I therefore determined, first, to use the greatest number of troops practicable against the armed force of the enemy; preventing him from using the same force at different seasons against first one and then another of our armies, and the possibility of repose for refitting and producing necessary supplies for carrying on resistance. Second, to hammer continuously against the armed force of the enemy and his resources, until by mere attrition, if in no other way, there should be nothing left to him but an equal submission with the loyal section of our common country to the Constitution and laws of the land.

. . . . . .

It has been my fortune to see the armies of both the West and East fight battles, and from what I have seen I know there is no difference in their fighting qualities. All that it was possible for men to do in battle they have done. The Western armies commenced their battles in the Mississippi Valley, and received the final surrender of the remnant of the principal army opposed to them in North Carolina. The armies of the East commenced their battles on the river from which the Army of the Potomac derived its name, and received the final surrender of their old antagonist at Appomattox Court House, Virginia. The splendid achievements of each have nationalized our victories, removed all sectional jealousies, (of which we have unfortunately experienced too much,) and the cause of crimination and recrimination that might have followed had either section failed in its duty. All have a proud record, and all sections can well congratulate themselves and each other for having done their full share in restoring the supremacy of law over every foot of territory belonging to the United States. Let them hope for perpetual peace and harmony with that enemy, whose manhood, however mistaken the cause, drew forth such herculean deeds of valor.

[When, August 17, 1867, President Johnson ordered General Grant to remove from command at New Orleans General Sheridan, and at the same time asked him to make suggestions in regard to the order, General Grant replied]:

I am pleased to avail myself of this invitation to urge, earnestly urge, in the name of a patriotic people who have sacrificed hundreds of thousands of loyal lives, and thousands of millions of treasure, to preserve the integrity and union of this country, that this order be not insisted on. It is unmistakably the expressed wish of the country that General Sheridan should not be removed from his present command.

This is a republic where the will of the people is the law of the land. I beg that their voice may be heard.

General Sheridan has performed his civil duties faithfully and intelligently. His removal will only be regarded as an effort to defeat the laws of Congress.

[During the suspension, for political reasons, of Mr. Stanton as Secretary of War, by President Johnson, General Grant was appointed Secretary of War, *ad interim*. When the Senate, January 13, 1868, passed a resolution of non-concurrence with the suspension, General Grant immediately surrendered the keys of the office, which offended Mr. Johnson. A correspondence between them ensued. General Grant's closing letter is as follows]:

The course you understood I agreed to pursue was in violation of law, and that without orders from you; while the course I did pursue, and which I never doubted you fully understood, was in accordance with law, and not in disobedience of any orders of my superior.

And now, Mr. President, when my honor as a soldier, and integrity as a man, have been so violently assailed, pardon me for saying that I can but regard this whole matter, from beginning to end, as an attempt to involve me in the resistance of law for which you hesitated to assume the responsibility, in order thus to destroy my character before the country. I am in a measure confirmed in this conclusion by your recent orders directing me to disobey orders from the Secretary of War, my superior, and your subordinate, without having countermanded his authority. I conclude with the assurance, Mr. President, that nothing less than a vindication of my personal honor and character could have induced this correspondence on my part.

[From his Inaugural Address, March 4, 1869.]

CITIZENS OF THE UNITED STATES: Your suffrages having elected me to the office of President of the United States, I have, in conformity with the Constitution of our country, taken the oath of office prescribed therein. I have taken this oath without mental reservation, and with a determination to do, to the best of my ability, all that it requires of me.

The responsibilities of the position I feel, but accept them without fear. The office has come to me unsought; I commence its duties untrammelled. I bring to it a conscious desire and determination to fill it, to the best of my ability, to the satisfaction of the people. On all leading questions agitating the public mind I will always express my views to Congress, and urge them according to my judgment, and when I think it advisable, will exercise the constitutional privilege of interposing a veto to defeat measures which I oppose. But all laws will be faithfully executed, whether they meet my approval or not.

I shall on all subjects have a policy to recommend, none to enforce against the will of the people. Laws are to govern all alike — those opposed to as well as those in favor of them. I know no method to secure the repeal of bad or obnoxious laws so effectual as their strict execution. . . . . .

A great debt has been contracted in securing to us and our posterity the Union. The payment of this, principal and interest, as well as the return to a specie basis as soon as it can be accomplished without material detriment to the debtor class or to the country at large, must be provided for. To protect the national honor, every dollar of the government indebtedness should be paid in gold, unless otherwise especially stipulated in the contract. Let it be understood that no repudiation of one farthing of our public debt will be trusted in public places, and it will go far towards strengthening a credit which ought to be the best in the world, and will ultimately enable us to replace the debt with bonds bearing less interest than we now pay.

[From a Message, December, 1870.]

..... As soon as I learned that a Republic had been proclaimed at Paris, and the people of France had acquiesced in the change, the minister of the United States was directed by telegraph to recognize it, and to tender my congratulations and those of the people of the United States. The re-establishment in France of a system of government disconnected with the dynastic traditions of Europe appeared to be a proper subject for the felicitations of Americans. Should the present struggle result in attaching the hearts of the French to our simpler form of representative government, it will be a subject of still further satisfaction to our people. While we make no effort to impose our institutions upon the inhabitants of other countries, and while we adhere to our traditional neutrality in civil contests elsewhere, we cannot be indifferent to the spread of American political ideas in a great and highly civilized country like France.

[From a Message, December, 1871.]

..... In Utah there still remains a remnant of barbarism repugnant to civilization, to decency, and to the laws of the United States. . . . Neither polygamy nor any other violation of existing statutes will be permitted within the territory of the United States. It is not with the religion of the self-styled Saints that we are now dealing, but with their practices. They will be protected in the worship of God according to the dictates of their own consciences, but they will not be permitted to violate the laws under the cloak of religion.

[From a Message, December 7, 1875.]

..... As we are now about to enter upon our second centennial — commencing our manhood as a nation — it is well to look back upon the past, and study what will be best to preserve and advance our future greatness. . . . . .

We should look to the dangers threatening us,

and remove them as far as lies in our power. We are a republic whereof one man is as good as another before the law. Under such a form of government, it is of the greatest importance that all should be possessed of education and intelligence enough to cast a vote with a right understanding of its meaning. A large association of ignorant men cannot, for any considerable period, oppose a successful resistance to tyranny and oppression from the educated few, but will inevitably sink into acquiescence to the will of intelligence, whether directed by the demagogue or by priestcraft. Hence the education of the masses becomes of the first necessity for the preservation of our institutions. They are worth preserving, because they have secured the greatest good to the greatest proportion of the population of any form of government yet devised. All other forms of government approach it in proportion to the general diffusion of education and independence of thought and action. As the principal step, therefore, to our advancement in all that has marked our progress in the past century, I suggest for your earnest consideration, and most earnestly recommend it, that a constitutional amendment be submitted to the legislatures of the several States for ratification, making it the duty of each of the several States to establish and forever maintain free public schools adequate to the education of all the children in the rudimentary branches within their respective limits, irrespective of sex, color, birthplace or religions; forbidding the teaching in said schools of religious, atheistic, or pagan tenets; and prohibiting the granting of any school funds or school taxes, or any part thereof, either by legislative, municipal, or other authority, for the benefit or in aid, directly or indirectly, of any religious sect or denomination, or in aid or for the benefit of any other object of any nature or kind whatever.

. . . . . .

[From a Speech at the Annual Reunion of the Army of the Tennessee, at Des Moines, Iowa, September 29, 1875.]

Comrades: It always affords me much gratification to meet my old comrades in arms of ten or fourteen years ago, and to live over again in memory the trials and hardships of those days — hardships imposed for the preservation and perpetuation of our free institutions. We believed then, and believe now, that we had a good government, worth fighting for, and, if need be, dying for. How many of our comrades of those days paid the latter price for our preserved Union! Let their heroism and sacrifices be ever green and in our memory. Let not the results of their sacrifices be destroyed. The Union and the free institutions for which they fell, should be held more dear for their sacrifices. We will not deny to any of those who fought against us any privileges under the government which we claim for ourselves; on the contrary, we honor all such who come forward in good faith to help build up the waste places, and to perpetuate our institutions against all enemies, as brothers in full interest with us in a common heritage; but we are not prepared to apologize for the part we took in the war. It is to be hoped that like trials will never again befall our country. In this sentiment no class of people can more heartily join than the soldier, who submitted to the dangers, trials, and hardships of the camp and the battlefield. On whichever side they may have fought, no class of people are more interested in guarding against a recurrence of those days.

Let us then begin by guarding against every enemy threatening the perpetuity of free republican institutions. I do not bring into this assemblage politics, certainly not partisan politics; but it is a fair subject for soldiers in their deliberations to consider what may be necessary to secure the prize for which they battled in a republic like ours. Where the citizen is sovereign and the official the servant, where no power is exercised except by the will of the people, it is important that the sovereign — the people — should possess intelligence.

The free school is the promoter of that intelligence which is to preserve us as a free nation. If we are to have another contest in the near future of our national existence, I predict that the dividing line will not be Mason and Dixon's, but between patriotism and intelligence on the one side, and superstition, ambition, and ignorance on the other. Now in this centennial year of our national existence, I believe it a good time to begin the work of strengthening the foundation of the house commenced by our patriotic forefathers one hundred years ago, at Concord and Lexington. Let us all labor to add all needful guarantees for the more perfect security of free thought, free speech, and free press, pure morals, unfettered religious sentiments, and of equal rights and privileges to all men, irrespective of nationality, color, or religion. Encourage free schools, and resolve that not one dollar of money appropriated to their support, no matter how raised, shall be appropriated to the support of any sectarian school. Resolve that the State or Nation, or both combined, shall furnish to every child growing up in the land, the means of acquiring a good common-school education, unmixed with sectarian, pagan, or atheistic tenets. Leave the matter of religion to the family altar, the church, and the private school supported entirely by private contributions. Keep the church and state forever separate. With these safeguards, I believe the battles which created the Army of the Tennessee will not have been fought in vain.

[From a Letter explanatory of a passage in the above Speech.]

I feel no hostility to free education going as high as the state or national government feels able to provide, protecting, however, every child in the privilege of a common-school education before public means are applied to a higher education for the few.

[From a Message.]

In a former Message to Congress I had occasion to consider this question, [the recognition of belligerent rights,] and reached the conclusion that the conflict in Cuba, dreadful and devastating as were its incidents, did not rise to the fearful dignity of war.

[From a Message, December, 1876.]

..... The compulsory support of the free schools, and the disfranchisement of all who cannot read and write the English language, after a fixed probation, would meet my hearty approval.*

[Veto Message of the Senate Currency Bill.]

I am not a believer in any artificial method of making paper money equal to coin when the coin

* He would not have this action retrospective. It should apply only to future voters.

is not owned or held ready to redeem the promise to pay, for paper money is nothing more than promises to pay.

[From a Speech at a banquet in the Town-hall, Birmingham, October 17.]

..... He [Mr. Chamberlain, M. P.] alluded to the great merit of retiring a large army at the close of a great war. If he had ever been in my position for four years, and undergone all the anxiety and care that I had in the management of those large armies, he would appreciate how happy I was to be able to say that they could be dispensed with. I disclaim all credit and praise for doing that one thing. . . . Further, we Americans claim to be so much of Englishmen, and to have so much general intelligence, and so much personal independence and individuality, that we do not quite believe that it is possible for any one man there to assume any more right and authority than the constitution of the land gave to him. Among the English-speaking people we do not think these things possible. We can fight among ourselves, and dispute and abuse each other, but we will not allow ourselves to be abused outside; nor will those who look on at our little personal quarrels in our own midst permit us to interfere with their own rights. —*Around the World with General Grant,* by John Russell Young.

[From a Speech, in reply to an Address on behalf of the International Arbitration Union, Birmingham.]

..... I am conscientiously, and have been from the beginning, an advocate of what the society represented by you is seeking to carry out; and nothing would afford me greater happiness than to know, as I believe will be the case, that, at some future day, the nations of the earth will agree upon some sort of Congress, which shall take cognizance of international questions of difficulty, and whose decisions will be as binding as the decision of our Supreme Court is binding on us. It is a dream of mine that some such solution may be found for all questions of great difficulty that may arise between different nations. In one of the addresses reference was made to the dismissal of the army to the pursuit of peaceful industry. I would gladly see the millions of men who are now supported by the industry of the nations return to industrial pursuits, and thus become self-sustaining, and take off the tax upon labor which is now levied for their support. — *Around the World.*

[In reply to an Address of the Iron-Founders' Society, July 3, 1877.]

..... I recognize the fact that whatever there is of greatness in the United States, or indeed in any other country, is due to the labor performed.

The laborer is the author of all greatness and wealth. Without labor there would be no government, or no leading class, or nothing to preserve. With us labor is regarded as highly respectable. — *Around the World.*

[At a lunch in the Guild hall, London, June 16, 1877. After having spoken once before, he said]:

Habits formed in early life and early education press upon us as we grow older. I am not aware that I ever fought two battles on the same day in the same place, and that I should be called upon to make two speeches on the same day under the same roof is beyond my understanding. What I do understand is, that I am much indebted to all of you for the compliments you have paid me. All I can do is to thank the Lord Mayor for his kind words, and to thank the citizens of Great Britain here present in the name of my country and for myself.

[Later in the day, at a dinner in the Crystal Palace, Mr. Thomas Hughes proposed the health of General Grant, adding that he did not impose the burden of a reply. General Grant, however, said]:

Mr. Hughes, I must none the less tell you what gratification it gives me to hear my health proposed in such hearty words by Tom Brown, of Rugby. — *Around the World.*

[A Speech at a dinner-party at Hamburg, of American ladies and gentlemen, July 4, 1878.]

Mr. Consul and Friends: I am much obliged to you for the kind manner in which you drink my health. I share with you in all the pleasure and gratitude which Americans so far from home should feel on this anniversary. But I must dissent from one remark of our consul, to the effect that I saved the country during the recent war. If our country could be saved or ruined by the efforts of any one man we should not have a country, and we should not be now celebrating our Fourth of July. There are many men who would have done far better than I did under the circumstances in which I found myself during the war. If I had never held command; if I had fallen; if all our generals had fallen, there were ten thousand behind us who would have done our work just as well, who would have followed the contest to the end, and never surrendered the Union. Therefore it is a mistake, and a reflection upon the people, to attribute to me, or to any number of men who held high command, the salvation of the Union. We did our work as well as we could, and so did hundreds of thousands of others. We deserve no credit for it, for we should have been unworthy of our country and of the American name, if we had not made every sacrifice to save the Union. What saved the Union was the coming forward of the young men of the nation. They came from their homes and fields, as they did in the time of the Revolution, giving everything to the country. To their devotion we owe the salvation of the Union. The humblest soldier who carried a musket is entitled to as much credit for the results of the war as those who were in command. So long as our young men are animated by this spirit there will be no fear for the Union.—*Around the World.*

With a people as honest and proud as the Americans, and with so much common-sense, it is always a mistake to do a thing not entirely right for the sake of expediency.—*Around the World.*

When I was in the army I had a physique that could stand anything. Whether I slept on the ground or in a tent, whether I slept one hour or ten in the twenty-four, whether I had one meal or three, or none, made no difference. I could lie down and sleep in the rain without caring. But I was many years younger, and I could not hope to do that now.—*Around the World.*

The only eyes a general can trust are his own. —*Around the World.*

I never saw the President [Lincoln] until he gave me my commission as Lieutenant-general.

Afterwards I saw him often, either in Washington or at head-quarters. Lincoln, I may almost say, spent the last days of his life with me. I often recall those days. He came down to City Point in the last month of the war, and was with me all the time. He lived on a dispatch-boat in the river, but was always around head-quarters. He was a fine horseman, and rode my horse Cincinnati. He visited the different camps, and I did all I could to interest him. He was very anxious about the war closing; was afraid we could not stand a new campaign, and wanted to be around when the crash came.

I have no doubt that Lincoln will be the conspicuous figure of the war; one of the great figures of history. He was a great man, a very great man. The more I saw of him, the more this impressed me. He was incontestably the greatest man I ever knew. What marked him especially was his sincerity, his kindness, his clear insight into affairs. Under all this he had a firm will, and a clear policy. People used to say that Seward swayed him, or Chase, or Stanton. This was a mistake. He might appear to go Seward's way one day, and Stanton's another, but all the time he was going his own course, and they with him. It was that gentle firmness in carrying out his own will, without apparent force or friction, that formed the basis of his character. He was a wonderful talker and teller of stories. It is said his stories were improper. I have heard of them, but I never heard Lincoln use an improper word or phrase. I have sometimes, when I hear his memory called in question, tried to recall such a thing, but I cannot. I always found him pre-eminently, a clean-minded man. I regard these stories as exaggerations. Lincoln's power of illustration, his humor, was inexhaustible. He had a story or an illustration for everything.—*Around the World.*

I would deal with nations as equitable law requires individuals to deal with each other.

I knew Stonewall Jackson at West Point and in Mexico. At West Point he came into the school at an older age than the average, and began with a low grade. But he had so much courage and energy, worked so hard, and governed his life by a discipline so stern, that he steadily worked his way along and rose far above others who had more advantages. Stonewall Jackson at West Point was in a state of constant improvement. He was a religious man then, and some of us regarded him as a fanatic. Sometimes his religion took strange forms—hypochondria—fancies that an Evil Spirit had taken possession of him. But he never relaxed in his studies or his Christian duties. I knew him in Mexico. He was always a brave and trustworthy officer,—none more so in the army. I never knew him or encountered him in the rebellion. I question whether his campaigns in Virginia justify his reputation as a great commander. He was killed too soon, and before his rank allowed him a great command. It would have been a test of generalship if Jackson had met Sheridan in the Valley, instead of some of the men he did meet. From all I know of Jackson, and all I see of his campaigns, I have little doubt of the result. If Jackson had attempted on Sheridan the tactics he attempted so successfully upon others he would not only have been beaten but destroyed. Sudden daring raids, under a fine general like Jackson, might do against raw troops and inexperienced commanders, such as we had in the beginning of the war, but not against drilled troops and a commander like Sheridan. The tactics for which Jackson is famous, and which achieved such remarkable results, belonged entirely to the beginning of the war and to the peculiar conditions under which the earlier battles were fought. They would have ensured destruction to any commander who tried them upon Sherman, Thomas, Sheridan, Meade, or, in fact, any of our great generals. Consequently Jackson's fame as a general depends upon achievements gained before his generalship was tested, before he had a chance of matching himself with a really great commander. No doubt so able and patient a man as Jackson, who worked so hard at anything he attempted, would have adapted himself to new conditions and risen with them. He died before his opportunity. I always respected Jackson personally, and esteemed his sincere and manly character. He impressed me always as a man of the Cromwell stamp, a Puritan—much more of the New Englander than the Virginian. If any man believed in the rebellion, he did. And his nature was such that whatever he believed in became a deep religious duty, a duty he would discharge at any cost. It is a mistake to suppose that I ever had any feeling for Stonewall Jackson but respect. Personally we were always good friends; his character had rare points of merit, and although he made the mistake of fighting against his country, if ever a man did so conscientiously, he was the man.—*Around the World.*

The war, when it broke out, found me relieved from the army, and engaged in my father's business in Galena, Illinois. A company of volunteers were formed under the first call of the President. I had no position in the company, but having had military experience I agreed to go with the company to Springfield, the capital of the State, and assist in drill. When I reached Springfield I was assigned to duty in the Adjutant's Department, and did a good share of the detail work. I had had experience in Mexico. As soon as the work of mustering-in was over, I asked Gov. Gates for a week's leave of absence to visit my parents in Covington. The Governor gave me the leave. While I wanted to pay a visit home, I was also anxious to see McClellan. McClellan was then in Cincinnati in command. He had been appointed Major-General in the regular army. I was delighted with the appointment. I knew McClellan and had great confidence in him. I have, for that matter, never lost my respect for McClellan's character, nor my confidence in his loyalty and ability. I saw in him the man who was to pilot us through, and I wanted to be on his staff. I thought that if he would make me a major, or a lieutenant-colonel, I could be of use, and I wanted to be with him. So when I came to Cincinnati I went to the head-quarters. Several of the staff officers were friends I had known in the army. I asked one of them if the General was in. I was told he had just gone out, and was asked to take a seat. Everybody was so busy that they could not say a word. I waited a couple of hours. I never saw such a busy crowd — so many men at an army head-quarters with quills behind their ears. But I supposed it was all right, and was much encouraged by their industry. It was a great comfort to see the men so busy with the quills. Finally, after a long wait, I told an officer that I would come in again next day, and requested him to tell McClellan that I had called. Next day I came in. The same story. The general had just gone out, might be in at any moment. Would I wait? I sat and waited for two hours, watching the officers with their quills, and left. . . . McClellan never acknowledged my call, and, of course, after he knew I had been at his head-quarters I was bound to await his acknowledgment. I was older, had ranked him in the army, and could not hang around his head-quarters watching the men with the quills behind their ears. I went over to make a visit to an old army friend, Reynolds, and while there learned that Governor Gates, of Illinois, had made me a colonel of volunteers. Still I should like to have joined McClellan.

This pomp and ceremony was common at the beginning of the war. McClellan had three times as many men with quills behind their ears as I had ever found necessary at the head-quarters of a much larger command. Fremont had as much state as a Sovereign, and was as difficult to approach. His head-quarters alone required as much transportation as a division of troops. I was under his command a part of the time, and remember how imposing was his manner of doing business. He sat in a room in full uniform, with his maps before him.

When you went in, he would point out one line or another in a mysterious manner, never asking you to take a seat. You left without the least idea of what he meant or what he wanted you to do.

..... McClellan is to me one of the mysteries of the war. As a young man he was always a mystery. He had the way of inspiring you with the idea of immense capacity, if he would only have a chance. Then he is a man of unusual accomplishments, a student and a well-read man. I have never studied his campaigns enough to make up my mind as to his military skill, but all my impressions are in his favor. I have entire confidence in McClellan's loyality and patriotism. But the test which was applied to him would be terrible to any man, being made a major-general at the beginning of the war. It has always seemed to me that the critics of McClellan do not consider this vast and cruel responsibility — the war a new thing to all of us, the army new, everything to do from the outset, with a restless people and Congress. McClellan was a young man when this devolved upon him, and if he did not succeed, it was because the conditions of success were so trying. If McClellan had gone into the war as did Sherman, Thomas, or Meade, had fought his way along and up, I have no reason to suppose he would not have now as high a distinction as any of us. McClellan's main blunder was in allowing himself political sympathies, and in permitting himself to become the critic of the President, and in time his rival. This is shown in his letter to Mr. Lincoln on his return to Harrison's Landing, when he sat down and wrote out a policy for the government. He was forced into this by his associations, and that led to his nomination for the presidency. I remember how disappointed I was about this letter, and also in his failure to destroy Lee at Antietam. His friends say that he failed because of the interference from Washington. I am afraid the interference from Washington was not from Mr. Lincoln so much as from the enemies of the administration, who believed they could carry their point through the army of the Potomac. My own experience with Mr. Lincoln and Mr. Stanton, both in the western and eastern armies, was the reverse. I was never interfered with. I had the fullest support of the President and Secretary of War. No general could want better backing, for the President was a man of great wisdom and moderation, the Secretary a man of enormous character and will. Very often where Lincoln would want to say Yes, his Secretary would make him say No; and more frequently when the Secretary was driving on in a violent course, the President would check him. United, Lincoln and Stanton made about as perfect a combination as I believe could, by any possibility, govern a great nation in time of war. — *Around the World.*

A general who will never take a chance in a battle will never fight one. — *Around the World.*

Sherman is not only a great soldier, but a great man. He is one of the very great men in our country's history. He is a many-sided man. He is an orator with few superiors. As a writer he is among the first. As a general I know of no man I would put above him. Above all, he has a fine character — so frank, so sincere, so outspoken, so genuine. There is not a false line in Sherman's character — nothing to regret. . . . . .

The march to the sea was proposed by me in a letter to Halleck before I left the Western army; my objective point was Mobile. It was not a sudden inspiration, but a logical move in the game. It was the next thing to be done. We had gone so far into the South that we had to go to the sea. We could not go anywhere else, for we were certainly not going back. The details of the march, the conduct, the whole glory belong to Sherman. I never thought much as to the origin of the idea. I presume it grew up in correspondence with Sherman; that it took shape as those things always do. Sherman is a man with so many resources and a mind so fertile, that once an idea takes root it grows rapidly. My objection to Sherman's plan at the time, and my objection now, was his leaving Hood's army in the rear. I always wanted the march to the sea, but at the same time I wanted Hood. — *Around the World.*

[From his Speech in London, when presented with the freedom of the city, June 15, 1877.]

Although a soldier by education and profession, I have never felt any sort of fondness for war, and I have never advocated it except as a means of peace. — *Around the World.*

I was never more delighted at anything than the close of the war. I never liked service in the army — not as a young officer. I did not want to go to West Point. My appointment was an accident, and my father had to use his authority to make me go. If I could have escaped West Point without bringing myself into disgrace at home, I would have done so. I remember about the time I entered the Academy there were debates in Congress over a proposal to abolish West Point. I used to look over the papers and read the Congress reports with eagerness to see the progress the bill made, and hoping to hear that the school had been abolished, and that I could go home to my father without being in disgrace. I never went into a battle willingly or with enthusiasm. I was always glad when a battle was over. I never want to command another army. I take no interest in armies. When the Duke of Cambridge asked me to review his troops at Aldershot, I told his Royal

Highness that the one thing I never wanted to see again was a military parade. When I resigned from the army and went to a farm I was happy. When the rebellion came I returned to the service because it was a duty. I had no thought of rank; all I did was to try and make myself useful. My first commission as brigadier came on the unanimous indorsement of the delegation from Illinois. I do not think I knew any of the members but Washburne, and I did not know him very well. It was only after Donelson that I began to see how important was the work that Providence devolved upon me. . . . You see, Donelson was our first clear victory, and you will remember the enthusiasm that came with it. . . . When other commands came I always regretted them. When the bill creating the grade of Lieutenant-General was proposed, with my name as Lieutenant-General, I wrote Mr. Washburne opposing it. I did not want it. I found that the bill was right and I was wrong, when I came to command the Army of the Potomac—that a head was needed to the army. I did not want the Presidency, and have never quite forgiven myself for resigning the command of the army to accept it; but it could not be helped. I owed my honors and opportunities to the Republican party, and if my name could aid it I was bound to accept. The second nomination was almost due to me—if I may use the phrase—because of the bitterness of political personal opponents. My re-election was a great gratification, because it showed me how the country felt. — *Around the World.*

I always dreaded going to the Army of the Potomac. After the battle of Gettysburg I was told I could have the command, but I managed to keep out of it. I had seen so many generals fall, one after another, like bricks in a row, that I shrank from it. After the battle of Mission Ridge, and my appointment as Lieutenant-General, and I was allowed to choose my place, it could not be avoided. Then it seemed as if the time was ripe, and I had no hesitation. — *Around the World.*

The most troublesome men in public life, are those over-righteous people who see no motive in other people's actions but evil motives; who believe all public life is corrupt, and nothing is well done unless they do it themselves. They are narrow-headed men, their two eyes so close together that they can look out of the same gimlet-hole without winking. — *Around the World.*

Andrew Johnson, one of the ablest of the poor white class, tried to assert some independence; but as soon as the slaveholders put their thumb upon him, even in the Presidency, he became their slave. — *Around the World.*

I do not believe in luck in war any more than in luck in business. Luck is a small matter; may affect a battle or a movement, but not a campaign or a career.— *Around the World.*

Speaking of the notable men I have met in Europe, I regard Bismarck and Gambetta as the greatest. I saw a good deal of Bismark in Berlin, and later in Gastein, and had long talks with him. He impresses you as a great man.

Gambetta also impressed me greatly. I was not surprised, when I met him, to see the power he wielded over France. I should not be surprised at any prominence he might attain in the future. I was very much pleased with the Republican leaders in France. They seemed a superior body of men. My relations with them gave me great hopes for the future of the Republic. They were men apparently of sense, wisdom, and moderation. — *Around the World.*

I have always had an aversion to Napoleon and the whole family. When I was in Denmark the Prince Imperial was there, and some one thought it might be pleasant for me to meet him. I declined, saying I did not want to see him or any of his family. Of course the first emperor was a great genius, but one of the most selfish and cruel men in history. Outside of his military skill, I do not see a redeeming trait in his character. He abused France for his own ends, and brought incredible disasters upon his country to gratify his selfish ambition. I do not think any genius can excuse a crime like that. The third Napoleon was worse than the first, the especial enemy of America and liberty. Think of the misery he brought upon France by a war, which, under the circumstances, no one but a madman would have declared. I never doubted how the war would end, and my sympathies at the outset were entirely with Germany. I had no ill-will to the French people, but to Napoleon. After Sedan, I thought Germany should have made peace with France; and I think that if peace had been made then, in a treaty which would have shown that the war was not against the French people, but against a tyrant and his dynasty, the condition of Europe would now be different. Germany, especially, would be in a better condition, without being compelled to arm every man, and drain the country every year of its young men to arm against France. . . . There exists, and has since the foundation of our government always existed, a traditional friendship between our people and the French. I had this feeling in common with my countrymen. But I felt at the same time that no people had so great an interest in the removal of Napoleonism from France as the French people. — *Around the World.*

[From a Speech at Elgin, Scotland.]

I am happy to say, that during the eight years of my Presidency it was a hope of mine, which I am glad to say was realized, that all differences between the two nations should be settled in a manner honorable to both. All the questions, I am glad to say, were so settled, and in my desire for that result, it was my aim to do what was right, irrespective of any other consideration whatever. During all the negotiations, I felt the importance of maintaining the friendly relations between the great English-speaking people of this country and the United States, which I believe to be essential to the maintenance of peace principles throughout the world, and I feel confident that the continuance of those relations will exercise a vast influence in promoting peace and civilization throughout the world. — *Around the World.*

[From a Speech at Newcastle.]

. . . . . The President [of the Chamber of Commerce] in his remarks has alluded to the personal friendship existing between the two nations. I will not say the two peoples, because we are one people; but we are two nations having a common destiny, and that destiny will be brilliant in proportion to the friendship and co-operation of the brethren on the two sides of the water. . . . These are two nations which ought to be at peace with each other. We ought to strive to keep at peace with all the world besides, and by our example stop those wars which have devastated our own countries, and are now devastating some countries in Europe. — *Around the World.*

[From a Speech to the workingmen at Newcastle.]

I was always a man of peace, and I have always advocated peace, although educated a soldier. I never willingly, although I have gone through two wars, of my own accord advocated war. I advocated what I believed to be right, and I have fought for it to the best of my ability, in order that an honorable peace might be secured.—*Around the World.*

Now, there is one subject that has been alluded to here, that I do not know that I should speak upon at all,— I have heard it occasionally whispered since I have been in England,— and that is, the great advantages that would accrue to the United States if free trade should only be established. I have a sort of recollection, through reading, that England herself had a protective tariff until she had manufactories somewhat established. I think we are rapidly progressing in the way of establishing manufactories ourselves, and I believe we shall become one of the greatest free-trade nations on the face of the earth; and when we both come to be free-traders, I think that probably the balance of the nations had better stand aside, and not contend with us at all in the markets of the world. — *Around the World.*

[From a Conversation with Bismarck.]

I regard Sheridan as not only one of the great soldiers of our war, but one of the great soldiers of the world, — as a man who is fit for the highest commands. No better general ever lived than Sheridan.

. . . . . .

The truth is, I am more of a farmer than a soldier. I take little or no interest in military affairs, and, although I entered the army thirty-five years ago, and have been in two wars, in Mexico as a young lieutenant, and later, I never went into the army without regret, and never retired without pleasure. — *Around the World.*

[The following conversation took place between General Grant and Bismarck.]

"You had to save the Union just as we had to save Germany."

"Not only save the Union, but destroy slavery."

"I suppose, however, the Union was the real sentiment, the dominant sentiment?"

"In the beginning, yes; but as soon as slavery fired upon the flag, it was felt, we all felt, even those who did not object to slaves, that slavery must be destroyed. We felt that it was a stain to the Union that men should be bought and sold like cattle."

"I suppose if you had had a large army at the beginning of the war it would have ended in a much shorter time?"

"We might have had no war at all; but we cannot tell. Our war had many strange features; there were many things which seemed odd enough at the time, but which now seem providential. If we had had a larger regular army, as it was then constituted, it might have gone with the South. In fact, the Southern feeling in the army among high officers was so strong that when the war broke out the army dissolved. We had no army. Then we had to organize one. A great commander like Sherman or Sheridan even then might have organized an army and put down the rebellion in six months or a year, or, at the farthest, two years. But that would have saved slavery, perhaps, and slavery meant the germs of new rebellion. There had to be an end of slavery. Then we were fighting an enemy with whom we could not make a peace. We had to destroy him. No convention, no treaty was possible, only destruction."

"It was a long war, and a great work well done, and I suppose it means a long peace."
"I believe so." — *Around the World*.

[From a letter to Governor Chamberlain, of South Carolina, July 26, 1876.]

Too long denial of guaranteed right is sure to lead to revolution, bloody revolution, where suffering must fall upon the innocent as well as the guilty.

[From a Speech at Galveston, Texas, March 25, 1880.]

. . . ˙ . . It was my fortune, more than a third of a century ago, to visit Texas as Second Lieutenant, and to have been one of those who went into the conflict which was to settle the boundary of Texas. I am glad to come back now on this occasion to behold the territory which is an empire in itself, and larger than some of the empires of Europe. I wish for the people of Texas, as I do for the people of the entire South, that they may go on developing their resources, and become great and powerful, and in their prosperity forget, as the worthy Mayor expressed it, that there is a boundary between the North and South. I am sure we will all be happier and much more prosperous when the day comes that there shall be no sectional feeling. Let any American, who can travel abroad, as I have done, and with the opportunity of witnessing what there is to be seen that I have had, and he will return to

America a better American and a better citizen than when he went away. He will return more in love with his own country. Far be it from me to find fault with any of the European Governments. I was well received at their hands on every side, by every nation in Europe, but with their dense population and their worn-out soil it takes a great deal of government to enable the people to get from the soil a bare subsistence. Here we have rich virgin soil, with room enough for all of us to expand and live, with the use of very little government. I do hope we long may be able to get along happily and contentedly without being too much governed."

[From a Speech at Warren, Ohio, September 28, 1880.]

In view of the known character and ability of the speaker who is to address you to-day, and his long public career and association with the leading statesmen of this country for the past twenty years, it would not be becoming in me to detain you with many remarks of my own. But it may be proper for me to account to you on the first occasion of my presiding at political meetings for the faith that is in me.

I am a Republican, as the two great political parties are now divided, because the Republican party is a National party, seeking the greatest good for the greatest number of citizens. There is not a precinct in this vast Nation where a Democrat cannot cast his ballot and have it counted as cast. No matter what the prominence of the opposite party, he can proclaim his political opinions, even if he is only one among a thousand, without fear and without proscription on account of his opinions. There are fourteen States, and localities in some other States, where Republicans have not this privilege.

This is one reason why I am a Republican. But I am a Republican for many other reasons. The Republican party assures protection to life and property, the public credit and the payment of the debts of the Government, State, county, or municipality so far as it can control. The Democratic party does not promise this; if it does, it has broken its promises to the extent of hundreds of millions, as many Northern Democrats can testify to their sorrow. I am a Republican, as between the existing parties, because it fosters the production of the field and farm and of manufactories, and it encourages the general education of the poor as well as the rich. The Democratic party discourages all these when in absolute power. The Republican party is a party of progress and of liberality toward its opponents. It encourages the poor to strive to better their children, to enable them to compete successfully with their more fortunate associates, and, in fine, it secures an entire equality before the law of every citizen, no matter what his race, nationality, or previous condition. It tolerates no privileged class. Every one has the opportunity to make himself all he is capable of.

Ladies and gentlemen, do you believe this can be truthfully said in the greater part of fourteen of the States of this Union to-day which the Democratic party controls absolutely? The Republican party is a party of principles, the same principles prevailing wherever it has a foothold. The Democratic party is united in but one thing, and that is in getting control of the Government in all its branches. It is for internal improvement at the expense of the Government in one section and against this in another. It favors repudiation of solemn obligations in one section, and honest payment of its debts in another, where public opinion will not tolerate any other view. It favors fiat money in one place and good money in another. Finally, it favors the pooling of all issues not favored by the Republicans, to the end that it may secure the one principle upon which the party is a most harmonious unit, namely, getting control of the Government in all its branches.

I have been in some part of every State lately in rebellion, within the last year. I was most hospitably received at every place where I stopped. My receptions were not by the Union class alone, but by all classes, without distinction. I had a free talk with many who were against me in the war, and who have been against the Republican party ever since. They were in all instances reasonable men, judged by what they said. I believed then and believe now that they sincerely want a breakup in this "Solid South" political condition. They see that it is to their pecuniary interest as well as to their happiness that there should be harmony and confidence between all sections. They want to break away from the slavery which binds them to a party name. They want a pretext that enough of them can unite upon to make it respectable. Once started, the Solid South will go as Kukluxism did before, as is so admirably told by Judge Tourgee in his "Fool's Errand." When the break comes those who start it will be astonished to find how many of their friends have been in favor of it for a long time, and have only been waiting to see some one take the lead. This desirable solution can only be attained by the defeat and continued defeat of the Democratic party as now constituted.

[Speech in New York, November 20, 1880.]

Now, in regard to the future of myself, which has been alluded to here, I am entirely satisfied as I am to-day. I am not one of those who cry out against the republic, and charge it with being ungrateful. I am sure that, as regards the American people, as a nation and as individuals, I have every reason under the sun, if any person really has, to be satisfied with their treatment of me.

[Speech in New York, December 1, 1880.]

The government owes much to the service of its volunteer soldiers. Too much credit cannot be paid them. The very fact that the country can raise so great and good an army, in such an emergency as our late civil war, is a proof that we have institutions in which all the people have an equal part; that we have a government, not for the privileged class, but for the people and by the people. When the peaceful citizen changes to the soldier, he does so readily, feeling that he is fighting for himself when he is fighting for his government. I hope and feel that the country will not again have to call upon such numbers of its citizens for support. I am confident that we will not have another civil war, but should the menaces of a foreign foe cause a call to arms, we will find the same support and readiness in organizing an army as in 1861.

RUTHERFORD B. HAYES.

BORN, 1822. — GRADUATED AT KENYON COLLEGE, O., 1842. — MEMBER OF HARVARD COLLEGE LAW SCHOOL. — BEGAN PRACTICE OF LAW, 1845. — MAJOR IN THE UNION ARMY, JUNE 7, 1861. — JUDGE ADVOCATE OF THE MILITARY DEPARTMENT OF OHIO, 1861. — LIEUTENANT-COLONEL, OCTOBER 24, 1861. — BRIGADIER-GENERAL, MARCH 13, 1865. — ELECTED TO CONGRESS, 1865. — CHAIRMAN OF THE LIBRARY COMMITTEE. — RE-ELECTED, 1867. — GOVERNOR OF OHIO FOR THREE TERMS, 1868-1872. — PRESIDENT, 1877-1881.

GIVE me the popularity that runs after, not that which is sought for. — *College Diary.*

Judge [Stanley] Mathews and I have agreed to go into the service for the war — if possible, into the same regiment. I spoke my feelings to him, which he said were his own, that this was a just and a necessary war, and that it demanded the whole power of the country; that I would prefer to go into it, if I knew I was to be killed in the course of it, rather than to live through and after it without taking any part in it. — *May* 15, 1861.

[From a Speech in Ohio, 1867.]

The uniform lesson of history is, that unjust and partial laws increase and create antagonism, while justice and equity are the sure foundation of prosperity and peace. . . . . .

The truth is, that every step made in advance towards the standard of the right has in the event always proved a safe and wise step. Every step toward the right has proved a step toward the expedient; in short, that in politics, in morals, in public and private life, the right is always expedient.

[From a Speech, in 1867, during the political campaign.]

Our adversaries are accustomed to talk of the rebellion as an affair which began when the rebels attacked Fort Sumter in 1861, and which ended when Lee surrendered to Grant, in 1865. . . . But the causes, the principles, and the methods which produced the rebellion are of an older date than the generation which suffered from the fruit they bore, and their influence and power are likely to last long after that generation passes away. Ever since armed rebellion failed, a large party in the South have struggled to make participation in the rebellion honorable, and loyalty to the Union dishonorable. The lost cause with them is the honored cause. In society, in business, and in politics, devotion to treason is the test of merit, the passport to preferment. They wish to return to the old state of things, an oligarchy of race and the sovereignty of States.

To defeat this purpose, to secure the rights of man, and to perpetuate the national Union, are the objects of the congressional plan of reconstruction. . . . There are now within the limits of the United States about five millions of colored people. They are not aliens or strangers. They are not here by the choice of themselves or their ancestors. They are here by the misfortune of their fathers and the crime of ours. Their labors, privations, and sufferings, unpaid and unrequited, have cleared and redeemed one-third of the inhabited territory of the Union. Their toil has added to the resources and wealth of the nation untold millions. Whether we prefer it or not, they are our countrymen, and will remain so forever.

They are more than our countrymen — they are citizens. Free colored people were citizens of the colonies. The constitution of the United States, formed by our fathers, created no disablities on account of color. By the acts of our fathers and of ourselves, they bear equally the burdens, and are required to discharge the highest duties of citizens. They are compelled to pay taxes, and bear arms. They fought side by side with their white countrymen in the great struggle for independence, and in the recent war for the Union. . . . Slaves were never voters. It was bad enough that our fathers, for the sake of union, were compelled to allow masters to reckon three-fifths of their slaves for representation, without adding slave suffrage to the other privileges of the slaveholders. But free colored men were always voters in many of the colonies, and in several of the States, North and South, after independence was achieved. They voted for members of the Congress which declared independence, and for members of every Congress prior to the adoption of the federal constitution; for the members of the convention which framed the constitution; for the members of many of the State conventions which ratified it, and for every president, from Washington to Lincoln.

Our government has been called the white man's government. Not so. It is not the government of any class, or sect, or nationality, or race. It is a government founded on the consent of the governed. It is not the government of the native-born, or of the foreign-born, of the rich man, or of the poor man, of the white man, or of the colored man — it is the government of the freeman. And when colored men were made citizens, soldiers, and freemen, by our consent and votes, we were estopped from denying to them the right of suffrage.

To corrupt the ballot-box is to destroy our free institutions. — 1868.

[From the Annual Message, as Governor of Ohio. 1869.]

All agree that a Republican government will fail unless the purity of elections is preserved. Convinced that great abuses of the electoral franchise cannot be prevented under existing legislation, I have heretofore recommended the enactment of a registry law, and also some appropriate measure to secure to the minority, as far as practicable, a representation upon all boards of elections.

[From the Inaugural Address, as Governor, 1870.]

..... Our judicial system is plainly inadequate to the wants of the people of the State. Extensive alterations of existing provisions must be made. The suggestions I desire to present in this connection are as to the manner of electing judges, their terms of office, and their salaries. It is fortunately true that the judges of our courts have heretofore been, for the most part, lawyers of learning, ability, and integrity. But it must be remembered that the tremendous events and the wonderful progress of the last few years are working great changes in the condition of our society. Hitherto, population has been sparse, property not unequally distributed, and the bad elements which so frequently control large cities have been almost unknown in our State. But with a dense population crowding into towns and cities, with vast wealth accumulating in the hands of a few persons or corporations, it is to be apprehended that the time is coming when judges elected by popular vote, for short official terms, and poorly paid, will not possess the independence required to protect individual rights. Under the National Constitution judges are nominated by the Executive and confirmed by the Senate, and hold office during good behavior. It is worthy of consideration whether a return to the system established by the fathers is not the dictate of the highest prudence. I believe that a system under which judges are so appointed, for long terms and with adequate salaries, will afford to the citizen the amplest possible security that impartial justice will be administered by an independent judiciary.

[From a Speech at Columbus, Ohio, 1870.]

..... The sectarian agitation against the public schools was begun many years ago. During the last few years it has steadily and rapidly increased, and has been encouraged by various indications of possible success. It extends to all of the states where schools at the common expense have been long established. Its triumphs are mainly in the large towns and cities. It has already divided the schools, and in a considerable degree impaired and limited their usefulness.

The glory of the American system of education

has been, that it was so cheap that the humblest citizen could afford to give his children its advantages, and so good that the man of wealth could nowhere provide for his children anything better. This gave the system its most conspicuous merit. It made it a republican system. The young of all conditions of life are brought together, and educated on terms of perfect equality. The tendency of this is to assimilate and to fuse together the various elements of our population, to promote unity, harmony, and general good-will in our American society.

But the enemies of the American system have begun the work of destroying it. They have forced away from the public schools, in many towns and cities, one third or one fourth of their pupils, and sent them to schools, which, it is safe to say, are no whit superior to those they have left. These youths are thus deprived of the associations and the education in practical republicanism and American sentiment which they peculiarly need.

Nobody questions their constitutional and legal right to do this, and to do it by denouncing the public schools. Sectarians have a lawful right to say that these schools are "a relict of paganism — that they are "godless," and that "the secular school-system is a social cancer." But when, having thus succeeded in dividing the schools, they make that a ground for abolishing school taxation, dividing the school fund, or otherwise destroying the system, it is time that its friends should rise up in its defence.

We all agree that neither the government nor political parties ought to interfere with religious sects. It is equally true that religious sects ought not to interfere with the government or with political parties. We believe that the cause of good government and the cause of religion both suffer by all such interference. But if sectarians make demands for legislation, of political parties, and threaten a party with opposition at the elections in case the required enactments are not passed, and if the political party yields to such threats, then those threatenings, those demands, and that act of the political party become a legitimate subject of political discussion, and the sectarians who thus interfere with the legislation of the State are alone responsible for the agitation which follows.

[From his Annual Message, as Governor of Ohio, January, 1871. Civil Service Reform.]

. . . . . What the public welfare demands is a practical measure which will provide for a thorough and impartial investigation in every case of suspected neglect, abuse, or fraud. Such an investigation to be effective must be made by an authority independent, if possible, of all local influences. When abuses are discovered, the prosecution and punishment of offenders ought to follow. But even if prosecutions fail in cases of full exposure, public opinion almost always accomplishes the object desired. A thorough investigation of corruption and criminality leads with great certainty to the needed reform. Publicity is a great corrector of abuses.

[From a Speech at Glendale, Ohio, 1872.]

. . . . . We want a financial policy so honest that there can be no stain on the national honor, and no taint on the national credit; so stable that labor and capital and legitimate business of every sort can confidently count upon what it will be the next week, the next month, and the next year. We want the burdens of taxation so justly distributed, that they will bear equally upon all classes of citizens in proportion to their ability to sustain them. We want our currency gradually to appreciate until, without financial shock or any sudden shrinkage of values, but in the natural course of trade, it shall reach the uniform and permanent value of gold.

[From a Speech at Marion, Ohio, 1872.]

The objections to an inflated and irredeemable paper currency are so many that I do not attempt to state them all. . . . It promotes speculation and extravagance, and at the same time discourages legitimate business, honest labor, and economy. It dries up the true sources of individual and public prosperity. Overtrading and fast living always go with it; it stimulates the desire to incur debt; it causes high rates of interest; it increases importations from abroad; it has no fixed value; it is liable to frequent and great fluctuations, thereby rendering every pecuniary engagement precarious, and disturbing all existing contracts and expectations. It is the parent of panics. Every period of inflation is followed by a loss of confidence, a shrinkage of values, depression of business, panics, lack of employment, and wide-spread disaster and distress. The heaviest part of the calamity falls on those least able to bear it. The wholesale dealer, the middle-man, and the retailer, always endeavor to cover the risks of the fickle standards of value by raising their prices. But the men of small means and the laborer are thrown out of employment, and want and suffering are liable soon to follow.

When government enters upon the experiment of issuing irredeemable paper money, there can be no fixed limit to its volume. The amount will depend on the interest of leading politicians, on their whims, and on the excitement of the hour. It affords such facilities for contracting debt that extravagance and corrupt government expenditures are the sure result. Under the name of public improvements, the wildest enterprises, contrived for private gain, are undertaken. Indefinite expansion becomes the rule, and, in the end, bankruptcy, ruin, and repudiation.

[From an Address at the Dedication of a Soldiers' Monument in Findley, Ohio, 1875.]

..... I know not how many of them [the fallen soldiers] have been gathered into the cemeteries near their homes; I know not how many others have been gathered into the beautiful national cemeteries near the great battle-fields. I know not how many are lying in swamps, along the mountain sides, in nameless graves, — the unknown heroes of the Union; but wherever they are, and however many there may be, you people of Hancock County have erected your monument to all who fell, who left your county. All soldiers, I am sure, feel like thanking you for this.

I remember well the first of the saddest days of my life was after one of our great battles in the early period of the war. Recovering from wounds with other comrades who had been wounded there, we passed near the battle-field, as soon as we felt able to do so; and when we came there, what did we learn? Passing up the mountain, charging the line of the enemy, they fell; and everywhere were the shallow graves in which were deposited the remains of our seven hundred companions who had fallen. And how were they buried? and how was their last resting-place marked? Hastily, tenderly, no doubt, the parties detailed to bury them had gathered up their remains. You soldiers know how it was done. They placed upon the face of each man who died, whenever they could ascertain his name, a piece of an envelope, or a scrap of a letter, or something of the kind, containing his name, his company, his regiment, fastening it there, hoping some day his friends might come and find him, and learn who was there buried. And then, you remember, there were no coffins, nothing of the sort; but they took the blue overcoat and placed it around the man, and took the cape, and bringing it over the face, fastened it down. This was his shroud; this was his coffin; and he was placed away to rest until the resurrection morn. That was the manner of his burial. And strange, I may say, was the result of that woollen material over the face; saturated in the water and covered with the earth, it did so protect them from decay that months afterwards many were recognized by their friends, preserved as they were by the overcoat-cape. And how was the grave marked? With a pencil they scratched upon a piece of fine board — a thin piece of cracker-box — the name and company, which was placed at the grave. This was all then; and we did not know what the result would be. We did not know what friends would do, what monuments would be reared.

As we left that field, talking to each other, we said there must be a soldiers' monument for the soldiers of our regiment.

. . . . . After the famous Antietam campaign was fought, we called the men together—four hundred and fifty or five hundred men,—and from the scanty pay which was to support the men, and to some extent, their families, the majority of the remainder subscribed at least one dollar, and others more, according to their ability, and raised in the regiment two thousand dollars to build a monument, on which, it was agreed, should be inscribed the name of every man in the regiment who had fallen, and every man who should fall during the continuance of the war.

[From his Letter of Acceptance of the Nomination for the Presidency, by the Republican National Convention.]

COLUMBUS, OHIO, July 8, 1876.

. . . . . The fifth resolution adopted by the Convention is of paramount interest. More than forty years ago, a system of making appointments to office grew up based upon the maxim, "To the victors belong the spoils." The old rule,—the true rule,—that honesty, capability, and fidelity constitute the only real qualifications for office, and that there is no other claim, gave place to the idea that party services were chiefly to be considered. All parties in practice have adopted this system. It has been essentially modified since its first introduction. It has not, however, been improved.

At first, the President, either directly or through the heads of departments, made all the appointments. But gradually the appointing power, in many cases, passed into the control of members of Congress. The offices, in these cases, have become not merely rewards for party services, but rewards for services to party leaders. This system destroys the independence of the separate departments of the government; it tends directly to extravagance and official incapacity; it is a temptation to dishonesty; it hinders and impairs the careful supervision and strict accountability by which alone faithful and efficient public service can be secured; it obstructs the prompt removal and sure punishment of the unworthy. In every way it degrades the civil service and the character of the government. It is felt, I am confident, by a large majority of the members of Congress, to be an intolerable burden, and an unwarrantable hindrance to the proper discharge of their legitimate duties. It ought to be abolished. The reform should be thorough, radical, and complete.

We should return to the principles and practices of the founders of the government, supplying by legislation, when needed, that which was formerly established custom. They neither expected nor desired from the public officers any partisan service. They meant that public officers should owe their whole service to the government and to the people. They meant that the officer should be secure in his tenure as long as his personal character remained untarnished, and the performance of his duties satisfactory. If elected, I shall conduct the administration of the government upon these principles; and all constitutional powers vested in the executive will be employed to establish this reform. . . . . . .

With a civil service organized upon a system which will secure purity, experience, efficiency, and economy; with a strict regard to the public welfare, solely, in appointments; with the speedy, thorough, and unsparing prosecution and punishment of all public officers who betray official trusts; with a sound currency; with education unsectarian and free to all; with simplicity and frugality in public and private affairs; and with a fraternal spirit of harmony pervading the people of all sections and classes, we may reasonably hope that the second century of our existence as a nation will, by the blessing of God, be pre-eminent as an era of good feeling, and a period of progress, prosperity, and happiness.

[From his Message, vetoing the Silver Bill, February 28, 1878.]

National promises should be kept with unflinching fidelity. There is no power to compel a nation to pay its just debts. Its credit depends on its honor. The nation owes what it has led or allowed its creditors to expect. I cannot approve a bill which, in my judgment, authorizes the violation of sacred obligations. The obligation to the public faith transcends all questions of profit or public advantage. Its unquestionable maintenance is the dictate as well of the highest expediency as of the most necessary duty, and should ever be carefully guarded by the Executive, by Congress, and by the people.

[From the Message vetoing the Chinese Bill, restricting Chinese immigration.]

The principal feature of the Burlingame treaty was its attention to and its treatment of the Chinese immigration, and the Chinese as forming, or as they should form, a part of our population. Up to this time (1859) the uncovenanted hospitality to immigration, our fearless liberality of citizenship, our equal and comprehensive justice to all inhabitants, whether they abjured their foreign nationality or not, our civil freedom and our religious toleration had made all comers welcome, and under these protections the Chinese, in considerable numbers, had made their lodgment upon our soil. . . . . . .

Unquestionably the adhesion of the government of China to these liberal principles of freedom in emigration, with which we were so familiar, and with which we were so well satisfied, was a great advance toward opening that empire to our civilization and religion, and gave promise in the future of greater and greater practical results in the diffusion, throughout that great population, of our arts and industries, our manufactures, our material improvements, and the sentiments of government and religion which seem to us so important to the welfare of mankind. The first clause of this article [of the Treaty] secures this acceptance by China of the American doctrine of free emigration to and fro among the people and races of the earth.

[Veto Message—Military Bill, April 29, 1879.]

It is the right of every citizen, possessing the qualifications prescribed by law, to cast one unintimidated ballot, and to have his ballot honestly counted.

[From the Veto of the Bill "to prohibit military interference at elections," May 12, 1879.]

Under the sweeping terms of the bill, the national government is effectually shut out from the exercise of the right, and from the discharge of the imperative duty, to use its whole executive power, whenever and wherever required, for the enforcement of its laws, at the places and times when and where its elections are held. The employment of its organized armed forces for any such purpose would be an offence against the law, unless called for by, and, therefore, upon permission of, the authorities of the States in which the occasion arises. What is this but the substitution of the discretion of the State governments for the discretion of the government of the United States as to the performance of its own duties? In my judgment, this is an abandonment of its obligations by the national government; a subordination of national authority, and an intrusion of State supervision over national duties, which amounts, in spirit and tendency, to State supremacy.

[Veto of the Bill regulating the pay and appointment of United States Deputy Marshals, June 15, 1880.]

We hold it to be an incontrovertible principle that the Government of the United States may, by means of physical force, exercised through its official agents, execute in every foot of American soil the power and functions that belong to it.

[From the Veto Message — Army Appropriation Bill.]

. . . . . Upon the assembling of this [forty-sixth] Congress, in pursuance of a call for an extra session, which was made necessary by the failure of the Forty-fifth Congress to make the needful appropriations for the support of the government, the question was presented whether the attempt made in the last Congress to engraft, by construction, a new principle upon the Constitution, should be persisted in or not. This Congress has ample opportunity and time to pass the appropriation bills, and also to enact any political measures which may be determined upon in separate bills by the usual and orderly methods of proceeding. But the majority of both Houses have deemed it wise to adhere to the principles asserted and maintained in the last Congress by the majority of the House of Representatives. That principle is that the House of Representatives has the sole right to originate bills for raising revenue, and therefore has the right to withhold appropriations upon which the existence of the government may depend, unless the Senate and the President shall give their assent to any legislation which the House may see fit to attach to appropriation bills. To establish this principle is to make a radical, dangerous, and unconstitutional change in the character of our institutions. . . . . .

The enactment of this bill into a law will establish a precedent which will tend to destroy the equal independence of the several branches of the government. Its principle places, not merely the

Senate and the Executive, but the judiciary also, under the coercive dictation of the House. The House alone will be the judge of what constitutes a grievance, and also of the means and measures of redress.

[From an Address at the Annual Reunion of the 23d Regiment, Ohio Veteran Volunteer Infantry, at Youngstown, Ohio.]

. . / . . . .

No man has ever stated the issues of the civil war more fully, more clearly, or more accurately than Mr. Lincoln. In any inquiry as to what may fairly be included among the things settled by our victory, all just and patriotic minds instinctively turn to Mr. Lincoln. To him, more than to any other man, the cause of Union and liberty is indebted for its final triumph. Besides, with all his wonderful sagacity, and wisdom, and logical faculty, dwelling intently, and anxiously, and prayerfully, during four years of awful trial and responsibility, on the questions which were continually arising to perplex and almost confound him, he at last became the very embodiment of the principles by which the country and its liberties were saved. All good citizens may now well listen to and heed his words. None have more reason to do it with respect and confidence, and a genuine regard, than those whom he addressed in his first inaugural speech as "my dissatisfied fellow-countrymen." The leader of the Union cause was so just and moderate, and patient and humane, that many supporters of the Union thought that he did not go far enough or fast enough, and assailed his opinions and his conduct; but now all men begin to see that the plain people, who at last came to love him and to lean upon his wisdom and firmness with absolute trust, were altogether right, and that in deed and purpose he was earnestly devoted to the welfare of the whole country, and of all its inhabitants.

. . . . . .

Touching the remaining important controversy settled by the war, the public avowals of opinion are almost all in favor of the faithful acceptance of the new constitutional amendments. On this subject the speeches of public men and the creeds and platforms of the leading political parties have for some years past been explicit. In 1872, all parties in their respective National Conventions adopted resolutions recognizing the equality of all men before the law, and pledging themselves, in the words of the Democratic National Convention, "to maintain emancipation and enfranchisement, and to oppose the reopening of the questions settled by the recent amendments to the Constitution." In 1876, the great political parties again, in the language of the St. Louis National Convention, affirmed their " devotion to the Constitution of the United States, with its amendments *universally* accepted as a final settlement of the controversies that engendered the civil war." Notwithstanding these declarations, we are compelled to take notice that, while very few citizens anywhere would wish to re-establish slavery if they could, and no one would again attempt to break up the Union by secession, there still remains in some communities a dangerous practical denial to the colored citizens of the political rights which are guaranteed to them by the Constitution as it now is. In the crisis of the war Mr. Lincoln appealed to the colored people to take up arms. About two hundred thousand responded to the call, enlisted in the Union armies, and fought for the Union cause under the Union flag. Equality of rights for the colored people, from that time, thus became one of the essential issues of the war. General Sherman said, "when the fight is over, the hand that drops the musket cannot be denied the ballot." Jefferson said long before, " the man who fights for the country is entitled to vote." When, with the help of the colored men, the victory was gained, the Fifteenth Amendment followed naturally as one of its legitimate results. No man can truthfully claim that he faithfully accepts the true settlements of the war, who sees with indifference the Fifteenth Amendment practically nullified.

No one can overstate the evils which the country must suffer if lawless and violent opposition to the enjoyment of constitutional rights is allowed to be permanently successful. The lawlessness which to-day assails the rights of the colored people will find other victims to-morrow. This question belongs to no race, to no party, and to no section. It is a question in which the whole country is deeply interested.

Patriotism, justice, humanity, and our material interests, all plead on the right side of this question. The colored people are the laborers who produce the cotton which, going abroad to the markets of the world, gives us that favorable balance of trade which is now doing so much for the revival of all business. The whole fabric of society rests upon labor. If free laborers suffer from oppression and injustice, they will either become discontented and turbulent, destroyers of property, and not producers of property, or they will abandon the communities which deprive them of their inalienable rights. In either case, social order and the peaceful industries upon which prosperity depends, are imperilled and perhaps sacrificed. It will not do to say that this is an affair which belongs solely to the distant States of the South. The whole country must suffer if this question is not speedily settled, and settled rightly. Where the two races are numerous, prosperity can only exist by the united and harmonious efforts of both the white people and the colored people. The only solid foundations for peace and progress in such communities are equal and exact justice to both races. Consider the present situation. Whatever complaints may have been heard during the progress of reconstruction, candid men must admit that all sections and all States are now equally regarded, and share alike the rights, the privileges, and the benefits of the common Government. All that is needed for the permanent pacification of the country is the cordial co-operation of all well-disposed citizens to secure the faithful observance of the equal-rights amendments of the Constitution.

. . . .

To establish now the State rights doctrine of the supremacy of the States, and an oligarchy of race, is deliberately to throw away an essential part of the fruits of the Union victory. The settlements of the war in favor of equal rights and the supremacy of the laws of the nation are just and wise, and necessary. Let them not be surrendered. Let them be faithfully accepted and firmly enforced. Let them stand, and, with the advancing tide of business prosperity, we may confidently hope, by the blessing of Divine Providence, that we shall soon enter upon an era of harmony and progress such as has been rarely enjoyed by any people.

[An Address at the Soldiers' State Reunion.]
COLUMBUS, OHIO, August 11, 1880.

. . . . . The citizens of Ohio who were soldiers in the Union Army, and who have assembled here in such large numbers, have many reasons for mutual congratulations as they exchange greetings and renew old friendships at this State reunion. We rejoice that we had the glorious privilege of enlisting and serving on the right side in the great conflict for the Union and for equal rights. The time that has passed since the contest ended is not so great but that we can without effort recall freshly and vividly the events and scenes and feelings and associations of that most interesting period of our lives. We rejoice, also, that we have been permitted to live long enough to see and to enjoy the results of the victory we gained, and to measure the vast benefits which it conferred on our country and on the world. I shall not attempt to make a catalogue of those benefits, or to estimate their value. A single fact, to which I call your attention, will sufficiently illustrate, for my present purpose, the immeasurable blessing conferred upon the United States by the success of the Union arms. The statistics of emigration, showing the movements of population which are going on in the world, afford a very good test of the comparative advantages and prosperity of the various civilized nations. People leave their own country and seek new homes in foreign lands to better their condition. Immigration into a country, therefore, is an evidence of that country's prosperity. It is also a most efficient cause of the progress of the country which receives it. During our civil war, and during the disturbed and troubled years which immediately preceded and followed it, immigration fell off and became of comparatively small importance. But now, our country's prosperity, the stability of our government, and the permanent prevalence of peace at home and with foreign nations, blessings which could not have been enjoyed by this country if the Union arms had failed, have given to the world a confidence in the future welfare and greatness of the United States which is pouring upon our shores such streams of immigration as were never known before. This is a fact of the most pregnant significance in our present condition. If we take a survey of the globe, we shall find everywhere, among civilized nations especially, many people who are eagerly looking forward to the time when they can emigrate to some more favored land. Only one of the great nations is in no danger of losing its capital and labor and skill by emigration. We find only one which by immigration is gaining rapidly in numbers, wealth and power. All are losing by this cause except the United States. The United States alone is gaining. Other nations see their people going, going. We see, from every quarter, the people of other countries coming, coming, coming. There is one flag, and in all the world only one, whose protection good men and women born under it will never willingly leave. There is one flag, and only one in the world, whose protecting folds good men and women born under every other flag that floats under the whole heavens are eagerly and gladly seeking. That flag, so loved at home, so longed for by millions abroad, is the old flag under which we marched, to save, what in our soldier days we were fond of calling, "God's country!" It is easily seen what it is that chiefly attracts this immigration. It goes where good land is cheap; where labor and capital find profitable employment; where peace and social order prevail; and where civil and religious liberty are secure. If we draw nearer to the subject, and ask where in our own country does this immigration mainly go, the recent census, whose results we are now getting, gives us the answer. That census shows us parts of our own country, where land is cheap and where capital and labor are needed, that are not rapidly increasing in prosperity. In these States it will be found that two things are wanting — the means for popular education are not sufficiently provided, and the good order of society is disturbed by a practical popular refusal to accept the results of the war for the union.

These two defects, wherever they prevail in our American society, are hostile to the increase of population and to prosperity. They are found generally to exist together. Where popular education prevails, the equal rights "amendments to the Constitution of the United States, embodying the results of the war, are inviolable." It must, perhaps, be conceded that there was one great error in the measures by which it was sought to secure the results, to harvest the fruits of our Union victory. The system of slavery in the South of necessity kept in ignorance four millions of slaves. It also left unprovided with education a large number of non-slave-holding white people. With the end of the war the slaves inevitably became citizens. The uneducated whites remained as they had been, also citizens. Thus the grave duties and responsibilities of citizenship were devolved largely, in the States lately in rebellion, upon uneducated people, white and colored. And with what result? Liberty and the exercise of the rights of citizenship are excellent educators. In many respects we are glad to believe that encouraging progress has been made at the South. The labor system has been reorganized, material prosperity is increasing, race prejudices and antagonisms have diminished, the passions and animosities of the war are subsiding, and the ancient harmony and concord and patriotic national sentiments are returning. But, after all, we cannot fail to observe that immigration, which so infallibly and instinctively finds out the true condition of all countries, does not largely go into the late slaveholding region of the United States. A great deal of cheap and productive land can there be found where population is not rapidly increasing. When our Revolutionary fathers adopted the ordinance of 1787 for the government of the northwest territory, out of which Ohio and four other great States have been carved, they were not content with merely putting into that organic law a firm prohibition against slavery, and providing effectual guarantees of civil and religious liberty, but they established, as the corner-stone of the free institutions they wished to build, this article: "Religion, morality, and knowledge being necessary to good government and the happiness of mankind, schools and the means of education shall forever be encouraged." Unfortunately for the complete success of reconstruction in the South, this stone was rejected by its builders. Slavery has been destroyed by the war: but its evils live after it, and deprive many parts of the South of that intelligent self-government without which, in America at least, great and permanent prosperity is impossible. To perpetuate the Union and to abolish slavery were the work of the war. To educate the uneducated is the appropriate work of peace. As long as any considerable numbers of our countrymen are uneducated, the citizenship of every American in every State is impaired in value, and is constantly imperilled. It is plain that at the end of the war the tremendous change in the labor and social systems of the Southern States, and the ravages and impoverishment of the conflict, added to the burden of their debts, and the loss of their whole circulating medium, which died in their hands, left the people of those States in no condition to provide for universal popular education. In a recent memorial to Congress on this subject, in behalf of the trustees of the Peabody educational fund, Hon. A. H. H. Stuart of Virginia shows that "two millions of children in the Southern States are without the means of instruction"; and adds, with great force, "Where millions of citizens are growing up in the grossest ignorance, it is obvious that neither individual charity nor the resources of impoverished States will be sufficient to meet the emergency. Nothing short of the wealth and power of the Federal Government will suffice to overcome the evil." The principle applied by general consent to works of public improvement is in point. That principle is, that whenever a public improvement is of national importance, and local and private enterprise are inadequate to its prosecution, the General Government should undertake it. On this principle I would deal with the question of education by the aid of the National Government.

Wherever in the United States the local systems of popular education are inadequate, they should be supplemented by the General Government, by devoting to the purpose, by suitable legislation and with proper safeguards, the public lands, or, if necessary, appropriations from the treasury of the United States. The soldier of the Union has done his work, and has done it well. The work of the schoolmaster is now in order. Wherever his work shall be well done, in all our borders, it will be found that there, also, the principles of the Declaration of Independence will be cherished, the sentiment of nationality will prevail, the equal-rights amendments will be cheerfully obeyed, and there will be " the home of freedom and the refuge of the oppressed of every race and of every clime."

[From an Address at the Reunion of Ohio Soldiers and Sailors, at Canton, Ohio, September, 1880.]

At the Soldiers' State reunion in Columbus, last month, I made some remarks on the duty of the general government to complete the work of reconstruction by affording aid, wherever it is needed, for the education of the illiterate white and colored people in the late slaveholding States. I am firmly convinced that the subject of popular education deserves the earnest attention of the people of the whole country, with a view to wise and comprehensive action by the government of the United

States. The means at the command of the local and State authorities are, in many cases, wholly inadequate to deal with the question. The magnitude of the evil to be eradicated is not, I apprehend, generally and fully understood. Consider these facts:

1. In the late slaveholding States, under the system of slavery, education was denied to the colored people, and the education of the non-slaveholding white people was greatly neglected. By reason of this state of things, in 1870 more than four millions of people in the South of school age and over that age were unable to read and write, and more than three-quarters of a million of voters are too illiterate to prepare or even to read their own ballots. This evil is not rapidly diminishing. By the latest available statistics it appears that in 1878 the total school population, white and colored, in the late slaveholding States was 5,187,584, and that only 2,710,096 were during that year enrolled in any school. This leaves 2,477,488 — almost two and a half millions — of the young who are growing up without the means of education. Citizenship and the right to vote were conferred upon the colored people by the government and people of the United States. It is, therefore, the sacred duty, as it is the highest interest, of the United States to see that these new citizens and voters are fitted by education for the

grave responsibility that has been cast upon them. Dr. Ruffner, school superintendent of Virginia, in an argument that the general government should aid the public schools of the South, says: "I know not what is true of Northern or Western States, but I can say for my State, and for most of the Southern States, we are not able to educate our people in any tolerable sense. We are too poor to do it. A few years ago I showed this conclusively by statistics. . . . There has not been much increase in financial ability in these States since that time; no increase on an average of my own State, so far as I can judge, and every well-informed man knows that, whatever be the wants of a State, her power of taxation has a limit."

2. In the Territories of the United States it is estimated that there are over two hundred thousand Indians, almost all of whom are uncivilized. They have heretofore been hunters and warriors. But now no one who observes the rapid progress of railroads and settlements in the West can fail to see that the game and fish, on which the Indians have hitherto subsisted, are about to disappear. The solution of the Indian question will speedily be either the extinction of the Indians, or their absorption into American citizenship, by means of the civilizing influences of education. With the disappearance of game, there can no longer remain Indian hunters and warriors. The days of Indian wars

are drawing to a close. There will soon be no room for question as to the department to which the Indian will belong. In a few years all must agree that he should belong, like every other citizen, only to himself. The time is not distant when he should be chiefly cared for by the civilizing department of the government — the Bureau of Education.

3. The people of the Territory of New Mexico have never been provided with the means of education. The number of people in that Territory in 1870, ten years old and upward, who could not read and write, was fifty-two thousand two hundred and twenty. This is largely more than half of the population. The school population is now over thirty thousand, of whom only about one-sixth are enrolled in schools. It will not be questioned that the power of the general government to " make all needful rules and regulations respecting the Territory belonging to the United States," is sufficient to authorize it to provide for the education of the increasing mass of illiterate citizens growing up in New Mexico and in the other Territories of the United States.

4. The number of immigrants arriving in the United States is greater than ever before. It is not improbable, from present indications, that from this source alone there will be added during the current decade to the population of our coun-

try 5,000,000 of people. On one day last spring there arrived in New York 4,907 immigrants, — almost five thousand in a single day at that one port. During the quarter ending the 30th of June last, the number of immigrants into the United States averaged 80,000 a month, and during the four months ending the 31st of July last there were nearly 300,000.

Happily for the United States, several of the large elements of this immigration contain very few people who are wholly uneducated. The Germans and Scandinavians have for the most part been educated at public schools in their own country. But it is probable that from one-fourth to one-third of the present total immigration into our country is from foreign nations in which popular education is greatly neglected. It may reasonably be estimated that at least from twenty to twenty-five per cent. of the immigrants are illiterate. In the current decade we shall probably receive from abroad more than a million of people of school age and upward who are unable to read and write any language; and of these about a quarter of a million in a few years will share with us equally, man for man, the duties and responsibilities of the citizen and the voter. Jefferson, with his almost marvellous sagacity and foresight, declared, nearly a hundred years ago, that free schools were an essential part — one of the columns, as he expressed it — of the republican edifice, and that "without instruction free to all, the sacred flame of liberty could not be kept burning in the hearts of Americans." Madison said, almost sixty years ago, "A popular government, without popular information, or the means of acquiring it, is but a prologue to a farce or a tragedy, or perhaps to both." Already, in too many instances, elections have become the farce which Madison predicted; and the tremendous tragedy which we saw when we were soldiers of the Union, and in which we bore a part, could never have occurred, if in all sections of our country there had been universal suffrage based upon universal education. In our country, as everywhere else, it will be found that, in the long run, ignorant voters are powder and ball for the demagogues. The failure to support free schools in any part of our country tends to cheapen and degrade the right of suffrage, and will ultimately destroy its value in every other part of the Republic. The unvarying testimony of history is, that the nations which win the most renowned victories in peace and war are those which provide ample means for popular education. Without free schools there is no such thing as affording to "every man an unfettered start and a fair chance in the race of life." In the present condition of our country universal education requires the aid of the general government. The authority to grant such aid is established by a line of precedents beginning with the origin of the Republic, and running down through almost every administration to the present time. Let this aid be granted wherever it is essential to the enjoyment of free popular instruction. In the language of Mr. Webster: "The census of these States shows how great a proportion of the whole population occupies the classes between infancy and manhood. These are the wide fields, and here is the deep and quick soil, for the seeds of knowledge and virtue, and this is the favored season,— the very springtime for sowing them. Let them be disseminated without stint; let them be scattered with a bountiful hand broadcast. Whatever the government can fairly do toward these objects, in my opinion, ought to be done."

[From an Address at the Anniversary of the Hampton Institute, Virginia, May 20, 1880.]

The President said that he should be glad if he could speak to all who are entitled to the credit of establishing and sustaining the Institute—the feeling of all who have listened to the exercises of the day; but the stream of congratulation and encouragement for the Institute flows so deep and strong that it is hardly necessary to add anything to it. He desired only to thank the principal, Gen. Armstrong, who has done so much, the trustees, the teachers, the pupils, and these who were now to go out, and to express to them all the gratitude and the satisfaction which he felt in what had been done. The question you are dealing with is the oldest and one of the most difficult, and indeed one of the most vital — how to deal with the seemingly repugnant elements which make up our population. When I remember the diversity of climate and soil and natural resources which characterize our country, it seems to me that these conditions required, if they did not create, the diverse elements of the population. The great task is, how to fuse a people differing so widely in race and nationality into one harmonious whole? — and this is the problem which Hampton Institute is solving. It is teaching us to deal with all these diverse races and classes as children of the same great Father. It is helping to wipe out sectionalism and race prejudice — and these are the only two enemies America has ever had to fear. We do not wish to repeal or change the laws of nature; what God has made separate and distinct, we do not mean to interfere with. We do not wish to abolish the distinctions between the races. We are willing that they should remain distinct and separate as the fingers of the hand; but we want them, for effectiveness in every good work, and for the national defence, to be united, to become one as the hand. This is the problem, so hard and difficult, which has caused so much anxiety, and so much suffering and affliction, which Hampton is solving. The question is settled, and there is no need of making a speech about it.

[From an Address to the Citizens of Detroit, Michigan, September 18, 1880.]

. . . . . .

The practice of creating public debts, as it prevails in this country, especially in municipal governments, has long attracted very serious attention. It is a great and growing evil. States, whose good name and credit have been hitherto untarnished, are threatened with repudiation. Many towns and cities have reached a point where they must soon face the same peril. I do not now wish to discuss the mischiefs of repudiation. My purpose is merely to make a few suggestions as to the best way to avoid repudiation. But, in passing, let me observe: Experience in this country has shown that no State or community can, under any circumstances, gain by repudiation. The repudiators themselves cannot afford it. The community that deliberately refuses to provide for its honest debts, loses its good name and shuts the door to all hope of future prosperity. It demoralizes and degrades all classes of its citizens. Capital and labor and good people will not go to such communities, but will surely leave them. If I thought my words could influence any of my countrymen who are so unfortunate as to be compelled to consider this question, I would say, let no good citizen be induced, by any prospect of advantage to himself or to his party, to take a single step toward repudiation. Let him set his face like flint against the first dawning of an attempt to enter upon that downward pathway. It has been well said that the most expensive way for a community to get rid of its honest debts is repudiation.

[From a Message to Congress, February, 1881.]

The Indians should be prepared for citizenship by giving to their young of both sexes that industrial and general education which is requisite to enable them to be self-supporting and capable of self-protection in civilized communities.

Lands should be allotted to the Indians in severalty, inalienable for a certain period.

The Indians should have a fair compensation for their lands not required for individual allotments, the amount to be invested, with suitable safeguards, for their benefit.

With these prerequisites secured, the Indians should be made citizens, and invested with the rights and charged with the responsibilities of citizenship.

. . . . . .

Nothing should be left undone to show to the Indians that the government of the United States regards their rights as equally sacred with those of its citizens.

[With reference to the Poncas, and their alleged wrongs, he added]:

Whether the Executive, or Congress, or the public is chiefly in fault is not now a question of practical importance. As the chief Executive at the time when the wrong was consummated, I am deeply sensible that enough of the responsibility for that wrong justly attaches to me to make it my personal duty and earnest desire to do all I can to give these Indian people that measure of redress which is required alike by justice and by humanity.

JAMES A. GARFIELD.

BORN, 1831. — GRADUATED AT WILLIAMS COLLEGE, MASS, 1856. — PROFESSOR OF ANCIENT LANGUAGES IN HIRAM INSTITUTE, OHIO, 1856. — PRESIDENT OF HIRAM COLLEGE, 1857. — ELECTED TO THE STATE SENATE, OHIO, 1859. — ADMITTED TO THE BAR, 1860. — COLONEL OF AN OHIO REGIMENT, 1861. — BRIGADIER-GENERAL, 1862. — MEMBER OF THE FITZ-JOHN PORTER COURT-MARTIAL, 1862. — CHIEF OF STAFF UNDER GENERAL ROSECRANS, 1863. — ELECTED TO CONGRESS, 1863. — MEMBER OF THE MILITARY COMMITTEE. — RE-ELECTED TO CONGRESS, 1865. — MEMBER OF COMMITTEE OF WAYS AND MEANS. — VISITED EUROPE, 1867. — CHAIRMAN OF THE COMMITTEE ON THE TARIFF, 1870. — ON APPROPRIATIONS, 1871-1875. — RE-ELECTED TO CONGRESS, 1878. — MEMBER OF THE ELECTORAL COMMISSION, 1876. — ELECTED TO THE SENATE OF THE UNITED STATES FROM OHIO, 1880. — PRESIDENT, 1881.

[Speech on the Currency. — 46th Congress.]

No man can doubt that within recent years, and notably within recent months, the leading thinkers of the civilized world have become alarmed at the attitude of the two precious metals in relation to each other; and many leading thinkers are becoming clearly of the opinion that, by some wise, judicious arrangement, both the precious metals must be kept in service for the currency of the world. And this opinion has been very rapidly gaining ground within the past six months to such an extent, that England, which for more than half a century has stoutly adhered to the single gold standard, is now seriously meditating how she may harness both these metals to the monetary car of the world. And yet outside of this capital, I do not this day know of a single great and recognized advocate of bi-metallic money who regards it prudent or safe for any nation largely to increase the coinage standard of silver at the present time beyond the limits fixed by existing laws. . . . Yet we, who during the past two years have coined far more silver dollars than we ever before coined since the foundation of the Government; ten times as many as we coined during half a century of our national life; are to-day ignoring and defying the enlightened universal opinion of bi-metallism, and saying that the United States, single-handed and alone, can enter the field and settle the mighty issue. We are justifying the old proverb that "fools rush in where angels fear to tread." It is sheer madness, Mr. Speaker. I once saw a dog on a great stack of hay that had been floated out into the wild overflowed stream of a river, with its stack-pen and foundation still holding together, but ready to be wrecked. For a little while the animal appeared to be perfectly happy. His hay-stack was there, and the pen around it, and he seemed to think the world bright and his happiness secure, while the sunshine fell softly on his head and hay. But by and by he began to discover that the house and the barn, and their surroundings were not all there, as they were when he went to sleep the night before; and he began to see that he could not command all the prospect, and peacefully dominate the scene as he had done before.

So with this House. We assume to manage this mighty question which has been launched on the wild current that sweeps over the whole world, and we bark from our legislative hay-stacks as though we commanded the whole world. In the name of common sense and sanity, let us take some account of the flood; let us understand that a deluge means something, and try if we can to get our bearings before we undertake to settle the affairs of all mankind by a vote of this House. To-day we are coining one-third of all the silver that is being coined in the round world. China is coining another third; and all other nations are using the remaining one-third for subsidiary coin. And if we want to take rank with China, and part company with all of the civilized nations of the Western world, let us pass this bill, and then "bay the moon" as we float down the whirling channel to take our place among the silver mono-metallists of Asia.

[Letter to B. A. Kimball.]
COLUMBUS, OHIO, February 16, 1861.

Mr. Lincoln has come and gone. The rush of people to see him at every point on the route is astonishing. The reception here was plain and republican, but very impressive. He has been raising a respectable pair of dark-brown whiskers, which decidedly improve his looks, but no appendage can ever render him remarkable for beauty. On the whole, I am greatly pleased with him. He clearly shows his want of culture, and the marks of western life; but there is no touch of affectation in him, and he has a peculiar power of impressing you that he is frank, direct, and thoroughly honest. His remarkable good sense, simple and condensed style of expression, and evident marks of indomitable will, give me great hopes for the country. And, after the long, dreary period of Buchanan's weakness and cowardly imbecility, the people will hail a strong and vigorous leader.

[To the Same.]

A monarchy is more easily overthrown than a rebublic, because its sovereignty is concentrated, and a single blow, if it be powerful enough, will crush it.

As an abstract theory, the doctrine of Free Trade seems to be universally true, but as a question of practicability, under a government like ours, the protective system seems to be indispensable.

[Speech on a Draft Bill, June 21, 1864.]

It has never been my policy to conceal a truth *merely* because it is unpleasant. It may be well to smile in the face of danger, but it is neither well nor wise to let danger approach unchallenged and unannounced. A brave nation, like a brave man, desires to see and measure the perils which threaten it. It is the right of the American people to know the necessities of the Republic when they are called upon to make sacrifices for it. It is this lack of confidence in ourselves and the people, this timid waiting for events to control us when they should obey us, that makes men oscillate between hope and fear; now in the sunshine of the hill-tops, and now in the gloom and shadows of the valley. To such men the bulletin which heralds success in the army gives exultation and high hope; the evening dispatch, announcing some slight disaster to our advancing columns, brings gloom and depression. Hope rises and falls by the accidents of war, as the mercury of the thermometer changes by the accidents of heat and cold. Let us rather take for our symbol the sailor's barometer, which faithfully forewarns him of the tempest, and gives him unerring promise of serene skies and peaceful seas.

[Speech in New York City, 1865, on the Assassination of President Lincoln.]

By this last act of madness it seems as though the Rebellion had determined that the President of the soldiers should go with the soldiers who have laid down their lives on the battle-field. They slew the noblest and gentlest heart that ever put down a rebellion upon this earth. In taking that life they have left "the iron" hand of the people to fall upon them. Love is on the front of the throne of God, but justice and judgment, with inexorable dread, follow behind; and where law is slighted and mercy despised, when they have rejected those who would be their best friends, then comes justice with her hoodwinked eye, and with the sword and scales. From every gaping wound of your dead chief, let the voice go up for the people to see to it that our house is swept and garnished. I hasten to say one thing more. For mere vengeance I would do nothing. This nation is too great to look for mere revenge. But for security of the future I would do everything.

[Speech in Congress on the Constitutional Amendment to abolish slavery, January 13, 1865.]

On the 21st day of June, 1788, our national sovereignty was lodged, by the people, in the Constitution of the United States, where it still resides, and for its preservation our armies are to-day in the field. In all these stages of development, from colonial dependence to full-orbed nationality, the people, not the States, have been omnipotent. *They* have abolished, established, altered, and amended, as suited their sovereign pleasure. *They* made the Constitution. That great charter tells its own story best:

"We, *the people* of the United States, in order to form a more perfect Union, establish justice, insure domestic tranquillity, provide for the common defence, promote the general welfare, and secure the blessings of liberty to ourselves and our posterity, do ordain and establish this Constitution for the United States of America."

. . . . . .

That Constitution, with its amendments, is the latest and the greatest utterance of American sovereignty. The hour is now at hand when that majestic sovereign, for the benignant purpose of securing still farther the 'blessings of liberty,' is about to put forth another oracle; is about to declare that universal freedom shall be the supreme law of the land. Show me the power that is authorized to forbid it. . . . They made the Constitution what it is. They could have made it otherwise then; they can make it otherwise now.

. . . . . .

In the very crisis of our fate, God brought us face to face with the alarming truth, that we must lose our own freedom, or grant it to the slave. In the extremity of our distress, we called upon the black man to help us save the Republic, and amidst the very thunder of battle we made a covenant with him, sealed both with his blood and ours, and witnessed by Jehovah, that when the nation was redeemed, he should be free, and share with us the glories and blessings of freedom. In the solemn words of the great proclamation of emancipation, we not only declared the slaves forever free, but we pledged the faith of the nation "to maintain their freedom"—mark the words, "*to maintain their freedom.*" The Omniscient witness will appear in judgment against us if we do not fulfil that covenant. Have we done it? Have we given freedom to the black man? What is freedom? Is it a mere negation? the bare privilege of not being chained, bought, and sold, branded, and scourged? If this be all, then freedom is a bitter mockery, a cruel delusion, and it may well be questioned whether slavery were not better.

But liberty is no negation. It is a substantive,

tangible reality. It is the realization of those imperishable truths of the Declaration, "that all men are created equal," that the sanction of all just government is "the consent of the governed." Can these truths be realized until each man has a right to be heard on all matters relating to himself?

Mr. Speaker, we did more than merely to break off the chains of the slaves. The abolition of slavery added four million citizens to the Republic. By the decision of the Supreme Court, by the decision of the attorney-general, by the decision of all the departments of our government, those men made free are, by the act of freedom, made citizens.

. . . . . .

If they are to be disfranchised, if they are to have no voice in determining the conditions under which they are to live and labor, what hope have they for the future? It will rest with their late masters, whose treason they aided to thwart, to determine whether negroes shall be permitted to hold property, to enjoy the benefits of education, to enforce contracts, to have access to the courts of justice — in short, to enjoy any of those rights which give vitality and value to freedom. Who can fail to foresee the ruin and misery that await this race to whom the vision of freedom has been presented only to be withdrawn, leaving them without even the aid which the master's selfish, commercial interest in their life and service formerly afforded them? Will these negroes, remembering the battle-fields on which nearly two hundred thousand of their number have so bravely fought, and many thousands have heroically died, submit to oppression as tamely and peaceably as in the days of slavery? Under such conditions there could be no peace, no security, no prosperity. The spirit of slavery is still among us; it must be utterly destroyed before we shall be safe.

. . . . . .

Mr. Speaker, I know of nothing more dangerous to a Republic than to put into its very midst four million people, stripped of every attribute of citizenship, robbed of the right of representation, but bound to pay taxes to the government. If they can endure it, we can not. The murderer is to be pitied more than the murdered man; the robber more than the robbed. And we who defraud four million citizens of their rights are injuring ourselves vastly more than we are injuring the black man whom we rob.

Throughout the whole web of national existence we trace the golden thread of human progress toward a higher and better estate.

The life and light of a nation are inseparable.

We confront the dangers of suffrage by the blessings of universal education.

We should do nothing inconsistent with the spirit and genius of our institutions. We should do nothing for revenge, but everything for security: nothing for the past; everything for the present and future.

There are two classes of forces whose action and reaction determine the condition of a nation — the forces of Repression and Expression. The one acts from without; limits, curbs, restrains. The other acts from within; expands, enlarges, propels. Constitutional forms, statutory limitations, conservative customs, belong to the first. The free play of individual life, opinion, and action, belong to the second. If these forces be happily balanced, if there be a wise conservation and correlation of both, a nation may enjoy the double blessing of progress and permanence.

It matters little what may be the forms of National institutions, if the life, freedom, and growth of society are secured.

There is no horizontal stratification of society in this country like the rocks in the earth, that hold one class down below forevermore, and let another come to the surface to stay there forever. Our stratification is like the ocean, where every individual drop is free to move, and where from the sternest depths of the mighty deep any drop may come up to glitter on the highest wave that rolls.

The Union and the Congress must share the same fate. They must rise or fall together.

Real political issues cannot be manufactured by the leaders of political parties, and real ones cannot be evaded by political parties. The real political issues of the day declare themselves and come out of the depth of that deep which we call public opinion. The nation has a life of its own as distinctly defined as the life of an individual. The signs of its growth and the periods of its development make issues declare themselves; and the man or the political party that does not discover this, has not learned the character of the nation's life.

[Reply to Mr. Lamar, in a Committee of the Whole.]

Mr. Chairman, great ideas travel slowly, and for a time noiselessly, as the gods, whose feet were shod with wool. Our war of independence was a war of ideas, of ideas evolved out of two hundred years of slow and silent growth. When, one hundred years ago, our fathers announced as self-evident truths the declaration that all men are created equal, and the only just power of governments is derived from the consent of the governed, they uttered a doctrine that no nation had ever adopted, that not one kingdom on the earth then believed. Yet to our fathers it was so plain that they would not debate it. They announced it as a truth "self-evident."

Whence came the immortal truths of the Declaration? To me this was for years the riddle of our history. I have searched long and patiently through the books of the *doctrinaires* to find the germs from which the Declaration of Independence sprang. I find hints in Locke, in Hobbes, in Rousseau, and Fénelon; but they were only the hints of dreamers and philosophers. The great doctrines of the Declaration germinated in the hearts of our fathers, and were developed under the new influences of this wilderness world, by the same subtile mystery which brings forth the rose from the germ of the rose-tree. Unconsciously to themselves, the great truths were growing under the new conditions, until, like the century-plant, they blossomed into the matchless beauty of the Declaration of Independence, whose fruitage, increased and increasing, we enjoy to-day.

It will not do, Mr. Chairman, to speak of the gigantic revolution through which we have lately passed as a thing to be adjusted and settled by a change of administration. It was cyclical, epochal, century-wide, and to be studied in its broad and grand perspective — a revolution of even wider scope, so far as time is concerned, than the Revolution of 1776. We have been dealing with elements and forces which have been at work on this continent more than two hundred and fifty years. I trust I shall be excused if I take a few moments to trace some of the leading phases of the great struggle. And in doing so, I beg gentlemen to see that the subject itself lifts us into a region where the individual sinks out of sight and is absorbed in the mighty current of great events. It is not the occasion to award praise or pronounce condemnation. In such a revolution men are like insects that fret and toss in the storm, but are swept onward by the resistless movements of elements beyond their control. I speak of this revolution not to praise the men who aided it, or to censure the men who resisted it, but as a force to be studied, as a mandate to be obeyed.

In the year 1620 there were planted upon this continent two ideas irreconcilably hostile to each other. Ideas are the great warriors of the world; and a war that has no ideas behind it is simply brutality. The two ideas were landed, one at Plymouth Rock, from the *Mayflower*, and the other from a Dutch brig at Jamestown, Virginia. One was the old doctrine of Luther, that private judgment, in politics as well as religion, is the right and duty of every man; and the other, that capital should own labor, that the negro had no rights of manhood, and the white man might justly buy, own, and sell him and his offspring forever. Thus freedom and equality on the one hand, and on the other the slavery of one race and the domination of another, were the two germs planted on this continent. In our vast expanse of wilderness, for a long time, there was room for both; and their advocates began the race across the continent, each developing the social and political institutions of their choice. Both had vast interests in common; and for a long time neither was conscious of the fatal antagonisms that were developing.

For nearly two centuries there was no serious collision; but when the continent began to fill up, and the people began to jostle against each other; when the Roundhead and the Cavalier came near enough to measure opinions, the irreconcilable character of the two doctrines began to appear. Many conscientious men studied the subject, and came to the belief that slavery was a crime, a sin, or, as Wesley said, 'the sum of all villanies.' This belief dwelt in small minorities for a long time. It lived in the churches and vestries, but later found its way into the civil and political organizations of the country, and finally found its way into this chamber. A few brave, clear-sighted, far-seeing men announced it here, a little more than a generation ago. A predecessor of mine,

Joshua R. Giddings, following the lead of John Quincy Adams, of Massachusetts, almost alone held up the banner on this floor, and from year to year comrades came to his side. Through evil and through good report he pressed the question upon the conscience of the nation, and bravely stood in his place in this House, until his white locks, like the plume of Henry of Navarre, showed where the battle of freedom raged most fiercely.

And so the contest continued; the supporters of slavery believing honestly and sincerely that slavery was a divine institution; that it found its high sanctions in the living oracles of God and in a wise political philosophy; that it was justified by the necessities of their situation; and that slave-holders were missionaries to the dark sons of Africa, to elevate and bless them. We are so far past the passions of that early time that we can now study the progress of the struggle as a great and inevitable development, without sharing in the crimination and recrimination that attended it. If both sides could have seen that it was a contest beyond their control; if both parties could have realized the truth that "unsettled questions have no pity for the repose of nations," much less for the fate of political parties, the bitterness,-the sorrow, the tears, and the blood might have been avoided. But we walked in the darkness, our paths obscured by the smoke of the conflict, each following his own convictions through ever-increasing fierceness, until the debate culminated in " the last argument to which kings resort."

This conflict of opinion was not merely one of sentimental feeling; it involved our whole political system; it gave rise to two radically different theories of the nature of our government; the North believing and holding that we were a nation, the South insisting that we were only a confederation of sovereign States, and insisting that each State had the right, at its own discretion, to break the Union, and constantly threatening secession where the full rights of slavery were not acknowledged.

Thus the defence and aggrandizement of slavery, and the hatred of abolitionism, became not only the central idea of the Democratic party, but its master passion, — a passion intensified and inflamed by twenty-five years of fierce political contest, which had not only driven from its ranks all those who preferred freedom to slavery, but had absorbed all the extreme pro-slavery elements of the fallen Whig party. Over against this was arrayed the Republican party, asserting the broad doctrines of nationality and loyalty, insisting that no State had a right to secede, that secession was treason, and demanding that the institution of slavery should be restricted to the limits of the States where it already existed. But here and there many bolder and more radical thinkers declared, with Wendell Phillips, that there never could be union and peace, freedom and prosperity, until we were willing to see John Hancock under a black skin.

Mr. Chairman, ought the Republican party to surrender its truncheon of command to the Democracy? The gentleman from Mississippi says, if this were England, the ministry would go out in twenty-four hours with such a state of things as we have here. Ah, yes! that is an ordinary case of change of administration. But if this were England, what would she have done at the end of the war? England made one such mistake as the gentleman asks this country to make, when she threw away the achievements of the grandest man that ever trod her highway of power. Oliver Cromwell had overturned the throne of despotic power, and had lifted his country to a place of masterful greatness among the nations of the earth; and when, after his death, his great sceptre was transferred to a weak though not unlineal hand, his country, in a moment of reactionary blindness, brought back the Stuarts. England did not recover from that folly until, in 1689, the Prince of Orange drove from her island the last of that weak and wicked line. Did she afterward repeat the blunder?

* * * * * * *

I am aware that there is a general disposition "to let by-gones be by-gones," and to judge of parties and of men, not by what they have been, but by what they are and what they propose.

That view is partly just and partly erroneous. It is just and wise to bury resentments and animosities. It is erroneous in this, that parties have an organic life and spirit of their own — an individuality and character which outlive the men who compose them; and the spirit and traditions of a party should be considered in determining their fitness for managing the affairs of a nation.

. . . .

I will close by calling your attention again to the great problem before us. Over this vast horizon of interests North and South, above all party prejudices and personal wrong-doing, above our battle hosts and our victorious cause, above all that we hoped for and won, or you hoped for and lost, is the grand, onward movement of the Republic to perpetuate its glory, to save liberty alive, to preserve exact and equal justice to all, to protect and foster all these priceless principles, until they shall have crystalized into the form of enduring law, and become inwrought into the life and the habits of our people.

And, until these great results are accomplished, it is not safe to take one step backward. It is still more unsafe to trust interests of such measureless value in the hands of an organization whose members have never comprehended their epoch, have never been in sympathy with its great movements, who have resisted every step of its progress, and whose principal function has been

"'To lie in cold obstruction'

across the pathway of the nation.

"No, no, gentlemen, our enlightened and patriotic people will not follow such leaders in the rearward march. Their myriad faces are turned the other way; and along their serried lines still rings the cheering cry, 'Forward! till our great work is fully and worthily accomplished.'"

[From a Speech in Congress, 1866.]

Duties should be so high that our manufacturers can fairly compete with the foreign product, but not so high as to enable them to drive out the foreign article, enjoy a monopoly of the trade, and regulate the price as they please. This is my doctrine of protection. . . . I am for a protection that leads to ultimate free trade. I am for that free trade which can only be achieved through a reasonable protection.

[Letter to A. B. Hinsdale.]
WASHINGTON, January 1, 1867.

I am less satisfied with the present aspect of public affairs than I have been for a long time. . . .

Really there seems to be a fear on the part of many of our friends that they may do some absurdly extravagant thing to prove their radicalism. I am trying to do two things: dare to be a radical and not be a fool, which, if I may judge by the exhibitions around me, is a matter of no small difficulty. . . . My own course is chosen, and it is quite probable it will throw me out of public life.

We provide for the common defence by a system which promotes the general welfare.

[From an Address at Hiram College, June 14, 1867.]

It is to me a perpetual wonder how any child's love of knowledge survives the outrages of the school-house. I, for one, declare that no child of mine shall ever be *compelled* to study one hour, or to learn even the English alphabet, before he has deposited under his skin at least seven years of muscle and bone.

[From the Same.]

The student should study himself, his relations to society, to nature, and to art, and above all, in all, and through all these, he should study the relations of himself, society, nature, and art, to God, the Author of them all.

[From the Same.]

It is well to know the history of those magnificent nations whose origin is lost in fable, and whose epitaphs were written a thousand years ago — but if we cannot know both, it is far better to study the history of our own nation, whose origin we can trace to the freest and noblest aspirations of the human heart — a nation that was formed from the hardiest, purest, and most enduring elements of European civilization — a nation that, by its faith and courage, has dared and accomplished more for the human race in a single century than Europe accomplished in the first thousand years of the Christian era. The New England township was the type after which our Federal Government was modelled; yet it would be rare to find a college student who can make a comprehensive and intelligible statement of the municipal organization of the township in which he was born, and tell you by what officers its legislative, judicial, and executive functions were administered. One half of the time which is now almost wasted, in district schools, on English Grammar, attempted at too early an age, would be sufficient to teach our children to love the Republic, and to become its loyal and life-long supporters. After the bloody baptism from which the nation has arisen to a higher and nobler life, if this shameful defect in our system of education be not speedily remedied, we shall deserve the infinite contempt of future generations. I insist that it should be made an indispensable condition of graduation in every American college, that the student must understand the history of this continent since its discovery by Europeans, the origin and history of the United States, its constitution of government, the struggles through which it has passed, and the rights and duties of citizens who are to determine its destiny and share its glory.

Having thus gained the knowledge which is necessary to life, health, industry, and citizenship, the student is prepared to enter a wider and grander field of thought. If he desires that large and liberal culture, which will call into activity all his powers, and make the most of the material God has given him, he must study deeply and earnestly the intellectual, the moral, the religious, and the æsthetic nature of man; his relations to nature, to civilization, past and present, and above all, his relations to God. These should occupy nearly, if not fully, half the time of his college course. In connection with the philosophy of the mind, he should study logic, the pure mathematics, and the general laws of thought. In connection with moral philosophy, he should study political and social ethics — a science so little known either in colleges or congresses. Prominent among all the rest should be his study of the wonderful history of the human race, in its slow and toilsome march across the centuries — now buried in ignorance, superstition and crime; now rising to the sublimity of heroism and catching a glimpse of a better destiny; now turning remorselessly away from, and leaving to perish, empires and civilizations in which it had invested its faith, and courage, and boundless energy for a thousand years, and plunging into the forests of Germany, Gaul, and Britain, to build for itself new empires, better fitted for its new aspirations; and, at last, crossing three thousand miles of unknown sea, and building in the wilderness of a new hemisphere its latest and proudest monuments.

[Speech in the House of Representatives, February 12, 1867.]

I cannot forget that we have learned slowly. . . . I cannot forget that less than five years ago I received an order from my superior officer commanding me to search my camp for a fugitive slave, and if found, to deliver him up to a Kentucky captain who claimed him as his property; and *I had the honor to be perhaps the first officer in the army who peremptorily refused to obey such an order.* We were then trying to save the Union without hurting slavery. . . . It took us two years to reach a point where we were willing to do the most meagre justice to the black man, and to recognize the truth that

"A man's a man for a' that!"

Sir, the hand of God has been visible in this work, leading us by degrees out of the blindness of our prejudices, to see that the fortunes of the Republic and the safety of the party of liberty are inseparably bound up with the rights of the black man. At last our party must see that if it would preserve its political life, or maintain the safety of the Republic, we must do justice to the humblest man in the Nation, whether black or white. I thank God that to-day we have struck the rock; we have planted our feet upon solid earth. Streams of light will gleam out from the luminous truth embodied in the legislation of this day. This is the *ne plus ultra* of reconstruction, and I hope we shall have the courage to go before our people everywhere with "This or nothing" for our motto.

Now, sir, as a temporary measure, I give my support to this military bill properly restricted. It is severe. It was written with a steel pen made out of a bayonet; and bayonets have done us good service hitherto. All I ask is that Congress shall place civil governments before these people of the rebel States, and a cordon of bayonets behind them.

Now, what does this bill propose? It lays the hands of the Nation upon the rebel State governments, and takes the breath of life out of them. It puts the bayonet at the breast of every rebel murderer in the South to bring him to justice. It commands the army to protect the life and property of citizens whether black or white. It places in the hands of Congress absolutely and irrevocably the whole work of reconstruction.

With this thunderbolt in our hands shall we stagger like idiots under its weight? Have we grasped a weapon which we have neither the courage nor the wisdom to wield?

WILLIAM H. SEWARD.*

When in' Europe in 1867, my attention was particularly drawn to the significant fact that the pictures of Lincoln and Seward were the only portraits of American statesmen that were notably prominent, and that these were everywhere seen together. I asked a Frenchman of distinction why

---

* "Another talk that I recall was at a social gathering. It was at a dinner-party, after the failure of Greeley's campaign. The host was, perhaps, the most original genius in Washington. He was an old companion of Greeley at Brook Farm. He was giving the dinner in payment of a bet he had lost by reason of Greeley's defeat. The conversation embraced all the topics of the day, and, in the course of it, turned to Seward. A member of the company thought that Seward had been dead years before he was put

Seward was held in such high estimation; and his answer most seriously impressed me with the thought that perhaps, after all the slanders of his detractors, Mr. Seward had builded for the future more wisely than we knew. This gentleman said: "Mr. Seward is the American statesman who looms up the most prominently from over the water. His diplomacy in Mexico has placed the imprint of greatness upon his name. Halting for a moment in the midst of the turmoil of the civil war, with his pen he dismembered the coalition organized to place Maximilian upon the Mexican throne, and thus placed the first mine under the throne of the Third Bonaparte. He has undertaken what the combined powers of Europe have not ventured to essay — to break the sceptre of the Second Empire." The views entertained by this distinguished Frenchman seem also to have been held in Mexico, for upon the occasion of the death of Mr. Seward, the press of that country all made the most grateful mention of his services in that regard.

into the grave. General Garfield thought differently, and delivered, on the spur of the moment, a remarkable eulogy on the dead statesman. Soon afterward, I reduced to notes the outlines of that eulogy, so far as my memory served me, and I reproduce it here. General Garfield possesses rare conversational powers, and uses, in social discourse, a diction not less eloquent and elegant than that to which he is accustomed in the forum." — *Washington Correspondent of the Chicago Tribune.*

The enthusiasm of this Frenchman, continued General Garfield, had not perished from my memory later when public duties called me to the State Department. The Alaska treaty had just been signed. I found the Sage of Auburn alone, in the thoughtful mood so common to him when meditating upon great subjects. Our conversation fell upon himself, and I found that he had been meditating upon his withdrawl from public life. He had been eight years in the second highest place in this Nation. He had almost had the Presidency within his grasp; but the displeasure of his party had fallen upon him, and he was about to retire from the political arena. He told me that power was sweet to him; that he clung even then fondly to its shadow; and that he relinquished his sceptre with regret. His exact language, in speaking of his past career was: "It is unpleasant to yield up power." The conversation turned upon Alaska. The Secretary fell into the dream-like attitude that was never seen except by those who were familiar with him, and commenced to explain his theory of the Alaska purchase in forcible, prophetic, almost pathetic words which I never shall forget. I left the room then with grander ideas of the man than I had ever entertained before. His conversation indicated that he had been following a particular course of study, for he remarked that, to his notion, the two greatest books of the century were Marsh's "Man in Nature," and the Duke of Argyll's "Reign of Law." The application of Argyll's theory of law as applied to political development, Mr. Seward had evidently studied with much care. He had been reasoning upon natural laws as they affect a nation. He had been speculating upon the elementary forces of a nation's grandeur, and upon the contrivance in combining them to make them operate in a direction desired. This theory was founded upon the possibility of tracing these forces in history, and of discovering the operation of these laws under conditions which had actually determined the course of mankind and nations in definite directions. The text of his theory was the history of the world's seas. History had taught him that the grandest achievements of man had been associated with the shores of the world's seas. To go back no further than the beginning of the Christian era, the most sacred, solemn story of the hopes of man had been written in wanderings on the banks of the Sea of Galilee. With the progress of Christian civilization, thus sea-born, the advancing tide of human progress was staid by the banks of the Mediterranean. It was along the borders of this sea that the Byzantine Empire flourished and was destroyed; that Rome attained her supremacy, and fell. With the progress of time, and the advance of civilization westward, the Atlantic took the place of the Galilean

Sea and of the Mediterranean. It is the sea of the present. But unless the laws of political geography are false, the contests of the future are to be around the shores of the "still sea," now our own Pacific. The nation of the future is the nation that holds the key of those waters. The purchase of Alaska has given our Republic a foothold on both sides of that sea. It is a geographical impossibility that any other nation can occupy a position in its own territory upon both sides of the Pacific. This is the theory of the purchase. It secures the control of the Pacific to the young Republic. It assures the future of the world's dominion to Yankee civilization. This was the theory.

And his outlook, said General Garfield, with enthusiasm, was grand. In his political horoscope, he saw the Republic enjoying a prosperity of which the annals of human affairs had furnished no example; he saw our country rising to the place of umpire among the world's powers; he saw how, by wise statesmanship, our material prosperity and peaceful conquests grew together; how our increasing commerce made us mistress of the seas; how Western civilization and Oriental decrepitude were staid upon the borders of that Pacific sea, and compelled to render homage to Young America, who had become the keeper of the world's keys.

These were the grand thoughts of Mr. Seward as he was about to relinquish the mantle of his power, and, continued General Garfield, his views have left a lasting impression upon me. Mr. Seward could not have died more successfully than he did. He passed away in the lull between two elections, and received the merited eulogiums of both parties. He bore success followed by failure better than any American I know. He was for nearly a decade next to the source of power, and missed the place which was the goal of his later years, retiring from public life suffering the displeasure of his party. But he quietly retired to private life, and never lost his genial spirit or his noble ways.

[This report of the conversation is indorsed by General Garfield as " in the main correct."

J. C.]

[Speech on the Currency Question, 1868.]

As a medium of exchange, money is to all business transactions what ships are to the transportation of merchandise. If a hundred vessels, of a given tonnage, are just sufficient to carry all the commodities between two ports, any increase of the number of vessels will correspondingly decrease the value of each as an instrument of commerce; any decrease below one hundred will correspondingly increase the value of each. If the number be doubled, each will carry but half its usual freight, will be worth but half its former value for that trade. There is so much work to be done, and no more. A hundred vessels can do it all. A thousand can do no more than all.

. . . .

When the money of the country is gold and silver, it adapts itself to the fluctuations of business without the aid of legislation. If at any time we have more than is needed, the surplus flows off to other countries through the channels of international commerce. If less, the deficiency is supplied through the same channels. Thus the monetary equilibrium is maintained. So immense is the trade of the world, that the golden streams pouring from California and Australia into the specie circulation are soon absorbed in the great mass, and equalized throughout the world, as the waters of all the rivers are spread upon the surface of all the seas.

Not so, however, with an inconvertible paper currency. Excepting the specie used in payment of customs and the interest on our public debt, we are cut off from the money currents of the world. Our currency resembles rather the waters of an artificial lake, which lie in stagnation or rise to full banks at the caprice of the gate-keeper.

[A Speech on Currency and the Banks, 1870.]

The business of the country is like the level of the ocean, from which all measurements are made of heights and depths. Though tides and currents may for a time disturb, and tempests vex and toss its surface, still through calm and storm the grand level rules all its waves and lays its measuring-lines on every shore. So the business of the country, which, in the aggregated demands of the people for the exchange of values, marks the ebb and flow, the rise and fall of the currents of trade, and forms the base-line from which to measure all our financial legislation, and is the only safe rule by which the volume of our currency can be determined.

. . . .

The State bank system was a chaos of ruin, in which the business of the country was again and again ingulfed. The people rejoice that it has been swept away, and they will not consent to its re-establishment. In its place we have the National-bank system, based on the bonds of the United States, and sharing the safety and credit of the government. Their notes are made secure, first, by a deposit of government bonds, worth at least ten per cent. more than the whole value of the notes; second, by a paramount lien on all the assets of the banks; third, the personal liability of all the shareholders to an amount equal to the capital they hold; and, fourth, the absolute guarantee by the government to redeem them at the

National Treasury if the banks fail to do so. Instead of seven thousand different varieties of notes, as in the State system, we have now but ten varieties, each uniform in character and appearance. Like our flag, they bear the stamp of nationality, and are honored in every part of the Union.

[From a Speech in the House, April 1, 1870.]

As an abstract theory of political economy free-trade has many advocates, and much can be said in its favor; nor will it be denied that the scholarship of modern times is largely on that side; that a large majority of the great thinkers of the present day are leading in the direction of what is called free-trade.

While this is true, it is equally undeniable that the principle of protection has always been recognized and adopted in some form or another by all nations, and is to-day, to a greater or less extent, the policy of every civilized government. . . . . .

Protection, in its practical meaning, is that provident care for the industry and development of our own country which will give our own people an equal chance in the pursuit of wealth, and save us from the calamity of being dependent upon other nations with whom we may any day be at war.

In so far as the doctrine of free-trade is a protest against the old system of oppression and prohibition, it is a healthy and worthy sentiment. But underlying all theories, there is a strong and deep conviction in the minds of a great majority of our people in favor of protecting American industry. . . . . . .

[Speech on the Fourteenth Amendment to the Constitution, April 4, 1871.]

. . . . . Nothing more aptly describes the character of our Republic than the solar system, launched into space by the hand of the Creator, where the central sun is the great power around which revolve all the planets in their appointed orbits. But while the sun holds in the grasp of its attractive power the whole system, and imparts its light and heat to all, yet each individual planet is under the sway of laws peculiar to itself.

Under the sway of terrestrial laws, winds blow, waters flow, and all the tenantries of the planet live and move. So, sir, the States move on in their orbits of duty and obedience, bound to the central government by this Constitution, which is their supreme law; while each State is making laws and regulations of its own, developing its own energies, maintaining its own industries, managing its local affairs in its own way, subject only to the supreme but beneficent control of the

Union. When State-rights ran mad, put on the form of secession, and attempted to drag the States out of the Union, we saw the grand lesson, taught in all the battles of the late war, that a State could no more be hurled from the Union, without ruin to the nation, than could a planet be thrown from its orbit without dragging after it, to chaos and ruin, the whole solar universe.

In 1865 we had a debt of two billions seven hundred and seventy-two millions of dollars upon our hands, the debt accumulated from the great results of the war; we were compelled to pay from that debt one hundred and fifty-one millions of dollars in coin a year as interest, and that was a dreadful annual burden. In the year after the war ended, we paid five hundred and ninety millions of dollars over our counter in settling the business of the war and maintaining the ordinary expenses of the government. These tremendous burdens it seemed for a time we could not carry, and there were wicked men, and despairing men, and men who said we ought not to try to carry the burdens; but the brave nation said, This burden is the price of our country's life, all through it there is the price of blood and the price of liberty, and, therefore, we will bow our knees to the burden, we will carry it upon the stalwart shoulders of the nation.

[Letter to Professor Demmon, December 16, 1871.]

..... Since I entered public life, I have constantly aimed to find a little time to keep alive the spirit of my classical studies, and to resist that constant tendency, which all public men feel, to grow rusty in literary studies, and particularly in the classical studies. I have thought it better to select some one line of classical reading, and, if possible, do a little work on it each day. For this winter I am determined to review such parts of the Odes of Horace as I may be able to reach. And, as preliminary to that work, I have begun by reading up the bibliography of Horace.

The Congressional Library is very rich in materials for this study, and I am amazed to find how deep and universal has been the impress left on the cultivated mind of the world by Horace's writings.

The Student should study himself, his relation to Society, to Nature and to Art — and above all, in all, and through all these, he should study the relations of Himself, Society, Nature, and Art to God the Author of them all.

Greek is perhaps the most perfect instrument of Thought ever invented by Man, and its Literature has never been equalled in purity of style and boldness of expression.

History is but the unrolled scroll of Prophecy. The world's history is a divine Poem, of which the history of every nation is a canto, and every man a word. Its strains have been pealing along down the centuries, and though there have been mingled the discords of warring cannon and dying men, yet to the Christian, Philosopher, and Historian — the humble listener — there has been a divine melody running through the song which speaks of hope and halcyon days to come.

The lesson of History is rarely learned by the actors themselves.

Theologians in all ages have looked out admiringly upon the material universe, and from its inanimate existences demonstrated the Power, Wisdom, and Goodness of God; but we know of no one who has demonstrated the same attributes from the History of the human race.

Mankind have been slow to believe that order reigns in the universe, that the world is a Cosmos, not a chaos.

The assertion of the reign of Law has been stubbornly resisted at every step. The divinities of Heathen superstition still linger in one form or another in the faith of the ignorant, and even many intelligent men shrink from the contemplation of one Supreme Will acting regularly, not fatuitously, through laws beautiful and simple, rather than through a fitful and capricious Providence.

English liberty to-day rests not so much on the government as on those rights which the people have wrested from the government. The rights of the Englishman outnumber the rights of the Englishman's king.

Poetry is the language of Freedom.

Liberty can be safe only when Suffrage is illuminated by education.

[Speech on the last Census.]

The developments of statistics are causing history to be re-written. Till recently the historian studied nature in the aggregate, and gave us only the story of princes, dynasties, sieges, and battles. Of the people themselves — the great social body, with life, growth, forces, elements, etc. — he told us nothing. Now, statistical inquiry leads us into the hovels, houses, workshops, mines, fields, prisons, hospitals, and all places where human nature displays its weakness and strength. In these explorations he discovers the seeds of national growth and decay, and thus becomes the prophet of his generation.

Statistical science is indispensable to modern statesmanship. In legislation, as in physical science, it is beginning to be understood that we can control terrestrial forces only by obeying their laws. The legislator must formulate in his statistics not only the national will but also those great laws of social life revealed by statistics. He must study society rather than black-letter learning. He must learn the truth that " society usually prepares the crime, and the criminal is only the instrument that completes it," that statesmanship consists rather in removing causes than in punishing, or evading results.

[Speech on National Aid to Education, February 6, 1872.]

We look sometimes with great admiration at a government like Germany, that can command the light of its education to shine everywhere, that can enforce its school laws everywhere throughout the Empire. Under our system we do not rejoice in that, but we rather rejoice that here two forces play with all their vast power upon our system of education. The first is that of the local municipal power under our State government. There is the centre of responsibility. There is the chief educational power. . . . . . .

But there is another force even greater than that of the State and the local governments. It is the force of private voluntary enterprise, that force which has built up the multitude of private schools, academies, and colleges throughout the United States, not always wisely, but always with enthusiasm and wonderful energy.

. . . . . .

I am considering what is the best system of organizing the educational work of a nation, not from the political stand-point alone, but from the stand-point of the school-house itself. This work of public education partakes in a peculiar way of the spirit of the human mind in its efforts for culture. The mind must be as free from extraneous control as possible; must work under the inspiration of its own desires for knowledge;' and while instructors and books are necessary helps, the fullest and highest success must spring from the power of self-help.

So the best system of education is that which draws its chief support from the voluntary effort of the community, from the individual effort of citizens, and from those burdens of taxation which they voluntarily impose upon themselves. . . . Government shall be only a help to them, rather than a commander, in the work of education.

I would rather be beaten in Right than succeed in Wrong.

Present evils always seem greater than those that never come.

Poverty is uncomfortable, as I can testify; but nine times out of ten the best thing that can happen to a young man is to be tossed overboard and compelled to sink or swim for himself. In all my acquaintance I never knew a man to be drowned who was worth the saving.

For the noblest man that lives there still remains a conflict.

No man can make a speech alone. It is the great human power that strikes up from a thousand minds that acts upon him and makes the speech.

After the battle of Arms comes the battle of History.

There is a fellowship among the Virtues by which one great, generous passion stimulates another.

Growth is better than Permanence, and permanent growth is better than all.

The principles of Ethics have not changed by the lapse of years.

The possession of great power no doubt carries with it a contempt for mere external show.

[From a Speech on Repealing the Salary Clause, 1873.]

One of the brightest and greatest of men I know in this nation [Louis Agassiz], a man who, perhaps, has done as much for its intellectual life as any other, told me not many months ago that he had made it the rule of his life to abandon any intellectual pursuit the moment it became commercially valuable; that others would utilize what he had discovered; that his field of work was above the line of commercial values, and when he brought down the great truths of science from the upper heights to the level of commercial values, a thousand hands would be ready to take them, and make them more valuable in the markets of the world. He entered upon his great career, not for the salary it gave him, for that was meagre compared with the pay of those in the lower walks of life; but he followed the promptings of his great nature, and worked for the love of truth and the instruction of mankind.

[Letter to B. A. Hinsdale, 1874.]

The worst days of darkness through which I have ever passed have been greatly alleviated by throwing myself with all my energy into some work relating to others.

[Speech on the Currency and the Public Faith, April 8, 1874.]

There never did exist on this earth a body of men wise enough to determine by any arbitrary rule how much currency is needed for the business of a great country. The laws of trade, the laws of credit, the laws of God impressed upon the elements of this world, are superior to all legislation; and we can enjoy the benefits of these immutable laws only by obeying them.

. . . . . .

It has been demonstrated again and again that upon the artisans, the farmers, the day-laborers falls at last the dead weight of all the depreciation and loss that irredeemable paper-money carries in its train. Let this policy be carried out, and the day will surely and speedily come when the nation will clearly trace the cause of its disaster to those who deluded themselves and the people with what Jefferson fitly called "legerdemain tricks of paper-money."

[Speech on the Railway Problem, June 22, 1874.]

We are so involved in the events and movements of society that we do not stop to realize — what is undeniably true — that during the last forty years all modern societies have entered upon a period of change more marked, more pervading, more radical than any that has occurred during the last three hundred years. In saying this, I do not forget our own political and military history, nor the French Revolution of 1793. The changes now taking place have been wrought, and are being wrought, mainly, almost wholly, by a single mechanical contrivance, the steam locomotive. Imagine, if you can, what would happen if to-morrow morning the railway locomotive, and its corollary, the telegraph, were blotted from the earth. At first thought, it would seem impossible to get on at all with the feeble substitutes we should be compelled to adopt in place of these great forces. To what humble proportions mankind would be compelled to scale down the great enterprises they are now pushing forward with such ease! But were this calamity to happen, we should simply be placed where we were forty-three years ago.

There are many persons now living who well remember the day when Andrew Jackson, after four weeks of toilsome travel from his home in Tennessee, reached Washington and took his first oath of office as President of the United States. On that day the railway locomotive did not exist. During that year Henry Clay was struggling to make his name immortal by linking it with the then vast project of building a national road — a turnpike — from the national capital to the banks of the Mississippi.

In the autumn of that very year George Stephenson ran his first experimental locomotive, the "Rocket," from Manchester to Liverpool and back. The rumble of its wheels, redoubled a million times, is echoing to-day on every continent.

. . . . . .

The American people have done much for the locomotive, and it has done much for them. We have already seen that it has greatly reduced, if not wholly destroyed, the danger that the government will fall to pieces by its own weight. The railroad has not only brought our people and their industries together, but it has carried civilization into the wilderness, has built up States and Territories, which, but for its power, would have remained deserts for a century to come. "Abroad and at home," as Mr. Adams tersely declares, "it has equally nationalized people and cosmopolized nations." It has played a most important part in the recent movement for the unification and preservation of nations.

It enabled us to do what the old military science had pronounced impossible — to conquer a revolted population of eleven millions, occupying a territory one-fifth as large as the continent of Europe. In an able essay on the railway system, Mr. Charles F. Adams, Jr. has pointed out some of the remarkable achievements of the railroad in our recent history. For example, a single railroad track enabled Sherman to maintain eighty thousand fighting men three hundred miles beyond his base of supplies. Another line, in a space of seven days, brought a re-enforcement of two fully equipped army corps around a circuit of thirteen hundred miles, to strengthen an army at a threatened point. He calls attention to the still more striking fact that for ten years past, with fifteen hundred millions of our indebtedness abroad, an enormous debt at home, unparalleled public expenditures, and a depreciated paper currency, in defiance of all past experience, we have been steadily conquering our difficulties, have escaped the predicted collapse, and are promptly meeting our engagements; because, through energetic railroad development, the country has been producing real wealth, as no country has produced it before. Finally, he sums up the case by declaring that the locomotive has "dragged the country through its difficulties in spite of itself."

. . . . . .

In the darkness and chaos of that period, the feudal system was the first important step toward the organization of modern nations. Powerful chiefs and barons intrenched themselves in castles, and, in return for submission and service, gave to their vassals rude protection and ruder laws. But as the feudal chiefs grew in power and wealth, they became the oppressors of their people, taxed and robbed them at will, and finally, in their arrogance, defied the kings and emperors of the Mediæval States. From their castles, planted on the great thoroughfares, they practised the most capricious extortions on commerce and travel, and thus gave to modern language the phrase, "levy blackmail."

The consolidation of our great industrial and commercial companies, the power they wield, and the relations they sustain to the State and to the industry of the people, do not fall far short of Fourier's definition of commercial or industrial feudalism. The modern barons, more powerful than their military prototypes, own our greatest highways, and levy tribute at will upon all our vast industries. And, as the old feudalism was finally controlled and subordinated only by the combined efforts of the kings and the people of the free cities and towns, so our modern feudalism can be subordinated to the public good only by the great body of the people, acting through their governments by wise and just laws.

I shall not now enter upon the discussion of methods by which this great work of adjustment may be accomplished. But I refuse to believe that the genius and energy which have developed these new and tremendous forces, will fail to make them, not the masters, but the faithful servants of society. It will be a disgrace to our age and to us, if we do not discover some method by which the public functions of these organizations may be brought into full subordination to the public, and that, too, without violence, and without unjust interference with the rights of private individuals. It will be unworthy of our age, and of us, if we make the discussion of this subject a mere warfare against men. For in these great industrial enterprises have been, and still are engaged, some of the noblest and worthiest men of our time. It is the system — its tendencies and its dangers — which society itself has produced, that we are now to confront. And these industries must not be crippled, but promoted. The evils complained of are mainly of our own making. States and communities have willingly and thoughtlessly conferred these great powers upon railways; and they must seek to rectify their own errors without injury to the industries they have encouraged.

. . . . . .

It depends upon the wisdom, the culture, the self-control of our people and their representatives, to determine how wisely and how well this question shall be settled. But that it will be solved, and solved in the interest of liberty and justice, I do not doubt. And its solution will open the way to a solution of a whole chapter of similar questions that relate to the conflict between capital and labor.

[From a Speech in the House of Representatives, June, 1874.]

The division between church and state ought to be so absolute that no church property anywhere, in any State or in the nation, should be exempt from taxation; for, if you exempt the property of any church organization, to that extent you impose a church-tax upon the whole community.

Occasion may be the bugle-call that summons an army to battle, but the blast of a bugle can never make soldiers or win victories.

Things don't turn up in this world until somebody turns them up.

We cannot study nature profoundly without bringing ourselves into communion with the spirit of art which pervades and fills the universe.

If there be one thing upon this earth that mankind love and admire better than another, it is a brave man; it is a man who dares to look the devil in the face, and tell him he is a devil.

It is one of the precious mysteries of sorrow, that it finds solace in unselfish thought.

True art is but the anti-type of nature, the embodiment of discovered beauty in utility.

In order to have any success in life, or any worthy success, you must resolve to carry into your work a fulness of knowledge; not merely a sufficiency, but more than a sufficiency.

Be fit for more than the thing you are now doing.

If you are not too large for the place, you are too small for it.

What the arts are to the world of matter, literature is to the world of mind.

Many books we can read in a railroad car, and feel a harmony between the rushing of the train and the haste of the author; but to enjoy standard works, we need the quiet of a winter evening; an easy-chair before a cheerful fire, and all the equanimity of spirits we can command.

He who would understand the real spirit of literature should not select authors of any one period alone, but rather go to the fountain-head, and trace the little rill as it courses along down the ages, broadening and deepening into the great ocean of thought which the men of the present are exploring.

The true literary man is no mere gleaner, following in the rear and gathering up the fragments of the world's thought; but he goes down deep into the heart of humanity, watches its throbbings; analyzes the forces at work there; traces out, with prophetic foresight, their tendencies, and thus, standing out far beyond his age, holds up the picture of what it is and is to be.

[Letter to A. B. Hinsdale, 1876.]

I have followed this rule [as a lawyer] : whenever I have had a case, I have undertaken to work out thoroughly the principles involved in it; not for the case alone, but for the sake of comprehending thoroughly that branch of the law.

[From "Life and Character of Almeda A. Booth," June 22, 1876.]

We can study no life intelligently except in its relation to causes and results. Character is the chief element; for it is both a result and a cause — the result of all the elements and forces that combined to form it, and the chief cause of all that is accomplished by its possessor......

Every character is the joint product of nature and nurture. By the first, we mean those inborn qualities of body and mind inherited from parents, or rather from a long line of ancestors. Who shall estimate the effect of those latent forces, enfolded in the spirit of a new-born child, which may date back centuries, and find their origin in the unwritten history of remote ancestors — forces, the germs of which, enveloped in the solemn mystery of life, have been transmitted silently, from generation to generation, and never perish? All-cherishing Nature, provident and unforgetting, gathers up all these fragments that nothing may be lost, but that all may reappear in new combinations. Each new life is thus the "heir of all the ages," the possessor of qualities which only the events of life can unfold.

By the second element, nurture, culture, we designate all those influences which act upon this initial force of character, to retard or strengthen its development. There has been much discussion to determine which of these elements plays the more important part in the formation of character. The truth doubtless is, that sometimes the one and sometimes the other is the greater force; but so far as life and character are dependent upon voluntary action, the second is no doubt the element of chief importance.

[From the Same.]

Not enough attention has been paid to the marked difference between the situation and possibilities of a life developed here in the West, during the first half of .the present century, and those of a life nurtured and cultivated in an old and settled community like that of New England.

Consider, for example, the measureless difference between the early surroundings of John Quincy Adams and Abraham Lincoln. Both were possessed of great natural endowments. Adams was blessed with parents whose native force of character, and whose vigorous and thorough culture have never been surpassed by any married pair in America. Young Adams was thoroughly taught by his mother until he had completed his tenth year; and then, accompanying his father to France, he spent two years in a training-school at Paris and three years in the University at Leyden. After two years of diplomatic service, under the skilful guidance of his father's hand, he returned to America, and devoted three years to study at Harvard, where he was graduated at the age of twenty-one; and, three years later, was graduated in the law, under the foremost jurist of his time. With such parentage and such opportunities, who can wonder that by the time he reached the meridian of his life, he was a man of immense erudition, and had honored every great office in the gift of his country?

How startling the contrast, in every particular, between his early life and that of Abraham Lincoln. . . . Born to an inheritance of the extremest poverty, wholly unaided by his parents, surrounded by the rude forces of the wilderness, only one year at any school, never for a day master of his own time until he reached his majority, forcing his way to the profession of the law by the hardest and roughest road, and beginning its practice at twenty-eight years of age, yet, by the force of unconquerable will and persistent hard work, he attained a foremost place in his profession.

> "And, moving up from high to higher,
> Became, on fortune's crowning slope,
> The pillar of a people's hope,
> The centre of a world's desire."

[From the Same.]

It is one of the precious mysteries of sorrow, that it finds solace in unselfish work.

A pound of pluck is worth a ton of luck. Let not poverty stand as an obstacle in your way.

Here is the volume of our laws. More sacred than the twelve tables of Rome, this rock of the law rises in monumental grandeur alike above the people and the President, above the courts, above Congress, commanding everywhere reverence and obedience to its supreme authority.

That man makes a vital mistake who judges truth in relation to financial affairs from the changing phases of public opinion. He might as well stand on the shore of the Bay of Fundy, and from the ebb and flow of a single tide attempt to determine the general level of the sea, as to stand upon this floor, and from the current of public opinion on any one debate, judge of the general level of the public mind. It is only when long spaces along the shore of the sea are taken into account that the grand level is found from which the heights and depths are measured. And it is only when long spaces of time are considered, that we find at last that level of public opinion which we call the general judgment of mankind.

Bad faith on the part of an individual, a city, or even a State, is a small evil in comparison with the calamities which follow bad faith on the part of a sovereign government.

In the complex and delicately adjusted relations of modern society, confidence in promises lawfully made is the life-blood of trade and commerce. It is the vital air Labor breathes. It is the light which shines on the pathway of prosperity.

An act of bad faith on the part of a State or municipal corporation, like poison in the blood, will transmit its curse to succeeding generations.

We are accustomed to hear it said that the great powers of government in this country are divided into two classes; National powers and State powers. That is an incomplete classification. Our fathers carefully divided all governmental powers into three classes; one they gave to the

States, another to the Nation; but the third great class, comprising the most precious of all powers, they refused to confer on the State or Nation, but reserved to themselves. This third class of powers has been almost uniformly overlooked by men who have written and discussed the American system.

Congress must always be the exponent of the political character and culture of the people, and if the next centennial does not find us a great Nation with a great and worthy Congress, it will be because those who represent the enterprise, the culture, and the morality of the Nation do not aid in controlling the political forces which are employed to select the men who shall occupy the great places of trust and power.

There is scarcely a conceivable form of corruption or public wrong that does not at last present itself at the cashier's desk and demand money. The Legislature therefore, that stands at the cashier's desk and watches with its Argus eyes the demands for payment over the counter is most certain to see all the forms of public rascality.

A steady and constant Revenue drawn from sources that represent the prosperity of the nation, — a Revenue that grows with the growth of national wealth, and is so adjusted to the expenditures, that a constant and considerable surplus is annually left in the Treasury above all the necessary current demands, a surplus that keeps the Treasury strong, that holds it above the fear of sudden panic, that makes it impregnable against all private combinations, that makes it a terror to all stock-jobbing and gold-gambling, — this is financial health.

[From the "Atlantic Monthly," July, 1877.]

The most alarming feature of our situation is the fact, that so many citizens of high character and solid judgment pay but little attention to the sources of political power, to the selection of those who shall make their laws. . . . It is precisely this neglect of the first steps in our political processes that has made possible the worst evils of our system. Corrupt and incompetent presidents, judges, and legislators can be removed, but when the fountains of political power are corrupted, when voters themselves become venal, and elections fraudulent, there is no remedy except by awakening the public conscience, and bringing to bear upon the subject the power of public opinion and the penalties of the law. . . . In a word, our national safety demands that the fountains of political power shall be made pure by intelligence, and kept pure by vigilance; that the best citizens shall take heed to the selection and election of the worthiest and most intelligent among them to hold seats in the national legislature; and that when the choice has been made, the continuance of their representatives shall depend upon his faithfulness, his ability, and his willingness to work.

[Speech on the presentation to Congress of Carpenter's painting of President Lincoln and his Cabinet, at the time of his first reading of the Proclamation of Emancipation, January 16, 1878.]

Let us pause to consider the actors in that scene. In force of character, in thoroughness and breadth of culture, in experience of public affairs, and in national reputation, the cabinet that sat around that council-board has had no superior, perhaps no equal in our history. Seward, the finished scholar, the consummate orator, the great leader of the senate, had come to crown his career with those achievements which placed him in the first rank of modern diplomatists. Chase, with a culture and a frame of massive grandeur, stood as the rock and pillar of the public credit, the noble embodiment of the public faith. Stanton was there, a very Titan of strength, the great organizer of victory. Eminent lawyers, men of business, leaders of states, and leaders of men, completed the group.

But the man who presided over that council, who inspired and guided its determinations, was a character so unique that he stood alone, without a model in history, or a parallel among men. Born on this day, sixty-nine years ago, to an inheritance of extremest poverty, surrounded by the rude forces of the wilderness; wholly unaided by parents; only one year in any school; never, for a day, master of his own time until he reached his majority; making his way to the profession of the law by the hardest and roughest road; yet, by force of unconquerable will and persistent, patient work, he attained a foremost place in his profession,

> "And, moving up from high to higher,
> Became, on fortune's crowning slope,
> The pillar of a people's hope,
> The centre of a world's desire."

At first it was the prevailing belief that he would be only the nominal head of his administration; that its policy would be directed by the eminent statesmen he had called to his council. How erroneous this opinion was, may be seen from a single incident. Among the earliest, most difficult, and most delicate duties of his administration, was the adjustment of our relations with Great Britain. Serious complications, even hostilities, were apprehended. On the 21st day of May, 1861, the Secretary of State presented to the President his draught of a letter of instructions to Minister Adams, in which the position of the United States and the attitude of Great Britain were set forth with the clearness and force which long experience and great ability had placed at the command of the Secretary.

Upon almost every page of that original draught are erasures, additions, and marginal notes in the handwriting of Abraham Lincoln, which exhibit a sagacity, a breadth of wisdom, and a comprehension of the whole subject, impossible to be found except in a man of the very first order. And these modifications of a great state-paper were made by a man who, but three months before, had entered, for the first time, the wide theatre of executive action.

Gifted with an insight and a foresight which the ancients would have called divination, he saw, in the midst of darkness and obscurity, the logic of events, and forecast the result. From the first, in his own quaint, original way, without ostentation or offence to his associates, he was pilot and commander of his administration. He was one of the few great rulers whose wisdom increased with his power, and whose spirit grew gentler and tenderer as his triumphs were multiplied.

[From the "North American Review," May-June, 1878.]

The Secretary of War is a civil officer; one of the constitutional advisers of the President — his civil executive to direct and control military affairs, and conduct army administration for the President. . . . This was clearly understood in our early history, and it is worthy of note that our most eminent Secretaries of War have been civilians, who brought to the duties of the office great political and legal experience, and other high qualities of statesmanship.

Perhaps it was wise in Washington to choose as the first Secretary of War, a distinguished soldier, for the purpose of creating and setting in order the military establishment; but it may well be doubted if any subsequent appointment of a soldier to that position has been wise. In fact, most of the misadjustments between the Secretary of War and the army, so much complained of in recent years, originated with a Secretary of War who had been a soldier, and could hardly refrain from usurping the functions of command. . . .

No very serious conflict of jurisdiction and command occurred until Jefferson Davis became Secretary of War. His early training as a soldier, his spirit of self-reliance and habits of imperious command, soon brought him into collision with General Scott, and were the occasion of a correspondence, perhaps the most acrimonious ever carried on by any prominent public man of our country.

[From a Speech at Faneuil Hall, Boston, September 11, 1878.]

The Republican party of this country has said, and it says to-day, that, forgetting all the animosities of the war, forgetting all the fierceness and the passion of it, it reaches out both its hands to the gallant men who fought us, and offers all fellowship, all comradeship, all feelings of brotherhood, on this sole condition, and on that condition they will insist forever: That in the war for the Union we were right, forever right, and that in the war against the Union they were wrong, forever wrong. We never made terms, we never will make terms, with the man who denies the everlasting rightfulness of our cause. That would be treason to the dead and injustice to the living; and on that basis alone our pacification is complete. We ask that it be realized, and we shall consider it fully realized when it is just as safe and just as honorable for a good citizen of South Carolina to be a Republican there as it is for a good citizen of Massachusetts to be a Democrat here.

[From an Address at Hiram College.]

Our great dangers are not from without. We do not live by the consent of any other nation. We must look within to find elements of danger.

[From a Speech on the Ninth Census.]

Statesmanship consists rather in removing causes than in punishing, or evading results.

[From a Speech, December 10, 1878.]

The man who wants to serve his country must put himself in the line of its leading thought, and that is the restoration of business, trade, commerce, industry, sound political economy, hard money, and the payment of all obligations; and the man who can add anything in the direction of accomplishing any of these purposes is a public benefactor.

The scientific spirit has cast out the Demons and presented us with Nature, clothed in her right mind and living under the reign of law. It has given us for the sorceries of the alchemist, the beautiful laws of chemistry; for the dreams of the astrologer, the sublime truths of astronomy; for the wild visions of cosmogony, the monumental records of geology; for the anarchy of diabolism, the laws of God.

We no longer attribute the untimely death of infants to the sin of Adam, but to bad nursing and ignorance.

Truth is so related and correlated that no department of her realm is wholly isolated.

Truth is the food of the human spirit, which could not grow in its majestic proportions without clearer and more truthful views of God and his universe.

Ideas are the great warriors of the world, and a war that has no ideas behind it is simply brutality.

I love to believe that no heroic sacrifice is ever lost, that the characters of men are moulded and inspired by what their fathers have done; that, treasured up in American souls are all the unconscious influences of the great deeds of the Anglo-Saxon race, from Agincourt to Bunker Hill.

Eternity alone will reveal to the human race its debt of gratitude to the peerless and immortal name of Washington.

I doubt if any man equalled Samuel Adams in formulating and uttering the fierce, clear, and inexorable logic of the Revolution.

The last eight decades have witnessed an Empire spring up in the full panoply of lusty life, from a trackless wilderness.

In their struggle with the forces of nature, the ability to labor was the richest patrimony of the colonist.

The granite hills are not so changeless and abiding as the restless sea.

To him a battle was neither an earthquake, nor a volcano, nor a chaos of brave men and frantic horses involved in vast explosions of gunpowder. It was rather a calm rational combination of force against force. —*Oration on Geo. H.` Thomas.*

After the fire and blood of the battle-fields have disappeared, nowhere does war show its destroying power so certainly and so relentlessly as in the columns which represent the taxes and expenditures of the nation.

[From a Speech, June 2, 1879.]

The Resumption of Specie Payments closes the most memorable epoch in our history since the birth of the Union. Eighteen hundred and sixty-one and eighteen hundred and seventy-nine are the opposite shores of that turbulent sea whose storms so seriously threatened with shipwreck the prosperity, the honor, and the life of the nation. But the horrors and dangers of the middle-passage have at last been mastered; and out of the night and tempest the Republic has landed on the shore of this new year, bringing with it union and liberty; honor and peace.

Our country needs not only a national but an international currency.

Let us have equality of dollars before the law, so that the trinity of our political creed shall be — equal States, equal men, and equal dollars throughout the Union.

[Address, at the Memorial Meeting, in the House of Representatives, January 16, 1879.]

No page of human history is so instructive and significant as the record of those early influences which develop the character and direct the lives of eminent men. To every man of great original power, there comes in early youth, a moment of sudden discovery — of self recognition — when his own nature is revealed to himself, when he catches, for the first time, a strain of that immortal song to which his own spirit answers, and which becomes thenceforth and forever the inspiration of his life —

"Like noble music unto noble words."

More than a hundred years ago, in Strasbourg, on the Rhine, in obedience to the commands of his father, a German lad was reluctantly studying the mysteries of the civil law, but feeding his spirit as best he could upon the formal and artificial poetry of his native land, when a page of William Shakespeare met his eye, and changed the whole current of his life. Abandoning the law, he created and crowned with an immortal name the grandest epoch of German literature.

Recording his own experience, he says:

At the first touch of Shakespeare's genius, I made the glad confession that something inspiring hovered above me. . . . The first page of his that I read made me his for life; and when I had finished a single play, I stood like one born blind, on whom a miraculous hand bestows sight in a moment. I saw, I felt, in the most vivid manner that my existence was infinitely expanded.

This Old World experience of Goethe's was strikingly reproduced, though under different conditions and with different results, in the early life of Joseph Henry. You have just heard the incident worthily recounted; but let us linger over it a moment. An orphan boy of sixteen, of tough Scotch fibre, laboring for his own support at the handicraft of the jeweler, unconscious of his great power, delighted with romance and the drama, dreaming of a possible career on the stage, his attention was suddenly arrested by a single page of an humble book of science which chanced to fall into his hands. It was not the flash of a poetic vision which aroused him. It was the voice of great Nature calling her child. With quick recognition and glad reverence his spirit responded; and from that moment to the end of his long and honored life, Joseph Henry was the devoted student of science, the faithful interpreter of nature.

To those who knew his gentle spirit, it is not

surprising that ever afterward he kept the little volume near him, and cherished it as the source of his first inspiration. In the maturity of his fame he recorded on its fly-leaf his gratitude. Note his words:

> This book, under Providence, has exerted a remarkable influence on my life. . . . It opened to me a new world of thought and enjoyment, invested things before almost unnoticed with the highest interest, fixed my mind on the study of nature, and caused me to resolve, at the time of reading it, that I would devote my life to the acquisition of knowledge.

We have heard from his venerable associates with what resolute perseverance he trained his mind and marshalled his powers for the higher realms of science. He was the first American after Franklin who made a series of successful original experiments in electricity and magnetism. He entered the mighty line of Volta, Galvani, Oërsted, Davy, and Ampère, the great exploring philosophers of the world, and added to their work a final great discovery, which made the electro-magnetic telegraph possible.

It remained only for the inventor to construct an instrument and an alphabet. Professor Henry refused to reap any pecuniary rewards from his great discovery, but gave freely to mankind what nature and science had given to him. The venerable gentleman of almost eighty years, who has just addressed us so eloquently, has portrayed the difficulties which beset the government in its attempt to determine how it should wisely and worthily execute the trust of Smithson. It was a perilous moment for the credit of America when that bequest was made. In his large catholicity of mind, Smithson did not trammel the bequest with conditions. In nine words he set forth its object — "for the increase and diffusion of knowledge among men." He asked and believed that America would interpret his wish aright, and with the liberal wisdom of science. . . . . .

For ten years Congress wrestled with those nine words of Smithson, and could not handle them. Some political philosophers of that period held that we had no constitutional authority to accept the gift at all [laughter] and proposed to send it back to England. Every conceivable proposition was made. The colleges clutched at it; the libraries wanted it; the publication societies desired to scatter it. The fortunate settlement of the question was this: that, after ten years of wrangling, Congress was wise enough to acknowledge its own ignorance, and authorized a body of men to find some one who knew how to settle it. [Applause.] And these men were wise enough to choose your great comrade to undertake the task. Sacrificing his brilliant prospects as a discoverer, he undertook the difficult work. He drafted a paper, in which he offered an interpretation of the will of Smithson, mapped out a plan which would meet the demands of science, and submitted it to the suffrage of the republic of scientific scholars. After due deliberation it received the almost unanimous approval of the scientific world. With faith and sturdy perseverance, he adhered to the plan and steadily resisted all attempts to overthrow it.

In the thirty-two years during which he administered the great trust, he never swerved from his first purpose; and he succeeded at last in realizing the ideas with which he started.

The germ of our political institutions, the primary cell from which they were evolved, was in the New England town, and the vital force, the informing soul of the town, was the Town Meeting, which for all local concerns was king, lords, and commons in all.

It is as much the duty of all good men to protect and defend the reputation of worthy public servants as to detect public rascals.

Political parties, like poets, are born, not made. No act of political mechanics, however wise, can manufacture to order and make a platform, and put a party on it which will live and flourish.

[On the Relation of the Government to Science, February 11, 1879.]

What ought to be the relation of the National Government to science? What, if anything, ought we to do in the way of promoting science? For example, if we have the power, would it be wise for Congress to appropriate money out of the Treasury, to employ naturalists to find out all that is to be known of our American birds? Ornithology is a delightful and useful study; but would it be wise for Congress to make an appropriation for the advancement of that science? In my judgment, manifestly not. We would thereby make one favored class of men the rivals of all the ornithologists who, in their private way, following the bent of their genius, may be working out the results of science in that field. I have no doubt that an appropriation out of our Treasury for that purpose would be a positive injury to the advancement of science, just as an appropriation to establish a church would work injury to religion.

Generally, the desire of our scientific men is to be let alone to work in free competition with all the scientific men of the world; to develop their own results, and get the credit of them each for himself; not to have the Government enter the lists as the rival of private enterprise.

As a general principal, therefore, the United

States ought not to interfere in matters of science, but should leave its development to the free, voluntary action of our great third estate, the people themselves.

In this non-interference theory of the Government, I do not go to the extent of saying that we should do nothing for education—for primary education. That comes under another consideration—the necessity of the nation to protect itself, and the consideration that it is cheaper and wiser to give education than to build jails. But I am speaking now of the higher sciences.

To the general principle I have stated, there are a few obvious exceptions which should be clearly understood when we legislate on the subject. In the first place, the Government should aid all sorts of scientific inquiry that are necessary to the intelligent exercise of its own functions.

For example, as we are authorized by the Constitution and compelled by necessity to build and maintain light-houses on our coast and establish fog-signals, we are bound to make all necessary scientific inquiries ·in reference to light and its laws, sound and its laws—to do whatever in the way of science is necessary to achieve the best results in lighting our coasts and warning our mariners of danger. So, when we are building iron-clads for our navy or casting guns for our army, we ought to know all that is scientifically possible to be known about the strength of materials and the laws of mechanics which apply to such structures. In short, wherever in exercising any of the necessary functions of the Government scientific inquiry is needed, let us make it, to the fullest extent, and at the public expense.

There is another exception to the general rule of leaving science to the voluntary action of the people. Wherever any great popular interest, affecting whole classes, possibly all classes of the community, imperatively need scientific investigation, and private enterprise cannot accomplish it, we may wisely intervene and help where the Constitution gives us authority. For example, in discovering the origin of yellow-fever and the methods of preventing its ravages, the nation should do, for the good of all, what neither the States nor ·individuals can accomplish. I might perhaps include in a third exception those inquiries which, in consequence of their great magnitude and cost, cannot be successfully made by private individuals. Outside these three classes of inquiries, the Government ought to keep its hands off, and leave scientific experiment and inquiry to the free competition of those bright, intelligent men whose genius leads them into the fields of research.

And I suspect, when we read the report of our commissioner to the late Paris Exposition, which shows such astonishing results, so creditable to our country, so honorable to the genius of our people, it will be found, in any final analysis of causes, that the superiority of Americans in that great Exposition resulted mainly from their superior freedom, and the greater competition between mind and mind untrammelled by Government interference; I believe it will be found we are best serving the cause of religion and science, and all those great primary rights which we did not delegate to the Congress or the States, but left the people free to enjoy and maintain them.

[Speech on the National Election.]

The great danger which threatens this country is, that our sovereign may be dethroned or destroyed by corruption. In any monarchy of the world, if the sovereign be slain or become lunatic, it is easy to put another in his place, for the sovereign is a person. But our sovereign is the whole body of voters. If you kill, or corrupt, or render lunatic our sovereign, there is no successor, no regent to take his place. The source of our sovereign's supreme danger, the point where his life is vulnerable, is at the ballot-box, where his will is declared; and if we cannot stand by that cradle of our sovereign's heir-apparent and protect it to the uttermost against all assassins and assailants, we have no government and no safety for the future.

[Remarks, in the House of Representatives, February 11, 1879, on the Life and Character of Gustave Schleicher.]

We are accustomed to say, and we have heard to-night, that he [Gustave Schleicher] was born on foreign soil. In one sense that is true; and yet in a very proper historic sense he was born in our fatherland. One of the ablest of recent historians begins his opening volume with the declaration that England is not the fatherland of the English-speaking people, but the ancient home, the real fatherland of our race, is the ancient forests of Germany. The same thought was suggested by Montesquieu long ago, when he declared in his Spirit of Laws that the British constitution came out of the woods of Germany.

To this day the Teutonic races maintain the same noble traits that Tacitus describes in his admirable history of the manners and character of the Germans. We may therefore say that the friend whose memory we honor to-night is one of the elder brethren of our race. He came to America direct from our fatherland, and not, like our own fathers, by the way of England.

We who were born and have passed all our lives in this wide New World can hardly appreciate the influences that surrounded his early life. Born on the borders of that great forest of Germany, the Odenwald, filled as it is with the memories and traditions of centuries, in which are mingled Scandinavian mythology, legends of the middle ages, romances of feudalism and chivalry, histories of barons and kings, and the struggles of a brave people for a better civilization; reared under the institutions of a strong, semi-despotic government; devoting his early life to personal culture, entering at an early age the University of Giessen, venerable with its two and a half centuries of existence, with a library of four hundred thousand volumes at his hand, with a great museum of the curiosities and mysteries of nature to study, he fed his eager spirit upon the rich culture which that Old World could give him, and at twenty-four years of age, in company with a band of thirty-seven young students, like himself, cultivated, earnest, liberty-loving almost to the verge of communism — and who of us would not be communists in a despotism? — he came to this country, attracted by one of the most wild and romantic pictures of American history, the picture of Texas as it existed near forty years ago; the country discovered by La Salle at the end of his long and perilous voyage from Quebec to the northern lakes and from the lakes to the Gulf of Mexico; the country possessed alternately by the Spanish and the French and then by Mexico; the country made memorable by such names as Blair, Houston, Albert Sidney Johnson, and Mirabeau Lamar, perhaps as adventurous and daring spirits as ever assembled on any spot of the earth; a country that achieved its freedom by heroism never surpassed, and which maintained its perilous independence for ten years in spite of border enemies and European intrigues.

It is said that a society was formed in Europe embracing in its membership men of high rank, even members of royal families, for the purpose of colonizing the new Republic of the Lone Star, and making it a dependency of Europe under their patronage; but without sharing in their designs, some twenty thousand Germans found their way to the new Republic, and among these young Schleicher came.

[From the "North American Review," March, 1879.]

The ballot was given to the negro not so much to enable him to govern others as to prevent others from misgoverning him. Suffrage is the sword and shield of our law, the best armament that liberty offers to the citizen.

[From the Same, June, 1879.]

If our republic were blotted from the earth and from the memory of mankind, and if no record of its history survived, except a copy of our revenue laws and our appropriation bills for a single year, the political philosopher would be able from these materials alone to reconstruct a large part of our history, and sketch with considerable accuracy the character and spirit of our institutions.

[Speech in Congress, on the first anniversary of Mr. Lincoln's death.]

There are times in the history of men and nations when they stand so near the veil that separates mortals and immortals, time from eternity, and men from their God, that they can almost hear the breathings, and feel the pulsations of the heart of the Infinite. Through such a time has this nation passed. When two hundred and fifty thousand brave spirits passed from the field of honor through that thin veil to the presence of God, and when at last its parting folds admitted the martyred President to the company of the dead heroes of the republic, the nation stood so near the veil that the whispers of God were heard by the children of men. Awe-stricken by his voice, the American people knelt in tearful reverence, and made a solemn covenant with God and each other that this nation should be saved from its enemies; that all its glories should be restored, and on the ruins of slavery and treason the temples of freedom and justice should be built, and stand forever. It remains for us, consecrated by that great event, and under that covenant with God, to keep the faith, to go forward in the great work until it shall be completed. Following the lead of that great man, and obeying the high behests of God, let us remember

> "He has sounded forth his trumpet, that shall never call retreat;
> He is sifting out the hearts of men before his judgment-seat;
> Be swift, my soul, to answer him; be jubilant, my feet;
> For God is marching on."

Every great political party that has done this country any good has given to it some immortal ideas that have outlived all the members of that party.

[Speech at Cleveland, Ohio, October 11, 1879. — Resumption of Specie Payments.]

Now, what has been the trouble with us? 1860 was one shore of prosperity, and 1879 the other; and between these two high shores has flowed the broad, deep, dark river of fire and blood and disaster through which this nation has been compelled to wade, and in whose depths it has been almost suffocated and drowned. In the darkness of that terrible passage we carried liberty in our arms; we bore the Union on our shoulders; and we bore in our hearts and on our arms what was even better than liberty and Union — we bore the faith, and honor, and public trust of this mighty Nation. And never, until we came up out of the dark waters, out of the darkness of that terrible current, and planted our feet upon the solid shore of 1879 — never, I say, till then could this country look back to the other shore and feel that its feet were on solid ground, and then look forward to the rising uplands of perpetual peace and prosperity that should know no diminution in the years to come.

[Speech at Cleveland, October 11, 1879. — Appeal to Young Men.]

Now, I tell you, young man, don't vote the Republican ticket just because your father votes it. Don't vote the Democratic ticket, even if he does vote it. But let me give you this one word of advice, as you are about to pitch your tent in one of the great political camps. Your life is full and buoyant with hope now, and I beg you, when you pitch your tent, pitch it among the living and not among the dead. If you are at all inclined to pitch it among the Democratic people and with that party, let me go with you for a moment while we survey the ground where I hope you will not shortly lie. It is a sad place, young man, for you to put your young life into. It is to me far more like a graveyard than like a camp for the living. Look at it! It is billowed all over with the graves of dead issues, of buried opinions, of exploded theories, of disgraced doctrines. You cannot live in comfort in such a place. Why, look here! Here is a little double mound. I look down on it and I read, "Sacred to the memory of Squatter Sovereignty and the Dred Scott decision." A million and a half of Democrats voted for that, but it has been dead fifteen years — died by the hand of Abraham Lincoln, and here it lies. Young man, that is not the place for you.

But look a little farther. Here is another monument — a black tomb — and beside it, as our distinguished friend said, there towers to the sky a monument of four million pairs of human fetters taken from the arms of slaves, and I read on its little headstone this: " Sacred to the memory of human slavery." For forty years of its infamous life the Democratic party taught that it was divine — God's institution. They defended it, they stood around it, they followed it to its grave as a mourner. But here it lies, dead by the hand of Abraham Lincoln. Dead by the power of the Republican party. Dead by the justice of Almighty God. Don't camp there, young man.

But here is another — a little brimstone tomb — and I read across its yellow face in lurid, bloody lines these words: "Sacred to the memory of State Sovereignty and Secession." Twelve millions of Democrats mustered around it in arms to keep it alive; but here it lies, shot to death by the million guns of the Republic. Here it lies, its shrine burnt to ashes under the blazing rafters of the burning Confederacy. It is dead! I would not have you stay in there a minute, even in this balmy night air, to look at such a place.

But just before I leave it I discover a new-made grave, a little mound — short. The grass has hardly sprouted over it, and all around it I see torn pieces of paper with the word "fiat" on them, and I look down in curiosity, wondering what the little grave is, and I read on it: "Sacred to the memory of the Rag Baby nursed in the brain of all the fanaticism of the world, rocked by Thomas Ewing, George H. Pendleton, Samuel Cary, and a few others throughout the land." But it died on the 1st of January, 1879, and the one hundred and forty millions of gold that God made, and not fiat power, lie upon its little carcass to keep it down forever.

Oh, young man, come out of that! That is no place in which to put your young life. Come out, and come over into this camp of liberty, of order, of law, of justice, of freedom, of all that is glorious under these night stars.

Is there any death here in our camp? Yes! yes! Three hundred and fifty thousand soldiers, the noblest band that ever trod the earth, died to make this camp a camp of glory and of liberty forever.

But there are no dead issues here. There are

no dead ideas here. Hang out our banner from under the blue sky this night until it shall sweep the green turf under your feet! It hangs over our camp. Read away up under the stars the inscription we have written on it, lo! these twenty-five years.

Twenty-five years ago the Republican party was married to Liberty, and this is our silver wedding, fellow-citizens. A worthily married pair love each other better on the day of their silver wedding than on the day of their first espousals; and we are truer to Liberty to-day, and dearer to God than we were when we spoke our first word of liberty. Read away up under the sky across our starry banner that first word we uttered twenty-five years ago! What was it? "Slavery shall never extend over another foot of the territories of the great West." Is that dead or alive? Alive, thank God, forevermore! And truer to-night than it was the hour it was written! Then, it was a hope, a promise, a purpose. To-night it is equal with the stars — immortal history and immortal truth.

Come down the glorious steps of our banner. Every great record we have made we have vindicated with our blood and with our truth. It sweeps the ground, and it touches the stars. Come there, young man, and put in your young life where all is living, and where nothing is dead but the heroes that defended it! I think these young men will do that.

[From a Speech, January 14, 1880.]

I say, moreover, that the flowers that bloom over the garden-wall of party politics are the sweetest and most fragrant that bloom in the gardens of this world, and where we can fairly pluck them and enjoy their fragrance, it is manly and delightful to do so.

[Letter of Acceptance, July 10, 1880.]

Next in importance to freedom and justice is popular education, without which neither justice nor freedom can be permanently maintained. Its interests are intrusted to the States, and to the voluntary action of the people. Whatever help the Nation can justly afford should be generously given to aid the States in supporting common schools; but it would be unjust to our people, and dangerous to our institutions, to apply any portion of the revenues of the Nation or of the States to the support of sectarian schools. The separation of the Church and the State in everything relating to taxation should be absolute.

Our country cannot be independent unless its people, with their abundant natural resources, possess the requisite skill at any time to clothe, arm, and equip themselves for war, and in time of peace to produce all the necessary implements of labor. It was the manifest intention of the founders of the Government to provide for the common defence, not by standing armies alone, but by raising among the people a greater army of artisans, whose intelligence and skill should powerfully contribute to the safety and glory of the nation.

Over this vast horizon of interests, North and South, above all party prejudices and personal wrong-doing, above our battle hosts and our victorious cause, above all that we hoped for and won, or you hoped for and lost, is the grand onward movement of the Republic to perpetuate its glory, to save Liberty alive, to preserve exact and equal justice to all, to protect and foster all these priceless principles until they shall have crystallized into the form of enduring law and become inwrought into the life and habits of our People.

I look forward with joy and hope to the day when our brave people, one in heart, one in their aspirations for freedom and peace, shall see that the darkness through which we have travelled was but a part of that stern but beneficent discipline by which the great Disposer of events has been leading us on to a higher and nobler national life.

The hope of our National perpetuity rests upon

that perfect individual Freedom which shall forever keep up the circuit of perpetual change.

Whatever opinions we may now entertain of the Federalists as a party, it is unquestionably true that we are indebted to them for the strong points of the Constitution and for the stable government they founded and strengthened during the administration of Washington and Adams.

While it is true that no party can stand upon its past record alone, yet it is also true that its past shows the spirit and character of the organization, and enables us to judge what it will probably do in the future.

Parties have an organic life and spirit of their own — an individuality and character which outlive the men who compose them; and the spirit and traditions of a party should be considered in determining their fitness for managing the affairs of the nation.

It is a safe and wise rule to follow in all legislation, that whatever the people can do without legislation will be better done than by the intervention of the State and Nation.

[From a Speech, at the unveiling of a Soldiers' Monument, Painesville, Ohio, July 4, 1880.]

I once entered a house in old Massachusetts, where over its doors were two crossed swords. One was the sword carried by the grandfather of its owner on the field of Bunker Hill, and the other was the sword carried by the English grandsire of the wife on the same field, and on the other side of the conflict. Under those crossed swords, in the restored harmony of domestic peace, lived a happy and contented and free family, under the light of our republican liberties. I trust the time is not far distant when, under the crossed swords and the locked shields of Americans, north and south, our people shall sleep in peace and rise in liberty, love, and harmony, under the union of our flag of the stars and stripes.

[Speech to a Delegation of four hundred Young Men — First Voters — of Cleveland, Ohio, at Mentor, October 8, 1880.]

. . . . . I have not so far left the coast of youth to travel inland but that I can very well remember the state of young manhood, from an experience in it of some years, and there is nothing to me in this world so inspiring as the possibilities that lie locked up in the head and breast of a young man. The hopes that lie before him, the great inspirations around him, the great aspirations above him, all these things, with the untried pathway of life opening up its difficulties and dangers, inspire him to courage, and force, and work.

[From a Speech in New York, August 6, 1880.]

. . . . . Ideas outlive men. Ideas outlive all things, and you who fought in the war for the Union fought for immortal ideas, and by their might you crowned our war with victory. But victory was worth nothing except for the fruits that were under it, in it, and above it. We meet to-night as veterans and comrades, to stand sacred guard around the truths for which we fought, and while we have life to meet and grasp the hands of a comrade, we will stand by the great truths of the war; and, comrades, among the convictions of that war which have sunk deep in our hearts there are some that we can never forget. Think of the great elevating spirit of the war itself. We gathered the boys from all our farms, and shops, and stores, and schools, and homes, from all over the Republic, and they went forth unknown to fame, but returned enrolled on the roster of immortal heroes. They went in the spirit of those soldiers of Henry at Agincourt, of whom he said, "Who this day sheds his blood with me, to-day shall be my brother. Were he ne'er so vile, this day shall gentle his condition;" and it did gentle the condition and elevate the heart of every working soldier who fought in it, and he shall be our brother for evermore; and this thing we will remember; we will remember our allies who fought with us. Soon after the great struggle began we looked behind the army of white rebels and saw 4,000,000 of black people condemned to toil as slaves for our enemies, and we found that the hearts of this 4,000,000 were God-inspired with the spirit of freedom, and that they were our friends. We have seen white men betray the flag and fight to kill the Union, but in all that long, dreary war we never saw a traitor in a black skin. Our prisoners, escaping from the starvation of prison, and fleeing to our lines by the light of the North-star, never feared to enter the black man's cabin and ask for bread. In all that period of suffering and danger no Union soldier was ever betrayed by a black man or woman, and now that we have made them free, so long as we live we will stand by these black citizens. We will stand by them until the sun of liberty, fixed in the firmament of our Constitution, shall shine with equal rays upon every man, black or white, throughout the Union. Now, fellow-citizens, fellow-soldiers, in this there is all the beneficence of eternal justice, and by this we will stand forever.

[Remarks at Chatauqua, August 1, 1880.]

I would rather be defeated than make capital out of my religion.

[From an Address at the Anniversary of Hiram College, directly after the Chicago Convention, 1880.]

FELLOW-CITIZENS, NEIGHBORS, AND FRIENDS OF MANY YEARS: It always has given me pleasure to come back here and look upon these faces. It has always given me new courage and new friends. It has brought back a large share of that richness that belongs to those things out of which come the joys of life. While I have been sitting here this afternoon, watching your faces and listening to the very interesting address which has just been delivered, it occurred to me that the best thing you have that all men envy — I mean all men who have reached the meridian of life — is, perhaps, the thing that you care for less, and that is your leisure, — the leisure you have to think; the leisure you have to be let alone; the leisure you have to throw the plummet with your hand, and sound their depths and find out what is below; the leisure you have to walk about the towers of yourselves, and find how strong they are, or how weak they are, and determine what needs building up, and determine how to shape them, that you may make the final being that you are to be. Oh, these hours of building! If the superior beings of the universe would look down upon the world to find the most interesting object, it would be the unfinished, unformed character of young men, or of young women. These behind me have, probably, in the main settled such questions. Those who have passed into middle manhood and middle womanhood are about what they shall always be, and there is little left of interest or curiosity as to our development. But to your young and yet uninformed natures no man knows the possibilities that lie treasured up in your hearts and intellects; and while you are working up these possibilities with that splendid leisure, you are the most envied of all classes of men and women in the world. I congratulate you on your leisure. I commend you to keep it as your gold, as your wealth, as your means, out of which you can demand all the possible treasures that God laid down when He formed your nature, and unveiled and developed the possibility of your future. This place is too full of memories for me to trust myself to speak upon, and I will not; but I draw again to-day, as I have for a quarter of a century, evidences of strength and affection from the people who gather in this place, and I thank you for the permission to see you, and meet you, and greet you, as I have done to-day.

INDEX.

INDEX.

A.

Adams, John, 45, 66–68, 82, 85, 87, 124, 169, 189, 190.
Adams, John Quincy, 51, 133, 143, 144, 441.
Adams, Samuel, 52, 80, 110.
Agassiz, Louis, 430.
Alaska, 415.
Allied Powers, The, 130.
Amendment, The Fourteenth, 422.
Amendments to the Constitution, 367–370.
America and England, 318, 337.
Arbitration, International, 337.

B.

Bible, The, 67, 143.
Bi-metallism, 389.
Birmingham, England, 359, 360.
Bismarck, 335.
Bonaparte, Napoleon, 335, 336.
Books, 438.
Boston, 45, 47, 77–80.
British Constitution, 116.
Burlingame Treaty, 362.

C.

Calvinism, View of, 146.
Cass, Lewis, 199.
Cassel, Prince of Hesse-, 64.

Chaplain to Congress, 121.
Character, 98, 439.
Chase, S. P., 275, 446.
Chinese Immigration, 362, 363.
Christianity, 87, 109, 110, 164, 165.
Church-membership, 266.
Church and State, 437.
Civil Service, 109, 120, 142, 354, 359-361.
College Studies, 410.
Colored Citizens, 290, 349, 350, 368, 369, 374, 378, 465.
Colored Soldiers, 260, 270, 290, 294, 298, 477.
Commercial Reverses, 192.
Communism, 133.
Concentration of Power, 97, 117.
Concord, Battle at, 16.
Confederation, The, 170.
Congress, 444.
Congress, Organizing, in 1839, 166.
Congress, International, 319.
Consolidated Government, 97, 127.
Constitution, The U. S., 171-174, 177, 394.
Convention, Constitutional, 24, 172.
Credit, Expansion of, 221.
Currency, The, 184, 192, 317, 355, 356, 388, 418-420, 431.

D.

Davis, Jefferson, 449.
Debt, The National, 311, 423.
Debts, Public, 385.
Declaration of Independence, 102, 160-162, 170, 186, 189, 230-233, 240, 244, 400.
Declaration of Independence, Signers of, 59, 186.
Democratic Party, The, 343-345, 468.
Depravity, Human, 143.
Dissolution of the Union, 211, 219.
Divorce, 197.
Douglas, Stephen A., 226, 233, 236.

Draft Bill, 392.
Duché, Rev. Mr., 52-54.

E.

Education, Popular, 100, 107, 117, 141, 313, 314, 317, 352-354, 372-383, 376, 460, 472.
Education, Popular, National Aid to, 427.
Elections, Purity of, 351, 363, 462.
Elective Franchise, 351, 363.
Emancipation, 270.
Emancipation Proclamation, 248, 250, 257-259, 265, 275-278, 285, 294, 304, 446.
Emerson, Ralph Waldo, 223, 278.
England and America, 337.
English Constitution, The, 188.
Everett, Edward, 279.

F.

Federalists, The, 148, 474.
Fillmore, Millard, 212.
Finance, 355.
France, 62.
Franklin, Benjamin, 97, 124.
Free Trade, 338, 392, 421.
French Republic, 311.
Fourth of July, 61.
Fugitive Slaves, 411.
Future Life, The, 85.

G.

Gag-law, 168, 169.
Garfield, James A., 388, 411, 413.
Gambetta, 335.
Genius, 55, 66.
Georges, The, 148.
Gettysburg, Address at, 278, 279.

INDEX.   483

Goëthe, 454, 455.
Government, 118, 119, 177, 178, 187.
Grant, U. S., 280, 281, 292, 326, 332–334, 339, 345.
Greek Language, The, 424.
Greeley, Horace, 247.

H.

Habeas Corpus, 253–255.
Hadrian, Lines of, 138.
Hamilton, Alexander, 123.
Hampton Institute, 383.
Harrison, William Henry, 195.
Hayes, Rutherford B., 347.
Hayti, 163.
Henry, Joseph, 455.
Hereditary Succession, 149.
Hesse-Cassel, Prince of, 64.
History, 425.
Hodges, Colonel, 262.
Holmes, Oliver Wendell, 283.
Horace, 424.
Hughes, Thomas, 320.
Hutchinson, Governor, 68, 69, 79, 80, 82.

I.

Ideas, 399, 476.
Illinois, 127.
Immigration, 107, 371–373, 375, 381; Chinese, 362, 363.
Indians, The, 43, 196, 283, 379, 386.

J.

Jackson, Andrew, 163, 176, 284, 309.
Jackson, "Stonewall," 324.
Jefferson, Thomas, 88, 124, 170, 190, 381.
Johnson, Andrew, 234, 284, 308, 309.
Johnson, Richard M., 197, 200, 334.
Judiciary, The, 70, 72, 351.

L.

Labor, 319.
Laboulaye, E., 271.
Law, Reign of, 426.
Legislative Department, 187.
Leisure, 478.
Liberty, 46, 86, 171, 290, 406.
Lincoln, Abraham, 223, 271-273, 278, 279, 322-324, 330, 366, 367, 368, 391, 393, 413, 446-448, 466.
Literature in America, 104-107.
Locke, John, 174.
"Lost Cause, The," 348.
Louis XV., 149.
Louisiana, 195.

M.

Madison, James, 88, 111, 170, 382.
Manchester, England, 251.
Massachusetts, 12, 13.
Massacre, Boston, 77.
Mathews, Stanley, 347.
McClellan, George B., 327-330.
Metallic Basis, 184.
Military Academy, 129.
Militia, The, 129.
"Minute-men" of 1775, 169.
Miracles, 165.
Mississippi, The, 195.
Monroe, James, 100, 122, 127, 146, 147.
"Monroe Doctrine," 130, 207, 214.

N.

Napoleon Bonaparte, 335, 336.
Napoleon, Louis, 336.
National Authority, 364; and State Authority, 130.
National Credit, 213, 311, 322, 362.

National Debt, 311, 423.
National Morality, 115, 213, 322, 324, 348.
National Policy, 204.
Natural Bridge, The, 91.
Nature, Conformity to, 66.
Negroes, 93.
Neutrality, 207, 208, 214.
New England, 440.
New Jersey Delegation of 1839, 166.
New States, Admission of, 127
North Carolina, 173.
Nullification, 122, 123, 125, 163, 178-184.

O.

Orator, The, 134.
Oregon Territory, 206.
Otis, James, 83, 84.

P.

Parties, Origin of, 399, 458.
Party Spirit, 141.
Pemberton, General, 295.
People, The, 66, 394.
Perry, Oliver Hazard, 199.
Persecution, Religious, 112, 113.
Petition, Right of, 152-161, 168.
Pierce, Franklin, 217.
Polk, James K., 205.
Poncas, The, 387.
Pope, Alexander, 137.
Potomac, The, 90.
President and Senate, 138.
Presidential etiquette, 190; receptions, 268; title, 120.
Profanity, 22.
Property, 262.
Protective Duties, 407.
Public Schools, 141.
Punch, 224 *n*.

R.

Railway System, The, 431.
Randolph, John, 144.
Raynal, Abbé, 104.
Reason, a revelation, 68.
Rebellion, The, 348.
Rebel States, 296, 297.
Reconstruction, 412.
Religion, 44, 67, 266.
Religious Freedom, 42, 89, 101, 113, 114, 121, 171.
Republican Party, The, 342-345, 450, 470.
Repudiation, 311, 385.
Revenue, National, 444.
Revenue Bills, 364.
Revolution, The American, 186.
Rhetoric, 134.
Ruffner, Dr., 379.

S.

Sabbath, The, 22, 249, 250.
Schleicher, G., 463.
School-keeping, 46.
Schools, Public, 352-354; Sectarian, 352, 472.
Science, 451; relation of government to, 459.
Secession, 122, 125, 163, 179-182, 242, 243.
Secretary of War, 448.
Sectarian Schools, 472.
Self-government, 55, 109.
Senate, Functions of the, 120.
Separation from England, 54.
Seward, William H. 413, 446.
Shakespeare, 282.
Sheridan, Gen., 325, 339.
Sherman, Gen., 331.
Sin, Original, 59.

Slavery, 25, 26, 85, 93-97, 104, 126, 128, 132, 151-154, 160-162, 164, 184, 226, 231-236, 247, 263, 264, 267, 268, 270-275, 286, 287, 339, 340, 374, 375, 378, 394, 395-397, 401-4' ", 411.
Slave-trade, 126, 128.
Smithsonian Institute, 457.
"Solid South," The, 345.
South Carolina, 125, 163, 174, 178-183.
Special Privileges, 206.
Specie Payments, Resumption of, 453, 467.
Spectator, The London, 271.
"Spoils of Office," 125, 359.
"Squatter Sovereignty," 228.
Stanton, Secretary, 330, 446.
State Rights, 27, 243-246, 364, 370.
Statistics, 426.
Stuart, A. H. H., 376.
Student, The, 408-411, 424.
Suffrage, Negro, 465; unrestricted, 350.
"Surrender, Unconditional," 293.

T.

Tariff, The, 184, 338, 407.
Taylor, Zachary, 210.
Teutonic Races, 463.
Texas, 244, 245, 341, 465.
Thames, Battle of the, 197-200.
Thomas, Gen., 458.
Township, The New England, 409, 458.
Trade with Rebels, 296, 297.
Treason, 284, 288, 289.
Trinity, The, 146.
Tyler, John, 202.

U.

Union, Saving the, 247, 257-259, 339.
Union Soldiers, 321, 357-358, 371.
Utah, 312.

V.

Van Buren, Martin, 186.
Vicksburg, 280, 294-296.
Volunteer Soldiers, 346.

W.

Walpole, Memoirs of, 140.
War, 332, 335, 338.
War, Civil, Philosophy of the, 399, 400.
Washington, George, 11, 97, 119, 214.
Webster, Daniel, 383.
Wheatley, Phillis, 21
Wilderness, The, 302.
Woman, Political Influence of, 156-160.
Writs of Assistance, 81, 82.

Y.

Young man, Advice to a, 225.
Young Men, 475.

www.ingramcontent.com/pod-product-compliance
Lightning Source LLC
Chambersburg PA
CBHW021427300426
44114CB00010B/679